you
ONLY
live
ONCE...

...but if you do it
right, once is enough!
~Mae West~

Have a Happy Birthday Mr Bobman!
Go forth & enjoy (can I borrow
the book when you're done?!)

love
MacPhee! xx

June 2019

JUMP IN!

Because you
only live once...

'You only live once; but if you do it right, once is enough.'

Mae West

CONTENTS

Chapter 01

AN HOUR

In which we spend a couple of hours taking care of the little things – a shave, a shower, perhaps a cocktail or something to eat – before tackling the big stuff: sporting events, extreme feats, life-and-death spectacles, celestial phenomena and the ever-thought-provoking rituals of dawn and sunset.

Chapter 02

A DAY

In which we lose ourselves at festivals and carnivals, dine like kings, party all night in cities and fall asleep in some extraordinary settings. Then we spend a day or two in the outdoors, watching wildlife, walking by moonlight and seeking out the most silent places in the world. Finally, we face our greatest fears, whatever they may be.

Chapter 03
A WEEK

In which we take a week or two to drive the world's most exciting roads, spot the Big Five on safari, hail a helicopter, spend an adventure-packed week on an island and swap houses with someone. Closer to home, a week is time enough to discover delights on your doorstep and learn some dance steps to impress.

148–221

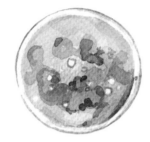

Chapter 04
A MONTH

In which, over a month or more, we venture to the Amazon, travel from one end of a country to the other, train for a marathon and celebrate the seasons. On the water we learn to surf and paddle. We also find time to volunteer and participate in a tradition. And to escape it all, we travel solo and build a log cabin in the wilds.

222–275

Chapter 05
A YEAR

In which we quit the desk job, take flying lessons, ski sweet powder for twelve months, uncover your family's roots, and resolve to learn a new language. Then, consider a sabbatical in the Caribbean or the south of France, or even a round-the-world journey with the perfect travel companion.

276–323

RO

you ONLY live ONCE

INTRODUCTION

Life's not a dress rehearsal. 'Carpe Diem.' 'Be happy while you're living for you're a long time dead.' Yes, there are *a lot* of motivational proverbs about living life to the max out there, including the title of this book. But that's probably because it's a big deal.

The average person has a lifespan of threescore years and ten, give or take. And there's a lot to pack in. Some people are born with a knack for sucking the marrow from the bones of life.

Sir Richard Burton, the Victorian explorer, soldier, spy, linguist, writer, ethnologist... we could go on, travelled to India with the British Army at the age of 20, where he learned more than half a dozen local languages, studied Hindu culture and kept a menagerie of monkeys. Later he explored Africa and the Middle East and translated *The Arabian Nights*.

A more contemporary example might be Keith Richards, Rolling Stones guitarist, writer of immortal riffs, and aspiring librarian. As both demonstrate, you can pack a lot into threescore years and ten if you try.

And that's what this book sets out to help you do. It is not just another bucketlist of big-ticket trips. We've all heard about Venice and, yes, it is probably worth going to Italy to see its waterways. Instead, hopefully you'll take away something more from this book: a resolve to live life to the fullest, to add a dash of *joie de vivre* to every day.

That doesn't just mean splashing out on exotic holidays but also seeking out and indulging in little pleasures – a new pair of handmade shoes, that simple dish of perfectly dressed pasta. And, while we feature a number of serious challenges – the Appalachian Trail,

you ONLY live ONCE

it's worth noting, doesn't get any easier the older you grow – there are just as many experiences that you can enjoy on your doorstep with a little lateral thinking.

Start by embracing spontaneity; experiences like sleeping under the stars, once in a while, remind you what an amazing privilege it is to be alive, to think and to enjoy the world around us.

And we've tried to suggest opportunities to learn and slake a little of that thirst for knowledge among these pages, with illustrations of how to mix cocktails, identify autumn leaves and train for a marathon with a difference. For hedonists and adventure-lovers we've also mapped once-in-a-lifetime experiences in cities and on islands.

Essentially, *You Only Live Once* is about experiences not places – though we travel to every corner of the planet. It is about those experiences that you will replay in your mind's eye years later; they may not feature the most spectacular destinations, they may even in fact have cost nothing, but they will be the travel experiences that changed you, the ones that still bring a smile to your face.

So, how does this book work? There are five chapters – for an Hour, Day, Week, Month and Year – and in each we suggest experiences that may take about that amount of time. Naturally, these definitions are as elastic as you want them to be. You might wish to spend one hour or several kitesurfing in Greece, you can stretch a day into a weekend, a week into a fortnight. You can spend one month or six working your passage abroad, take a year or more to travel around the world.

But what all these ideas have in common is that they're starting points. They will reignite long-forgotten desires – to learn an instrument or a language – or spark new and unexpected ambitions: why shouldn't you move to Provence for a year?

When you know what's stopping you, you can start working on a solution. Perhaps this book will be as useful in helping you identify obstacles as will be for refining your month's or your year's travel experiences. Then it's time to turn to Lonely Planet's extensive travel resources and begin planning the rest of your life. ●

London 2014

THE DARK HEDGES, COUNTY ANTRIM, NORTHERN IRELAND

Brian Glover

LET'S BEGIN

'Two roads diverged in a wood and I took the one less traveled by.'

Robert Frost

Chapter

01

In which we spend a couple of hours taking care of the little things

HOUR – a shave, a shower, perhaps a cocktail or something to eat – before tackling the big stuff: sporting events, extreme feats, life-and-death spectacles, celestial phenomena and the ever-thought-provoking rituals of dawn and sunset.

Chapter
01

BE AT THE BIRTH

IT ONLY TAKES A MOMENT OR TWO FOR A NEW LIFE TO BE BORN IN THE AFRICAN BUSH; AND JUST AS LONG FOR IT TO BE OVER. WITNESS THIS AWESOME LIFE-AND-DEATH SPECTACLE IN ZAMBIA'S SOUTH LUANGWA NATIONAL PARK.

They euphemistically call it the 'emerald season' – well, it sounds so much better than 'wet season'. But, from December to March, wet is undeniably what it is in Zambia's South Luangwa National Park. And yet, what life amid the water! The snap-crack dry bush and dusty trails are transformed into an almost blinding vivacity of green: trees sport their finest foliage, thickets thicken, grasses seem to grow before your eyes. Amid all that natural profusion – hiding somewhere – an array of African animals is entering the world.

They're clever, these creatures: it makes sense to give birth to your young when food is in abundance. And with the help of a good guide (and a good raincoat), you delve into the bustling jungle to see the circle of life begin. There! A fragile impala wobbles on unsteady legs. Over there! A family of warthogs, antennae-tails pointing skyward, trots down a burrow. In the river! A hefty hippo calf floats next to its massive mother.

There are rarities here too. Wild dogs – often a tough species to spot – have their puppies in the 'green'; at this time, the wide-roaming canines tend to stay closer to their dens, making them easier to find.

The added bonus of being here to see the baby critters is that you're not the only one watching – the predators descend too. For them, it's a succulent pick-n-mix. Hyenas, lions and leopards lurk (the latter particularly prevalent in South Luangwa), looking for an easy lunch as vulnerable newborns enter the world. ●

① Penguins, Antarctic Peninsula
After November's courtships, penguin chicks hatch in December. Cruise to the peninsula's rookeries to see new gentoo, chinstrap, Adélie and emperor parents feeding their newborn chicks.

② Wildebeest, Serengeti, Tanzania
The Great Migration circulates around the Serengeti. Head to the park's south to see a million wildebeest gather to give birth in February; an estimated 400,000 calves are born in one week.

③ Grey Whales, Baja California, Mexico
Practically the entire world population of grey whales comes to San Ignacio Lagoon to breed from February to April. Trips in small boats enable you to get close enough to stroke the curious calves.

④ Sea Turtles, Rekwa, Sri Lanka
Five turtle species nest on this southern beach from June to August. Contact the local Marine Conservation Society, which monitors when hatchlings will make their dash to the sea.

EMPEROR PENGUIN CHICKS ON ANTARCTIC PENINSULA   Getty/Wayne Lynch

An Hour

WITNESS THE DAWN

IT'S THE SIMPLE THINGS: TAKE JUST AN HOUR
TO STOP AND CONTEMPLATE THE INCREDIBLE
BEAUTY OF THE EVERYDAY AND IT'S BOUND TO BE A
MORNING TO REMEMBER.

Strange things happen in the dead of night. Worries worsen, trivial troubles assume disastrous proportions and the mind plays tricks. Strange sounds and shadowy flickers morph into ghosts, ghouls and villains. And then the sun comes up; funnily enough, it happens every day, yet always has the power to astonish. It's the combination of slow-burn build-up with sudden illumination – the anticipation with the guaranteed pay-off.

Picture this: you're in the Nepalese Himalaya and up at stupid o'clock to trek through the cold, coal-black night to reach that perfect perch, 3193m up Poon Hill. From here, come first light, the entire Annapurna Range will spread in perfect panorama. You sit and huddle against the altitudinous chill, to wait for nature to do her thing. First the sky's seams seem to tear, a fraying at the edge of the darkness. What was colourless turns off-black, then navy, then paler, paler blue. Purple-pinks begin to warm the horizon, a cheery backdrop for the jagged peaks. All around, rocks, boulders, faces begin to blush in the intensifying glow of pre-dawn. It is the golden hour, when the monsters of the night have slunk away and what lies ahead is enlightenment and fresh possibility.

And then, there it is – the sun itself bursts in. Once it's reared its radiant head, there's no stopping its speedy surge skywards. Golden becomes blazing – wakey, wakey, rise and shine. The world's best alarm clock has rung quite definitively: it's time to start a new day. ●

Gisborne, New Zealand

The North Island's easternmost city is the first big hub to see the sun rise. It's also within one of the few districts that permits 'freedom camping', so you can wild-camp away from the crowds to watch the new day dawn.

Mt Sinai, Egypt

Make a pre-dawn pilgrimage up this sacred mountain – where Moses allegedly received the Ten Commandments – to see the sun rise over the biblical landscape.

Dzibilchaltún, Mexico

At sunrise on the spring and autumn equinoxes, the sun shines directly between the doorposts of Dzibilchaltún's Temple of the Seven Dolls – testament to the architectural mastery of the Maya.

Longyearbyen, Svalbard

Polar night – when the sun doesn't rise above the horizon – lasts for over four months on this Arctic archipelago. The first time the sun makes an appearance in the capital Longyearbyen (around 8 March) is special indeed.

An Hour

You Only Live Once

OPEN YOUR EARS

PICK THE RIGHT VENUE AND YOU CAN GET LOST IN BOTH THE MUSIC AND THE MOMENT: A LIVE PERFORMANCE THAT REALLY MAKES YOU FEEL ALIVE.

The sense of awe begins well before the music starts playing. Just entering Verona's ancient Arena takes your breath away. Standing for almost 2000 years in the centre of this northern Italian city, the sheer size of the auditorium is astonishing.

Row after row of seats cling to the time-worn steps that line the inner edges of the Arena. The knowledge that Romans sat on these very steps to watch gruesome gladiatorial battles below is spine-tingling. In the centre, red velvet stalls offer yet more seating. The venue can entertain an immense 15,000 music-lovers in one performance.

As you take your seat, inhaling the mouth-watering aromas wafting over from the bustling restaurants nearby, the lights dim beneath the balmy evening sky. There is yet another surprise to come before the opera starts: first one, then another and soon most members of the audience have lit votive candles in what has become a traditional and incredibly pretty prelude to the performance. Thousands of tiny flickering flames illuminating this historical space is unforgettable.

And then the music starts. Tonight it is Georges Bizet's *Carmen*. All pomp and spectacle, the costumes are incredible and the singers sublime. It goes on for hours, but you don't really mind. It is all part of the experience. Although the sound quality here is less than ideal, especially if you are in the cheap seats up at the top, the visual extravaganza of the performance more than makes up for any imperfections in musical purity. It is an moment that stimulates all the senses. ●

You Only Live Once

THE MUSIKVEREIN IN VIENNA   Alamy/Epa European Pressphoto Agency B.V.

 1

Sydney Opera House, Sydney, Australia

Jørn Utzon created an icon when he designed one of the 20th century's greatest buildings. Thankfully what goes on inside is pretty special too. The two main halls are majestic, full of colour and shaped to achieve perfect acoustics.

 2

Wilton's Music Hall, London, England

One of the world's oldest surviving 'Grand Music Halls', this venue is one of London's best-kept secrets. The atmospheric building was left derelict for many years, but was mercifully saved from demolition and is being slowly restored to its former glory. Famous for offbeat and diverse performances, including jazz, cabaret and swing, Wilton's Music Hall is an unsung hero.

 3

Concertgebouw, Amsterdam, the Netherlands

Built in 1888, this Dutch venue is renowned for its incredible acoustics. However, no-one is quite sure how the designer, Dolf van Gendt, managed to create such a perfectly resonant hall, given that the science behind acoustics was relatively unknown at the time. Today it is home to some 900 concerts a year, attracting 700,000 visitors, making it one of the most visited concert halls in the world.

 4

The Musikverein, Vienna, Austria

Famous for the annual New Year concert in its Golden Hall, the Musikverein is widely acknowledged as one of the finest musical venues in the world. The Austrian capital is also home to two other world-class concert halls: the State Opera and the Konzerthaus, making Vienna a must-go destination for classical-music fans.

OPEN YOUR EARS

RODEO!

So, you've witnessed the running of the bulls in Pamplona, where next? Rodeos take place across the US and Canada, featuring bull and bronco riding, barrel racing (horse races over short circuits) and a lot of denim in one place. If you're inspired to take part, there are growing numbers of bull-riding courses around the continent, such as three-day clinics at Gary Leffew's Bull Riding World. Reassuringly, the veteran rodeo star says 'bull riding is 80 percent mental, 20 percent talent.'

An Hour

ADAM SKOLNICK FINDS SOLACE SWIMMING IN CALIFORNIA'S OPEN OCEAN

The colours soothe me. To be immersed in that aquamarine for more than an hour marinates the mind, opens it up and hushes my restless brain. I'll see JM's bubbles sometimes. The wake of his shallow kicks foaming white on the glassy surface.

Glinting balls of silver sardines swirl as we approach the rock reef just off Point Dume in Malibu, the stones crusted with spiny blue urchins and sprawling lavender starfish. There are striped bass and bright orange garibaldi, and when the sun is high, white bolts bounce off the sandy bottom, forming an underwater sundial.

We explore thick kelp forests, take deep nourishing breaths and follow the billowing light-green foliage to the floor. We slalom the giant stalks that recall a magic-beans fairy tale. Even on bright days, it's dark in the forest, patched together with sandy meadows saturated with turquoise light. I'll strain to make it all the way there and surface to deep breaths of relief, while waves thrash the sandstone cliffs, and the sun glistens gold on the tides.

On winter days we'll emerge on the beach shivering, our hands blue, teeth chattering. In the summer we'll stroll back to our starting point in the sun, warm and alive. We always laugh about something. No matter what else is going on in our lives, when the ocean has done its work, we always smile.

It took years for JM to get me in the water – and I had always previously had an excuse. Then came the summer of 2012. The Mayan apocalypse may never have materialised, but my personal apocalypse arrived right on time. I seriously injured my back and could no longer run. Couldn't even sit. The pain stayed with me for months. I was just 40

TO THE SEA!

I've swum with groups of sea lions 20-strong, with super-pods of dolphins, I've mingled with migrating whales

years old, and I couldn't move as well as most 70-year-olds. And it wasn't just my back that was wrecked, my marriage was on the verge of collapse. It was as if the emotional weight I was carrying was too much for my physiology and eventually everything blew up at once.

In the midst of the collapse, I met a clever massage therapist from northern Thailand, and she demanded I get in the water. So I found a pool at a nearby community college, and my back started to loosen. My lungs started working again, my body felt strong for the first time in forever. But there was no wild-nature love in the pool. There was never a deeper meaning.

JM called one day. I told him I was swimming and he convinced me to give the ocean a try. It was August. The water was 66°F (19°C) – warm enough to enjoy. The sea was crystal. We counted more than 50 bull rays gliding along the sandy bottom. After the swim, JM started talking about the positive ions, and how they funnel positivity into our cells by osmosis, or something. False or true, I was willing to believe. In those early days, the swim was the only good thing in my life.

Since then I've swum with groups of sea lions 20-strong, with super-pods of dolphins, I've mingled with migrating whales. We'll swim in stormy seas, navigate head-high surf and ride heavy currents sparked by swirling winds that lure in the kitesurfers. Sometimes we'll swim only a metre from one another and not make eye contact for a mile, each of us hidden in the trough of great swells.

We'll swim in soupy fog, we'll swallow bellyfuls of blue water, and watch flocks of pelicans skim the sea in formation. We've made friends with, and occasionally frightened, the lifeguards, who think we're mad. One confessed that he feels scared out by the rock reef: 'I prefer being at the top of the food chain.'

We know great white sharks patrol here, though we've never seen one. Occasionally they cross my mind on murky coldwater days, when we're outfitted like seals in our wetsuits. But usually I swim free and easy.

JM likes to tell a story about the 80-somethings he occasionally swims with at La Jolla Cove. There are a group of about a dozen of these wise, old masters – men and women who gather to swim year-round, without wetsuits. As JM was preparing to go out, one of those ladies came out of the drink with a goofy smile on her face. A bystander sipping coffee approached her and asked how it was.

'Amazing!' she said.

'Was there good visibility?' the bystander asked.

'Oh no, couldn't see anything out there.'

'Was it warm?'

'It was freezing,' said the swimmer. She was towel-drying and shivering by then.

'But you liked it?' asked the confused bystander.

'It was amazing!' she said, beaming gloriously. JM plans to be just like her one day. Me too. ●

TAKE A BATH

Hot or cold, clothed or not, nothing washes away the day like immersing yourself in a bath. Hungarians have long known this and the baths at the Gellert Hotel in Budapest are just one of several grand indoor and outdoor bathing spots in Hungary's capital. In volcanic Japan, steaming hot springs (onsens) are just as much part of the culture. Prefer a cold dip? Head to Finland in winter when 170 ice-holes are open for a post-sauna shock.

An Hour

HARNESS THE WIND

THE PERFECT DAY: A BOARD, A SAIL AND THE SEA, THE BEACH, THE SUN AND THE WAVES. KITE SURFING WILL BLOW YOU AWAY – LITERALLY.

A *giant, neon-coloured kite* is hovering above as you stand in a restless sea, a board under one arm and waves crashing around your legs. The lines connecting you to this awesome plaything appear to float upwards, powerless. And yet just a tweak of the bar in your hand sends the kite charging one way and then another. The strength of the wind is deceiving.

This is Pounda Beach in Paros, Greece, one of the best kitesurfing locations in Europe, thanks to the long, shallow shoreline and consistently strong winds. The air is sizzling with adrenalin-fuelled excitement.

Kitesurfers are zipping across the choppy water towards you at a frightening speed, seemingly about to crash into the beach. At the last minute they leap into the air and twist around, before speeding off in the other direction. They make it look easy. It is not.

It takes a few hours, and you spend most of your time being lifted violently out of the water and crashing face first into the sea. But eventually you learn how to dip the kite in a figure of eight formation, filling it with just the right amount of power. Suddenly you're up, skimming across the water on your board.

The feeling is one of exhilaration and unlike anything experienced before; as you lean back you're amazed by the force of the wind and the speed at which you're cutting through the waves. You laugh hysterically; you're instantly hooked. ●

You Only Live Once

HARNESS THE WIND

1 Ballooning

To really go where the wind blows, step into a balloon basket. There is no mechanism to steer, so you are literally at the mercy of whatever zephyrs you encounter. Fly over Cappadocia in Turkey, drift above the Serengeti's wildebeest in Tanzania or float above the Australian Outback.

2 Windsurfing

If speed is what you're after, then this is the sport for you. Top spots include Bonaire in the Caribbean, Tarifa in Spain and Maui in Hawaii. It can take a few years to master the skill, but its many devotees prove it is well worth the effort.

3 Ice sailing

An 18th-century Dutch commercial mode of transport, ice sailing has developed into a fast and exhilarating winter sport. It can be dangerous but this has not deterred people; it is currently practised in over 20 countries worldwide. All you need is a big expanse of thick ice, lots of wind – and no fear.

4 Kite flying

By far the easiest way to enjoy wind power is to fly a kite. To take this hobby to the next level, head to one of the many kite festivals around the world. Particularly popular in the East, there are huge, colourful gatherings every year in Japan, China, Indonesia and India.

TRIAL BY FIRE

FIND OUT WHERE TO TEST YOUR TASTE BUDS' TOLERANCE FOR EXTREME HEAT WITH THIS GUIDE TO THE WORLD'S HOTTEST CHILLIES. BUT CHECK THE HEAT-RATING SCOVILLE SCALE OF EACH FIRST...

Pure capsaicin
16 million units

Carolina Reaper
2,2 million

Pepper spray
2 million

Naga Bhut
Jolokia chilli
1 million

Habanero chilli
350,000

Bird Eye chilli
100,000

Jalapeno chilli
10,000

Tabasco sauce
2500

Trinidad Moruga Scorpion
Heat: *Hotter than the gates of hell*
Scoville heat units: *2 million*

The evil-looking Trinidad Moruga Scorpion has a fearsome sting in its tail, despite being knocked off the top spot by the Carolina Reaper. Sample this monster of a chilli pepper as hot sauce on the islands of Trinidad and Tobago.

Jalapeño
Heat: *Inglenook fireplace*
Scoville heat units: *10,000*

The original 'hot' chilli, this moderate scorcher is still grown in vast quantities in the Veracruz and Chihuahua districts of Mexico. Chipotles (smoked jalapeño peppers) are a key ingredient in Mexico's legendary adobo sauce.

Carolina Reaper
Heat: *Hotter than a thousand suns*
Scoville scale: *2.2 million*

More than 400 times hotter than Tabasco sauce, the world's hottest chilli will reduce body-building construction workers to tears. Order seeds from the PuckerButt Pepper Company of South Carolina and bring on the burn!

Naga Bhut Jolokia
Heat: *Napalm*
Scoville heat units: *1,001,300*

A key ingredient in Assamese curries, stir fries and chutneys, Naga 'ghost chillis' are also smeared over fences as a deterrent to wild elephants. To sample at source, visit food stalls at rural haat (tribal markets) in the central hills of Assam.

Habanero
Heat: *Incendiary*
Scoville heat units: *350,000*

When Mexicans want to turn up the heat, they reach for the habanero, an innocent-looking bell-shaped pepper containing the culinary equivalent of molten lava. Habaneros add pep to the scorching salsa served on the side with most meals in Mexico's Yucatan peninsula.

Bird Eye Chilli
Heat: *Eye-watering*
Scoville heat units: *100,000*

Compared to the record-breaking Carolina Reaper, Thailand's bird eye chilli is as weak as a kitten; try telling that to any traveller who has numbed their tongue on som tam, a fiery Thai salad made from raw bird eye chillies, lime juice and green papaya!

An Hour

TAKE A WATERFALL SHOWER

DON'T JUST CONTEMPLATE THE VIEW, TAKE THE PLUNGE! A DIP IN A WATERFALL POOL PROVIDES THE ULTIMATE WILD-SWIMMING EXPERIENCE.

Have you ever felt quite so refreshed? It's like being brushed all over with minty toothpaste or lightly slapped by a school of mermaids. You've been in cold water before; over the years, you've even been known to take several showers. But there's something about splashing alfresco beneath the spray of a real, rippling waterfall that makes you feel that bit more revived and alive.

Bursting up and breaking the surface like a model in a shampoo commercial, you survey your surroundings. This is Afu Aau Falls, a tempting water-tumble on Samoa's big island of Savaii. And, because Pacific-stranded Samoa is one of the remoter spots on the planet, there's no one else here. This ideal swim-spot seems to have been created just for you.

Rivulets drip over mossy rocks into the natural basin, and leafy vines drip down from the surrounding trees, as if in competition. Birds chirrup as you dip under, scramble out and leap back in. The pool is chill and clear – it makes your brain zing and your skin tingle. But swimming here isn't simply invigorating; it somehow makes you feel more a part of the place – as though, for a few hours only, you've been invited into Mother Nature's private club.

Of course, you can't just jump into any old waterfall. You don't want to stick your head under the 2832-tonnes-a-second that gushes over Niagara, or the heavy 108m-high splat of Victoria Falls. Plus all that plummeting power creates dangerous currents, froth and tumult at the bottom of a cascade. Some plunge pools are full of gnarly rocks or toothy crocs. But pick the right pool – perhaps a small stream-trickled mountain lake or a hidden gushing gorge (clothing optional) – and there's no finer nor more fun way to wash. ●

Tat Kuang Si Falls, Laos
These turquoise falls, 30km from Luang Prabang, are popular with locals and travellers alike. You can jump, dive or swing in by rope; a slippery jungle trail leads to the top.

Lower Ddwli Falls, Brecon Beacons, Wales
The clue's in the name: more than 20 pools dot a five-mile stretch of river in Waterfall Woods. Lower Ddwli has an arcing cascade, lots of swim space and, with luck, plentiful rainbows.

Rainbow Falls, Kerikeri, New Zealand
Walk the riverside trail, via kauri and totara trees, to reach this gorgeous gush, which tumbles over volcanic basalt into a perfect plunge pool.

Hot Springs Waterfall, Finca el Paraiso, Guatemala
A short hike leads to this natural spa: the sizzling thermal waters of the Rio Dulce (Sweet River) crash into an ice-cool pool, cloaked in luscious jungle.

An Hour

PUT IT ALL ON BLACK... NO, RED

In 2004, Briton Ashley Revell bet the sum total of all his worldy possessions – US$135,000 – on one spin of a roulette wheel in a Las Vegas casino. He put it all on red; the ball fell on no.7... red. But maybe black is the better bet? During a game of roulette at MonteCarlo's casino in 1913 the ball landed on black 26 times in a row. Gamblers lost millions of francs thinking it had to be red next... forgetting that the previous result has no influence on the next spin of the wheel.

MONTE CARLO CASINO IN MONACO   Getty/Steve Allen

An Hour

GET A CLOSE SHAVE

INDIAN BARBERS ARE THE SCOURGE OF FACIAL STUBBLE; SIT BACK AND LET A MAESTRO OF THE RAZOR WORK HIS MAGIC.

Before the invention of the disposable razor, shaving was an art form. The act of removing facial hair was an elegant dance, involving hogs' hair brushes, lashings of foam, delicate finger-work and a razor of the kind popularised by Sweeney Todd. Fortunately for travellers, this golden era of male grooming lives on in India, where a million backstreet barbers ply their trade with precision.

When sitting down for your first Indian shave, it pays to know the order of business. Step one is preparing the razor – most barbers use a cutthroat razor that takes a fresh disposable blade for every shave. Step two is the lather: shaving soap is whipped into a flurry of bubbles and applied liberally to chin and lip. Then the ballet begins. With gentle tugs and pinches, the barber will pull your facial skin taut and remove soap and stubble with graceful sweeps of the blade. Within minutes, you will make the transition from hairy caveman to well-groomed city gent.

Of course, once the shave begins, you are in the hands of the divine. If you have chosen a barber with homicidal tendencies, your journey ends here. Fortunately, the vast majority of barbers have worked out that slaying clients is a poor business model, and shaves are completed without so much as a nick. Removing stubble is just part of the process. Next comes a quick rub-down with astringent alum, a natural disinfectant that has been used since Vedic times, followed by a splash of cologne and a thorough face and head massage. The whole experience is surprisingly relaxing, if a little surreal. One essential tip – Indian men prefer moustaches so always remind the barber to trim the lip as well as the chin! ●

1 Havana, Cuba
If you want to live like Hemingway, begin the day with a dry martini and wet shave in a Havana barbers shop. In Cuba, the barber serves the multiple roles of hair-dresser, counsellor, gossip and confidant, and extra atmosphere is provided by whirling ceiling fans and salsa music on a crackling radio.

2 London, England
To make the most of a shave in London, it pays to have abundant facial hair like a Victorian pastor. Geo F Trumper of Curzon Street in Mayfair has been shaving the faces of well-heeled Londoners since 1875, and it even runs a shaving school where you can learn your own cutthroat technique.

3 Istanbul, Turkey
Moustaches don't happen all by themselves. They need to be groomed, as any moustachioed gentleman in Istanbul can confirm. A traditional Turkish shave extends to steam treatment with a hot towel, a snip of protruding nasal hair, and removal of offending ear hairs with a taut thread or a lit match.

4 Myanmar
In Myanmar, shaving has special significance. Enrolling as a Buddhist monk is a rite of passage for Burmese youngsters, and shaving the head is a milestone in that transition. Start your spiritual journey at one of Myanmar's forest monasteries; Pa-Auk has a long tradition of accepting foreign devotees.

An Hour

TAKE AN URBAN HIKE

WHILE AWAY A FEW HOURS ON THE SLOW PATH, AND SEE THE FAMILIAR ON FOOT. IT MAY NEVER LOOK THE SAME AGAIN.

Nobody walks in LA. A statement so true it's been immortalised in song. But walking in a city dominated by traffic and defined by freeways can give you a taste of the whole that's impossible at 35mph. Carved into a quilt of individuated neighborhoods, LA has a few connector boulevards that link these patchwork communities, and Sunset Boulevard is its most famous.

This sinuous 26-mile stroll from Union Station to the beach at Pacific Palisades takes about 15 hours to complete. Along the way, you'll skim downtown, and dodge the hipsters, immigrants and long-time locals who mingle in *taquerias* and *pananderías* of Echo Park. You'll glimpse the over-gentrified Silverlake, a 'hood Beck made famous, and wave at the Scientology complex in Hollywood. You'll be led along the famed Sunset Strip, punctuated by the landmark Château Marmont, all-powerful billboards, and the original House of Blues.

The rolling lawns, stately mansions and wide, empty sidewalks of Beverly Hills fade into paths that snake through the ivy where sidewalks should be. These trails are the exclusive domain of domestic workers as they hike between bus stops and their gigs in nearby Bel Air. Brentwood is next, then Dead Man's Curve, which Jan & Dean sang about in their 1966 tune based on Jan Berry's near-fatal wreck in his Stingray.

You'll climb the hills of the Pacific Palisades, home to folks like Dustin Hoffman and Tom Hanks, and then down you'll stroll toward the beach, stopping for some shade and perhaps a meditation in Paramahansa Yoganada's Lake Shrine, where George Harrison was eulogized in the Windmill Chapel.

In LA all things lead to the beach, and if you time it right, you can make it across town by sunset, where you may find yourself loving a city that you've never seen quite the same way. ●

LOS ANGELES BY NIGHT   Getty/GMG Software

You Only Live Once

WALK THIS WAY

 1

Sydney, Australia

Australia's largest city has one of the world's most spectacular urban coastlines. And you can walk the entire thing – all 94km of it – if you have a week to spare. The walk begins at Barrenjoey, at the tip of Sydney's northern beaches, and trips a sandy course to Manly before heading inland to the Harbour Bridge and southern shores of Sydney Harbour.

 2

New York City, USA

Everyone walks in NYC, and trying to single out a route might cause a fight. Still, we suggest starting at Washington Square Park in Greenwich Village and walking Fifth Ave, north past Bryant Park, into Midtown. Moving Uptown, skirt the perimeter of Central Park then continue to hike north through Marcus Garvey Park in Harlem, where that mythic street ends at the Harlem River.

 3

Berlin, Germany

Best known to cyclists, the Berlin Wall Trail follows the course of the wall that once divided West Berlin from East Germany. Seventeen years after the wall was famously breached (1989), it was transformed into a 160km hiking and cycling path. The trail is signposted and has interpretative boards detailing the 28-year story of the wall and Germany's division, including memorials to those who tried to escape.

4

Hong Kong, China

The Hong Kong Trail snakes 50km around Hong Kong Island, from Victoria Peak and its cracking views of Victoria Harbour to Tai Long Wan, a beautiful surf beach on the east coast. Take this route and you'll effectively be walking from the island's highest point to its lowest. The trail is divided into eight sections, some of which can be combined to turn the trail into a three- or four-day hike.

TOTAL ECLIPSE

NOTHING REMINDS US OF THE CELESTIAL BALLET UNFOLDING AROUND US AS WATCHING AN ECLIPSE OF THE SUN OR MOON. HERE'S WHEN AND WHERE TO SEE UPCOMING ECLIPSES.

TOTAL SOLAR ECLIPSES

When **8-9 March 2016**
Where **South and East Asia, West in Australia, much of Africa, Atlantic and Indian Oceans, Antarctica**

When **1 September 2016**
Where **South in Asia, North and East Australia, Pacific and Indian Oceans**

When **21 August 2017**
Where **West of Europe, North and East Asia, North and West of Africa, North America, north and west of South America, Pacific and Atlantic Oceans**

When **2 July 2019**
Where **South of North America, south and west of South America, Pacific Ocean**

When **4 December 2021**
Where **South of Australia, South of Africa, south of South America, Pacific, Atlantic and Indian Oceans, Antarctic**

TOTAL LUNAR ECLIPSES

When **26 February 2017**
Where **South and West Africa, much of South America, Pacific, Atlantic and Indian Oceans, Antarctica**

When **21 August 2017**
Where **South and East Asia, North and East Australia, Pacific and Indian Oceans**

When **31 January 2018**
Where **North and East of Europe, Asia, Australia, North and East of Africa, North America, north and west of South America, Pacific, Atlantic and Indian Oceans, Arctic and Antarctica**

When **27 July 2018**
Where **Europe, South and East of Asia, Australia, Africa, south of North America, South America, Pacific, Atlantic and Indian Oceans, Antarctica**

When **21 January 2019**
Where **Europe, Asia, North and South America, Pacific and Atlantic Oceans, Arctic**

SUN PICTURES CINEMA, BROOME, AUSTRALIA   Alamy/Hauke Dressler

STARLIT CINEMA

**KICK BACK FOR A COUPLE OF HOURS AT A THEATRE
WHERE THE BACKDROP IS AS DRAMATIC AS THE ACTION
ON SCREEN. CHOOSE YOUR SETTING WISELY AND YOU
CAN REALLY MAKE IT A MOVIE TO REMEMBER.**

E*very summer, all around the world,* you'll find cities setting up outdoor cinemas. But how many can promise you balmy nights under starry skies with virtually no chance of rain? And of those that can, how many can also deliver an illuminated ancient citadel on a giant rock catching your eye during a performance? Since 1935 the Cine Thisio in Athens, with the Acropolis towering in the background, has been doing just that, wooing tourists and locals alike.

You enter the oldest outdoor theatre in the city through its neon art deco entrance. Family-run since 1980, Cine Thisio shows a mix of classic films and new studio releases, and it takes the decision on what plays very seriously. Rather than distract, the 5th-century-BC Acropolis, and its flagship ruin the Parthenon, only enhance the experience, as does the old-school film projector and the rampant ivy that seems to cover everything except the seats and the screen.

In a world where you constantly view films on planes, phones, and all too often alone, the communal act of movie-watching feels magical, especially somewhere as stunning as this – it gives you goosebumps. You cosy up under your blanket, sup on a homemade sour-cherry drink and savour a freshly baked cheese pie, ready for the action to begin. ●

***Red Rocks Amphitheatre,
Colorado, USA***
At 2000m above sea level, the Red Rocks Amphitheatre sits in the shadow of two towering sandstone monoliths, providing both perfect acoustics and an awesome natural backdrop. Completed in 1941 and seating almost 10,000 people, its summer programme includes a mix of '80s, '90s and 2000s cult classics. Recent showings include *Point Break*, *The Blues Brothers* and *Mean Girls*.

Sun Pictures, Broome, Australia
The world's oldest outdoor cinema, Sun Pictures is located in the Chinatown district of Broome, in remotest Western Australia. The tin-fronted building started life as an Asian emporium, switching to showing silent movies in 1916. Now on the State Register of Heritage Places, it screens mainstream and indie movies under the stars. And it'll even provide mosquito repellent if you forget your own.

The Galileo, Cape Town, South Africa
From November to April each year, the super lush lawns of Kirstenbosch, Cape Town's oldest botanical garden, host cinephiles from all over the city. Set against the eastern slopes of Table Mountain, the site has gourmet food trucks or you can bring your own alcohol and pack a picnic.

Riviera Maya Film Festival, Mexico
Since 2012 the Riviera Maya Film Festival has sought to showcase Mayan people and culture with film screenings throughout the Quintana Roo region. These take place in various locations: actual cinemas; makeshift screens on the streets of Cancun and Tulum; and drive-in theatres, though the most enticing are the palm-fringed Caribbean beach screenings at Playa del Carmen, Tulum and Puerto Morelos.

GET A TATTOO*

HOLIDAY SNAPS FADE, SOUVENIRS ARE THROWN AWAY AND MEMORIES BECOME DISTANT. BUT GET INKED, AND YOU'LL REMEMBER THAT TRIP FOREVER.

Forget handicrafts or **Chang Beer T-shirts**, a tattoo is the only souvenir of Thailand that will literally last a lifetime. But why waste the opportunity by getting the same tribal armband as every Tom, Dick and Harry on Khao San Road? A tattoo is a commitment, and nothing shows more commitment than joining the queues of devotees at Wat Bang Phra for an intricate Buddhist *sak yant* tatt, etched by hand with a bamboo or metal spike.

Sak yant is more than just decoration. Every element of the design, from the depictions of tigers and elephants to the reams of blessings in Thai script and the complex grids of numbers and geometric forms, has profound spiritual meaning, designed to protect the bearer from harm. Consider it an amulet for good luck that you can't remove and lose after taking a shower.

The ritual is not for the faint hearted though. In *sak yant*, the customer is not king, and designs are selected by the monk administering the tattoos, intended as a blessing and a channelling of the divine. You will have to endure excruciating pain as the design is inked in a thousand tiny stabbing motions, and pay for the privilege with a Buddhist offering – either a bundle of incense or some flowers, candles or cigarettes, plus a few hundred baht to support the work of the monastery.

The reward is the feeling of shared human experience, as locals and foreigners, monks and businessmen are all united by the common thread of needle, ink and pain. Whether the tattoo renders you invulnerable to harm, as was believed in the days when Thai warriors were inked before heading into battle, is something only you can find out... ●

1

Sailor chic, Hawaii
Long before sleeves and tramp stamps, the tattoo was the mark of a sailor, with its own symbolic language of swallows, dice, snakes, eagles, daggers and damsels. Seek out veteran old-school tattooists on the island of Hawaii, where the legendary 'Sailor Jerry' Collins once practised his art on untold thousands of sailors and marines.

2

Samoan spectacular, Samoa
It was the Samoans who came up with the word tattoo – or more correctly 'tatau' – and the traditional art of *malofie* is still one of the benchmark tests of tattooing endurance. To adorn your body with a hand-tapped pattern of intricate lines from waist to knee, seek out members of the Sulu'ape family, hereditary tattoo masters since pre-colonial times.

3

Maori magic, New Zealand
In traditional Maori society, tattoos were the mark of a warrior, and it still takes a warrior's resolve to endure the pain of traditional *ta moko*, where designs are not so much etched as incised with a hammer and chisel. If that doesn't put you off, seek out trained *ta moko* artists in Rotorua and Auckland.

4

The Full Yakuza, Japan
In Japan, no self-respecting yakuza (gangster) would be seen dead in the steam room without a full-body *irezumi* tattoo. Applied by hand using a handmade needle brush, *irezumi* are the ultimate status symbol; a full-body design covering everything apart from the hands, feet and face can cost upwards of US$30,000.

69.3

miles per hour

speed that the fastest car ferry in the world, running between Montevideo in Uruguay and Buenos Aires in Argentina, can travel.

16:20:27

hours, minutes and seconds

current speed record for visiting all 270 London Underground stations, set by Geoff Marshall and Anthony Smith.

16.994

kilometres

distance covered in one hour while pulling a wheelie, performed by German bicycle rider Francesco Wiedemann in 2011.

43

minutes

duration that Brazilian surfer Picuruta Salazar spent riding the Pororoca, a tidal bore that creates a 4m-high wave that travels 800km inland up the Amazon River.

45

minutes

the time it can take venom of the Australian inland taipan to kill you. The snake grows up to length of 8 ft in length – don't tread on it.

206,864

number of bounces

performed on a pogo stick, achieved by James Roumeliotis, who bounced for 20 hours and 13 minutes in California in 2011.

6

hours

amount you need to subtract from international time in order to catch a bus if the timetable has been given to you in Swahili time.

68

minutes

the number of minutes you are looking back in time when observing Saturn through an Earth-based telescope.

7:18:55

hours, minutes and seconds

time it took Danial Jazaeri to complete the 1990 Prague City Marathon, while she was juggling a football with her feet without letting it touch the ground once.

14

hours

decompression stop time required by Jarrod Jablonski and Casey McKinlay after a 7-mile-long, 20-hour, point-to-point cave dive in Wakulla Springs, Florida in 2007.

360

maximum distance

in kilometres, you could travel by train in an hour – riding on an AGV Italo train (the Maglevs in China are faster but travel across short distances, taking less than an hour).

42

minutes

the time it takes to ski down Alpe d'Huez in France, which, at 16km, is the longest black run in the world.

ZIP IT!

Been bungy jumping? Zip lines should be next on your thrill-list. They're getting bigger and bolder; lines in Wales and Nepal run for more than 1.5km and send you flying at speeds of up to 160kph. But there's only one zip line where a passport is required: LimiteZero's zip line starts in Sanlúcar de Guadiana, Spain, but you'll land on the other side of the River Guadiana in Portugal. The whole experience takes 40 minutes but you'll gain an hour on landing due to Portugal's different time zone.

CROSSING THE RIVER GUADIANA WITH WWW.LIMITEZERO.COM   RFG Art Photography/R.F. Granada

COOK SOMETHING YOU CAUGHT

FORAGED FOOD IS THE ULTIMATE IN LOCAL FOOD. WHAT BETTER WAY IS THERE TO UNDERSTAND A PLACE THAN THROUGH YOUR STOMACH?

It's the antithesis to the ready meal: no premixed gloop, no additives (except maybe some soil); 'packaging' courtesy of Mother Nature. Foraging for food, and then magicking it into your own lunch, is simply the most satisfying way to eat. Not only do you get a wholesome feed but a primal reconnection with the earth, a sense that this is how eating used to be. Plus, there's also a cave-person smugness in knowing that, if all the supermarkets disappeared tomorrow, you could fend for yourself.

Autumn is bonanza time for foragers as fruits ripen on trees, berries appear as morsels of sweet delight on bushes – mind the thorns! – and mushrooms sprout from the damp ground. You need only keep your eyes open and a basket at the ready. In the seas and rivers, wild fish such as mackerel and salmon are readily caught.

Sometimes a professional guide will help point you in the right direction but usually asking locals for tips will be enough to get you harvesting the region's specialities for a couple of hours. ●

Pluck berries, Sweden
Swedes are serious about foraging. It's even written in their law: *allemansrätten* (every man's rights) grants permission to hike, camp and berry-pick on another's land, as long as it's done respectfully. Head out into the country's ample empty spaces in summer to find wild food – pick of the crops are sweet strawberries, golden cloudberries, blueberries and lingonberries.

Dive for scallops, Nova Scotia
Clinking masts, bright-painted huts, a salt-whiff on the breeze – the ocean defines Nova Scotia. Its waters are a veritable fish soup and, equipped with a Recreational Scallop Licence, you can dive down and take a portion for yourself. Scallop season runs from Easter to the end of July, and limits are set at 50 a day – quite enough for a magnificent mollusc feast. You can eat them straight from the shell.

Pick wild garlic, UK
Between March and May, many British woodlands start to stink. Wild garlic – or ransoms – grow rampant, their shiny green leaves and cheery white flowers cloaking many an undergrowth, and infusing the air with anti-vampiric fumes. Boot up and hike off with a pair of scissors – the leaves are best snipped carefully at the stem, and more flavoursome before the plants begin to bloom.

Funghi, France
In the great forests of eastern France autumn's seasonal delicacy is the mushroom, piles of which you will see in the town markets. If picking your own it's best to stick to a couple of varieties you can identify with certainty. Start with chanterelles, which are the colour and smell of apricots, and the bulbous cep. And don't be put off by the name of *trompettes de la mort* (trumpets of death) – they're tasty.

FRESHLY PICKED SCANDINAVIAN BERRIES   James Bedford

An Hour

WALK

OF

LIFE

NICOLA WILLIAMS RECALLS HER FRENCH WEDDING

It's fair to say my mother was horrified when I gently suggested, a few days before my marriage, that the groom and I might walk the 2km from church to wedding reception. On the day many guests were shocked too, so inbred is that impulse in our fast-paced lives to jump in the car for the shortest of journeys. Yet when my husband, beneath an exultant shower of rice on the church porch, grabbed my hand and jubilantly cried 'Join us in our first walk of life together!' stilettos, posh frocks and the wheels parked around the corner were momentarily forgotten. Everyone followed.

Two decades later, that slow celebratory walk through sun-baked vineyards in the softly rolling Beaujolais hills in France, remains one of the best walks of my life. Spontaneity and simplicity cast their spell that day, as we walked with best friends from two lives along a bewitching country lane. In a curvaceous sweep our path unfurled from the stone chapel, past a 19th-century marble fountain on the village square and uphill to the resplendent fairy-tale castle of Château de Varennes. Ancient milestones charted our route and the pace was no quicker than snail-slow as the wedding party processed serenely past serried rows of leafy green Gamay vines, pregnant with the promise of autumn's cherry-red wine. The sleek, white pencil dress sculpted to my frame by a Lyonnais designer and the strappy heels purchased a few weeks prior in Paris were *naturellement* as impractical as my mother had feared, but quite frankly, I could have been wearing hiking boots, so certain was my step.

The final curve in the road raised the curtain on a dazzling mirage of thick, gold-stone walls and richly decorated, Renaissance turrets – a fitting climax to a magnificent walk. An interlude between the hypnotic solemnity of the church service and the mad partying until dawn that was to ensue inside those sturdy castle walls, this short Beaujolais walk had been an unwitting celebration of love, life and friendship in glorious slow motion.

That slow celebratory walk through sun-baked vineyards in the softly rolling Beaujolais hills remains one of the best walks of my life

An Hour

You Only Live Once

SWIM WITH FISH

**VENTURE BENEATH THE SURFACE OF THE OCEANS TO SEE
HOW THE OTHER TWO-THIRDS OF THE PLANET LIVES.**

Everyone knows how the Jaws theme goes. You can guarantee it will be going through your mind as you plunge into the cold, choppy water of South Africa with only an aluminium cage between you and the ocean's apex predator. Diving with great white sharks, while controversial, remains one of the world's great adrenalin rushes and the Gansbaai in the Southern Cape is the ideal place to swim with the big fish. Numerous companies offer dives in Gansbaai's Shark Alley but look for the operators who invest some of their profits back into shark conservation.

Elsewhere in the world, there are sharks with which you can swim without the need for a cage. On either side of the Americas hammerhead sharks go about their business without taking too much notice of humans. Around Bimini in the Bahamas great hammerheads, some up to 6m in length, scour the shallow sea floor for stingrays. On the other side of Central America, lies Cocos Island, described by Jacques Cousteau as the most beautiful island in the world. It's a world-class dive location thanks to the schools of scalloped hammerhead sharks that gather on the edge of the island's seamount. Dive here in December and you'll witness one of nature's great wonders – but thanks to demand in Asia for their fins, hammerheads are highly threatened by illegal fishing so no-one knows for how much longer they will gather here. ●

① Whale sharks, Ningaloo Marine Park, Australia

This World Heritage-listed marine park protects the full 300km length of the exquisite Ningaloo Reef in Western Australia, often just 100m offshore. Over 220 species of coral have been recorded and their spawning attracts the park's biggest drawcard, the whale shark. These gentle giants can reach up to 18m long.

② Stingrays, Cayman Islands

Watch a dozen metre-wide rays, each armed with a venomous barb, glide towards you at Stingray City in Grand Cayman's North Sound. With water just 3m deep, visibility is superb; kit up and prepare to feel the rays' sucking kiss. The coolest season is December to April.

③ Tropical fish, Bora Bora

Strap on a snorkel and fins and you're equipped for one of the world's most most colourful wildlife show, just inches beneath the surface of the ocean. Tropical fish, including Sergeant Major fish, and Pacific double-saddle butterfly fish, swarm the fragile coral gardens beneath you.

④ Queensland groupers, Australia

Off the east coast of Australia, in the protected waters of the Great Barrier Reef, giant groupers up to 3m in length still lurk in dark corners, patrolling the reef for prey. Divers consider them intelligent and inquisitive fish; some are known to hang out at the renowned wreck dive at the SS Yongala, 22km from Alva Beach.

LOOK UP!

You don't have to be standing in Florence's Uffizi gallery to have your mind blown by simply looking up once in a while. We spend most of our time at eye level and a change of perspective opens up a new dimension of marvels: the architectural details of Glasgow, the abstract patterns of a forest canopy and, of course, the urban canyons of New York City.

PARK AVENUE, NEW YORK   Getty/Lotus Carroll

You Only Live Once

An Hour

CLASSIC COCKTAILS

TASTE IS A SHORTCUT TO MEMORY: DON'T JUST TRY AN ICONIC COCKTAIL IN THE CITY IT WAS INVENTED, TAKE THE RECIPE HOME FOR WHENEVER YOU WANT TO RETURN.

NEGRONI, FLORENCE

THE METHOD

1 part gin
1 part Martini Rosso
1 part Campari
orange peel for garnish

Combine all the ingredients in an ice-filled glass. Add a twist of orange peel to garnish.

THE TALE

The story goes that in 1919 Count Camillo Negroni of Florence asked for a more potent version of his favourite cocktail, the Americano. The barman switched soda water for gin and the lively little Negroni was born. Florence remains the ideal place to sample one as an aperitif.

MOJITO, HAVANA

THE METHOD
1 part lime juice
2 parts white rum
1 teaspoon of sugar
mint leaves
soda water

Muddle the lime juice, sugar and mint leaves in a glass. Fill the glass two-thirds full of ice and add the rum. Top up with soda water.

THE TALE
Ernest Hemingway would relieve the heat of Cuba with this refreshingly minty drink. It was a refinement of the mint-sugar-rum-and-lime 'Drake' and first recorded in the 1930s.

SINGAPORE SLING, SINGAPORE

THE METHOD
1 part gin
1 part cherry brandy
1 part Bénédictine
1 part fresh lime juice
2 parts soda water
1 dash of Angostura bitters
Mix all the ingredients, except the soda water
and bitters, in an ice-filled glass. Stir in the water then add a splash of bitters.

THE TALE
At the Long Bar in Raffles hotel, Singapore, the gin sling was the perfect antidote to the steamy climate; then a barman added a dash of fruitiness to invent the Singapore Sling.

64

SIDECAR, PARIS

THE METHOD

1 part Cointreau
1 part lemon juice
2 parts cognac

Pour all the ingredients into a cocktail shaker filled with ice. Shake well then strain into a chilled cocktail glass.

THE TALE

The Ritz Hotel in Paris, France claims the Sidecar as its own creation in the first decade or two of the 20th century. But after a couple of these punchy numbers it's no surprise that memories are hazy. The French School advocates equal parts of the ingredients; the English School prefers a little extra depth. ●

An Hour

THE PEAK DISTRICT NATIONAL PARK, ENGLAND   Justin Foulkes

PERFECT PARKS FOR PICNICS

YOU DON'T HAVE TO TRAVEL FAR FROM CITIES FOR GOOD TIMES OUTDOORS – JUST PACK A HEARTY LUNCH.

To the thousands of Manchester's industrial workers in the early 1930s, a walk in the Peak District was their only chance of getting any fresh air. Every Sunday – the one full day workers had off each week – Manchester London Road (now Piccadilly) railway station was packed full of ramblers excitedly waiting to explore the hills and moors. There was only one problem – they weren't allowed on most of them, least of all Kinder Scout, the highest hill in the Peaks.

What became known as the Kinder Trespass when, on 24 April 1932, 400 ramblers struck out across the fields, evaded Derbyshire's constabulary, and scrambled up the side of Kinder Scout, eventually led to the enshrining of Britain's first national park. And what was once an escape from the cramped, noisy factories below, remains a respite from a city's sound and fury.

Today, the sunlight seems to dance across the peak as it warms your back, picking out flashes of yellow moorland grass and rich green fern for a moment before skitting off to highlight a patch of purple heather. The clouds turn from black to white, before dissipating to reveal a widescreen blue sky, and Kinder turns with it. The dark, brooding moorland menace transforms into a glowing kaleidoscope of colour, beckoning you to clamber to the top. You've packed a pork pie for sustenance; sometimes it's the simple pleasures on your doorstep that are the most memorable. ●

You Only Live Once

HIKING IN ABRUZZO NATIONAL PARK, ITALY   Getty/Andrew Bain

PERFECT PARKS FOR PICNICS

Abruzzo National Park, Italy
Barely two hours from Rome, these granite peaks and beechwood forests rarely make it onto most people's Italy must-see lists. But they should: this is northern Italy at its most medieval, a wilderness where even short walks offer stupendous views. The main town is Pescasseroli, a jumble of pink stone houses nestled in a valley.

Shenandoah National Park, USA
One of the most spectacular national parks in the US, Shenandoah is just 120km west of Washington, DC. In spring and summer the wildflowers explode in a blaze of colour and in autumn the leaves burn a bright red and orange.

Ku-ring-gai Chase National Park, Australia
On Sydney's north shore, Ku-ring-gai Chase sits across Pittwater from the narrow peninsula of Palm Beach. On display is that classic Sydney cocktail of bushland, sandstone outcrops and water vistas, plus walking tracks, Aboriginal rock engravings and popular picnic areas.

The Black Forest, Germany
Between Strasbourg and Stuttgart, the Black Forest region is a vast nature playground featuring peaks and lakes irresistible to hikers, cyclists, bathers and boaters. Day trips are possible but stay for a weekend to explore the Panoramaweg and more scenic picnic spots.

STAND AT THE BOTTOM OF THE BURJ KHALIFA, THE WORLDS TALLEST SKYSCRAPER, IN DUBAI

SWIM WITH WHALE SHARKS OFF NINGALOO REEF ON THE CORAL COAST OF WESTERN AUSTRALIA

TREK TO EVEREST BASE CAMP AND TAKE IN VIEWS OF THE WORLDS HIGHEST MOUNTAIN

STARGAZE AT GALLOWAY FOREST PARK, SCOTLAND, THE FIRST DARK SKY PARK TO BE CREATED IN BRITAIN

HELP RENOWNED SCULPTOR ED JARRET BUILD A GIANT SANDCASTLE

WALK ALONG THE SOUTH RIM OF THE GRAND CANYON

WATCH THE SURFERS AT NAZAR, PORTUGAL

GO FOR A DRIVE IN THE MIDNIGHT RIDER, THE WORLDS LARGEST LIMOUSINE

SURF THE SAND DUNES OF NAMIBIA ON A TRADITIONAL SWAKOPMUN BOARD

LOSE YOURSELF IN THE DUBAI MALL, UNITED ARAB EMIRATES

EXPLORE THE VAST WILDERNESS OF SPARSELY POPULATED GREENLAND

FOLLOW IN THE FOOTSTEPS OF ERNEST SHACKLETON ON A TRIP TO ANTARCTICA

TAKE A HELICOPTER RIDE OVER FOZ DIGUACU, BRAZIL

DIVE THE GREAT BLUE HOLE, BELIZE, TO SEE THE MARINE STALACTITES

ROAM AMONGST CALIFORNIAS REDWOOD GIANTS

SWIM IN THE TRANSLUCENT WATERS OF AMORGOS, GREECE, WHERE THE BIG BLUE WAS FILMED

GET CLOSE TO ONE OF THE 70,000 KALAHARI ELEPHANTS IN CHOBE NATIONAL PARK, BOTSWANA

SIZE UP THE GIANT VEGETABLES AT THE NATIONAL GARDENING SHOW IN SOMERSET

PLAY A ROUND OF MINI-GOLF IN THE WORLDS LARGEST TENT, THE KHAN SHATYR, IN ASTANA, KAZAKHSTAN

SINK YOUR TEETH INTO THE ABSOLUTELY RIDICULOUS BURGER AT MALLIES SPORTS BAR, MICHIGAN, USA

GET LOST IN TRANSLATION IN TOKYO

ENJOY SOME RETAIL THERAPY IN MACYS, NEW YORK

50 WAYS TO FEEL SMALL
By Manfreda Cavazza

SPLASH OUT ON A VIRGIN GALACTIC SPACE FLIGHT

HEAD TO MONTEREY CANYON, OFF CALIFORNIA, TO SPOT BLUE WHALES

FALL IN LOVE WITH THE MARBLE WALLS, HIGH CEILINGS AND ELABORATE CHANDELIERS OF MOSCOWS IMPRESSIVE TUBE NETWORK

GO HIKING, RAFTING OR MOUNTAINEERING IN SOUTHERN SIBERIA, ONE OF THE LEAST TOURISTED AREAS IN ASIA

FIND THE REPLICA WILLYS WW2 JEEP ON DISPLAY IN THE EMIRATES NATIONAL AUTO MUSEUM

GO ON A CRUISE UP THE RIVER NILE

GO CAMEL TREKKING IN THE SAHARA DESERT

GO ON A TOUR OF BOEINGS EVERETT FACTORY, WASHINGTON, HOME TO THE 777 AND 787 DREAMLINER PRODUCTION LINES

GO PARAGLIDING IN TASMANIA

MARVEL AT THE LITTLE PEOPLE FAR BELOW ON A HOT AIR BALLOON RIDE OVER BAGAN, BURMA

SEARCH FOR DOROTHYS RUBY RED SLIPPERS ALONG THE ENDLESS CORRIDORS OF THE SMITHSONIAN INSTITUTE, WASHINGTON

WATCH THE SUN GO DOWN ON THE MUNDI MUNDI PLAINS IN NEW SOUTH WALES, AUSTRALIA

CLIMB MT KILIMANJARO

SAIL ACROSS THE PACIFIC OCEAN

DRIVE THE PAN-AMERICAN HIGHWAY, FROM PRUDHOE BAY, ALASKA TO USHUAIA, ARGENTINA

FLY OVER THE MUNDI MAN, THE WORLDS LARGEST ARTWORK, IN THE AUSTRALIAN OUTBACK

TAKE IN THE 360 DEGREE VIEWS OF LONDON FROM THE SHARD

SPOT EXOTIC BIRDS IN BRAZILS PANTANAL, THE WORLDS LARGEST (AND MOST COLOURFUL) SWAMP

BOOK A HOLIDAY ON BOARD ALLURE OF THE SEAS, THE BIGGEST CRUISE SHIP EVER BUILT

PAY HOMAGE TO THE SPRING TEMPLE BUDDHA IN HENAN, CHINA

DRIFT DOWN THE AMAZON RIVER ON A CANOE TOUR

MOVE INTO THE SUPERIOR HARBOR SOUTH BREAKWATER LIGHTHOUSE ON LAKE SUPERIOR, FREE TO ANYONE WILLING TO LOOK AFTER IT

VISIT SUE, THE SEVEN TONNE T-REX AT THE FIELD MUSEUM IN CHICAGO

DIVE THE GREAT BARRIER REEF, THE WORLDS LARGEST STRUCTURE COMPOSED OF LIVING ENTITIES

CLIMB THE 320 STEPS TO THE TOP OF THE DOME OF ST PETERS IN ROME AND TAKE IN THE VIEWS

LEAVE YOUR MARK ON THE NEW GRAFFITI SECTION OF THE GREAT WALL OF CHINA

HOLIDAY IN HOLLAND, HOME TO THE TALLEST POPULATION IN THE WORLD

EXPLORE THE NEVER-ENDING VINEYARDS OF CALIFORNIAS WINE COUNTRY

An Hour

BUY THOSE BOOTS

SOMETIMES IT DOESN'T PAY TO DITHER - WHAT MIGHT SEEM LIKE FRIVOLOUS FASHION MAY JUST BE SOMETHING YOU WALK THROUGH YOUR WHOLE LIFE IN.

The cowboy boots are standing on a shelf at the Boot Barn off I-65, just north of Nashville. They are dove grey with a subtle stitch pattern of curling vines, and they cost US$160, a fortune for you right now. Everything about them feels luxurious and long-lasting, from the cushioned footbed, to the thick rubber heels, to the heavy leather pull-straps.

When you return home, you wear them out to dinner with your new boyfriend, who pronounces them 'totally badass'. A year later, you wear them out to Utah to meet his parents for the first time, returning home with the toes covered in red desert dust. Every time you see your boyfriend's father after that, he asks you where your boots are. A year later, your boyfriend gets a fellowship in Australia, and you pack the boots off to Sydney in his suitcase before following a month later. Boyfriend, boots and you traverse the Sydney Harbour Bridge, circle Uluru, and trek through fields of curious marsupials on Kangaroo Island.

You aren't wearing your boots the night you decide to get married (you and your boyfriend, not you and the boots), but you had them on under your bias-cut silk wedding dress when you wed on a North Carolina goat farm six months later. Less than two years after that, your now-husband takes a job in Hong Kong. There's a photo of you on your first day in your new city, standing at the edge of Victoria Harbour before the splendid and terrifying skyline, wearing your (now-resoled) boots. When US$160 carries you through that much life, it's the definition of money well spent. ●

1

English brogues
Joseph Cheaney & Sons has been making classic men's shoes since 1886. Its five-eyelet wingcap Oxfords are the definition of timeless good taste, while the Imperial Sandringham wingtips have the same oak-bark leather soles British bankers and barristers have been wearing for nearly a century and a half.

2

Greek sandals
What better captures the warm weather, devil-may-care spirit of the Mediterranean than a pair of classic leather sandals? At Melissinos Art in Athens, sandals are oiled, shaved, and fitted to your feet on the spot. Just what you need for many years of sure-footed island-hopping.

3

Chinese slippers
Cheap, satin slippers are ubiquitous in China: you can buy them at any street market. But if you want lasting luxury, the designer Mary Ching offers a collection of slippers with a twist, in materials like cashmere, silk and suede, with embellishments from mink and mother-of-pearl to Swarovski crystal.

4

Australian riding boots
Founded in 1932 by the legendary bushman Reginald Murray Williams, RM Williams makes boots rough enough for ranch use and sleek enough to wear under a suit. Look for them in ostrich, kangaroo and crocodile, as well as the classic leather.

TAKE A SKYWALK

Walk above the clouds on the latest lofty lookouts. The Grand Canyon Skywalk was one of the first to allow visitors to walk on a glass platform cantilevered over the cliffside. In Jasper National Park, Alberta, Canada, the Glacier Skywalk has views over the Columbia Icefield. Or you can step into the void on Mont Blanc's Aiguille du Midi. Finally, the Aurland Lookout perches above Sognefjord in western Norway.

AURLAND LOOKOUT BY SAUNDERS ARCHITECTURE IN WESTERN NORWAY   ©Bent Renè Synnevåg

An Hour

You Only Live Once

FEEL THE PASSION

BE SWEPT ALONG BY THE WORLD'S MOST COMMITTED SPORTS FANS IN BELGIUM AND BEYOND FOR A COMMUNAL EXPERIENCE TO REMEMBER.

All around you there are men and women, young and old, waving the black-on-yellow flag of the Flemish Lion, waiting for the racers of the annual Liège-Bastogne-Liège bike race. You're standing, tight-packed, beside the road up the Cote de Saint-Roch, a short but steep (at 12% gradient) climb in the far east of Belgium. There's a misty drizzle – this is Belgium in April, after all – but the crowd is warmed by frites (potato chips) and beer brewed in the village of Achouffe nearby. The thrum of a helicopter in the distance means that the riders are approaching and the noise builds and the crowd pushes together ever more tightly along the narrow road. Here they come! A car and half a dozen motorbikes force their way through, then the leading riders emerge and are engulfed by the crowd so that it becomes hard to tell rider from fan.

In Belgium, cycling is the national sport, and nowhere are the crowds more numerous or passionate than at the Spring Classics, a series of early-season bike races of which the 250km Liège-Bastogne-Liège, founded in 1892, is the oldest. The heavenly triumvirate of beer, bikes and frites tempts vast numbers of fans; whatever the weather, Belgium's bleak cobbled roads are lined three or four deep with supporters, waving flags and yelling encouragement to their heroes. The Spring Classics, long, tough races over rough roads, favour a hardened breed of cyclist and the same is true of the spectators; this is free, boisterous, street-side entertainment, and it's a credit to cycling's working-class roots that it has been largely unchanged over the decades. ●

ESSENDON FANS ON GRAND FINAL DAY AT THE MCG, MELBOURNE   Getty/Phil Weymouth

FEEL THE PASSION

1
Kentucky Derby, USA
'The Most Exciting Two Minutes in Sport' occurs in Louisville, Kentucky, on the first Saturday of May. This horse race – 'decadent and depraved' according to Hunter S Thompson – sees the largest crowds in the infield area, fuelled by mint juleps and consumed by winning and losing on the 2km race.

2
Australian football, Melbourne
Winter is becoming spring and the Australian Rules footie season is drawing to a close at one of the world's great sporting stadiums, the MCG. It's Grand Final day in the AFL heartland of Victoria and the league's family-friendly vibe continues to the last kick of the season. No matter who you're barracking for, sport is the winner on this day.

3
Rugby, New Zealand
In the tiny nation of New Zealand rugby rules supreme. Here, 150,000 people lace up boots at the weekend to play, and this grassroots appeal spills out at grounds such as Yarrow Stadium in New Plymouth, Taranaki. Fans are close to the players, making for an intense atmosphere, with Mt Taranaki brooding in the background.

4
College American football, Georgia, USA
Forget the Superbowl, to find the most passionate American football fans you have to go to college gridiron games – and especially the great rivalry matches such as Georgia's Bulldogs against Florida's Gators – aka the 'World's Largest Outdoor Cocktail Party'.

FREEFALL!

What compels a person to jump out of a perfectly serviceable aircraft and fall to earth at 120mph? Skydivers give conflicting answers: it's the adrenalin rush and the sense of peace. It's the freedom and the responsibility. Find out for yourself by making a jump; most nations have a parachuting association that accredits schools.

An Hour

Chapter

02

In which we lose ourselves at festivals and carnivals, dine like kings, party all night in cities and fall asleep

DAY

in some extraordinary settings.

Then we spend a day or two in the outdoors,

watching wildlife, walking by moonlight

and seeking out the most silent places in the world.

Finally, we face our greatest fears, whatever they may be.

Chapter

02

LOST AND FOUND AT CARNIVAL

**LEAVE YOUR INHIBITIONS AT THE AIRPORT AND CLIMB
INTO A DESTINATION'S SKIN. SPEND A DAY WITH THE LOCALS,
LEARNING HOW TO REALLY LET YOUR HAIR DOWN.**

To get the most out of Carnival in Brazil's northeastern city of Olinda, you shouldn't so much go with the flow, as completely give in to it. Nowhere here will you find the regimented rows of security railings, ticket blockades and spectator seating that defines Carnival in Rio. In Olinda there are no spectators; people, processions, musicians and Carnival freaks all funnel through the town's narrow, cobbled, disorientating streets as one. If you're here, you are Carnival.

So give up on crowd control. Be irresponsible. Dance. Don't sleep. Find friends, then lose them again. Surrender to the insistent, comedic, skipping rhythm of frevo, the musical lifeblood of Olinda's Carnival; a high-speed military two-step-cum-polka (its name taken from the Brazilian word 'to boil'), it will have you flinging your limbs around like your flip-flops are on fire. Follow brass bands led by beaten-up trombones and tarnished trumpets. Bounce over cobbles holding a multicoloured umbrella – the symbol of the region – above your sun-addled head. And wonder not how the thing got into your hands.

Get drawn into a maracatu drumming procession and try, in vain, to shout for directions above the cacophony of cowbells, whistles and hundred-strong battery of alfaias (drums). You are lost. Embrace it. Embrace someone. Most people will be: arms and shoulders intertwined, jumping, dancing, losing integral parts of their homemade costumes, noting them being crumpled underfoot with a smile. Encounter everyone from Zorro to Thor during the 'superheroes parade', comprising costumed characters the surreal likes of which never graced the pages of a Marvel magazine. Stroll alongside 'Supermarket Man', riding in a shopping trolley wearing little more than a smile and an oversized papier-mâché carrot, and concede that what it lacks in sophistication, Olinda makes up for in genuine party spirit. ●

A Day

You Only Live Once

LOST AND FOUND AT CARNIVAL

 1

Lazarim Carnival, Portugal
14–17 February 2015
This pagan-rooted, pre-Lent Carnival pageant, in Portugal's northern interior is characterised not by a parade of semi-clad dancers but macabre hand-carved wooden masks sculpted with devil horns and skull-like faces. The festival's focal point is the ritual burning of male and female effigies and a theatrically read poem of judgement called The Testaments. Deliciously creepy, medieval mayhem.

 2

Junkanoo, Bahamas
26 December & 1 January
This Bahamian Carnival–Mardi Gras hybrid, said to date back to plantation-era Christmas parties, sees the nation's streets overrun with merenguing masses, dressed in rainbow costumes and headdresses like towering birds of paradise. Once midnight mass is finished, off roll the floats; musicians drive the crowd wild with goat-skin drums, cowbells, conch-shell horns and whistles.

 3

Ati-Atihan, Philippines
24–30 January 2015
This Christo-pagan beaded bacchanal, known as 'the mother of all Philippines festivals', is held on Kalibo, an island in a beach-fringed archipelago only an hour by plane from Manila. Expect tribal dance, fearsome face-paint and parades, all in celebration of Santo Niño (Infant Jesus). And on the last day, a tear-it-up, torchlit dance-off.

 4

Bon Om Tuk, Cambodia
Usually November
When the Tonle Sap River does an about-turn and flows in reverse, it signals party season for Cambodia. Honouring this annual hydro happening, coinciding with an auspicious Buddhist full moon, are three days of fireworks, feasting and dragon boat racing; the wildest celebrations are seen along Phnom Penh's Sisowath Quay.

ROAST ABERDEEN ANGUS BEEF AND YORKSHIRE PUDDING, BRITAINS BEST

FELAFEL, MIDDLE EAST CHICKPEAS

SAVOUR IRISH STEW, IRELANDS ONE-POT WONDER

BAOZI PILLOWY STEAMED AND BUNS FROM CHINA

PIRI-PIRI CHICKEN FLAME-GRILLED IN MOZAMBIQUE

LAYER LAMB AND EGGPLANT FOR GREECES MOUSSAKA

WIENER SCHNITZEL, VEAL CUTLETS FROM AUSTRIA

THEN SLOW-COOKED

JERK PORK MARINATED IN CHILLIES AND SPICES

HEART AND SOUL OF MEXICO FOOD

MOLE IS THE SMOKY SWEET SPICY

TRY BUN CHA, FRAGRANT GRILLED PORK, HERBS AND NOODLES FROM VIETNAM

BAO, A BEEFY BROTH, IS VIETNAMS ULTIMATE COMFORT FOOD

BAKLAVA, TURKISH FLO PASTRY WITH CHOPPED NUTS AND BUTTER

FOR AUTHENTIC PIZZA NO STUFFED CRUST YOU GOT TO GO TO ITALY

SOM TAM IS THAILANDS SPICY TART

CRUNCHY, SALTY AND SWEET PAPAYA SALAD

A LARGA OF SEAFOOD, COCONUT AND NOODLES, IS SOUTHEAST ASIA

THE RICE IS THE TRUE STAR OF SUSHI IN JAPAN

CHURRASCO CON CHIMICHURRI, ARGENTINAS STEAK WITH SPICY SAUCE OVER A FIRE

UMM ALI, A BREAD PUDDING, IS THE MIDDLE EASTS MOST SCRUMPTIOUS DESSERT

TAKE A TRIP TO TIBET FOR THE BEST MOMO DUMPLINGS

ENGLANDS LANCASHIRE HOT POT A WORKING-MANS CASSEROLE OF LAMB, LEEKS AND POTATOES

INDULGE YOUR SWEET TOOTH WITH A SLICE OF SHARLOTKA IN RUSSIA

GET TO GRIPS WITH CONCH, THE BAHAMAS GIANT SNAIL

TAPAS ARE SPAINS COMPANIONS TO A KILLER GLASS OF SHERRY

KUAYTIAW, THAILANDS FAST-FOOD NOODLE SOUP

BRIK IS A SAVOURY PASTRY PACKET FROM TUNISIA

GOULASH, HUNGARYS PAPRIKA- AND POTATO-RICH MEAT STEW

MIX RICE AND SEAFOOD IN A FLAT PLAN FOR SPANISH PAELLA

WRAP PORK IN LEAVES AND COOK SLOWLY FOR COCHINITA PIBIL IN MEXICO

50 DISHES TO TRY BEFORE YOU DIE
By Colin Eastwood

THE BURRITO, MEXICOS STREET-FOOD CLASSIC, IS FOUND AT FOOD TRUCKS AROUND THE WORLD

BOBOTIE IS SOUTH AFRICAS CUSTARDTOPPED MEAT CASSEROLE

CHIVITO IS URUGUAYS BASIC BEEFY SANDWICH

PHAT THAI, NOODLES, CRUNCHY PEANUTS, LIME AND CHILLI

PIEROGI ARE POLANDS CRESCENT-SHAPED DOUGHY DELIGHTS

FEAST ON FEIJOADA, BRAZILS NATIONAL DISH OF BEANS AND BEEF

FRESH BREAD FROM FRANCES BAKERS DOESNT DISAPPOINT

BIRYANI IS INDIAS REGAL RICE DISH

CULLEN SKINK, A SMOKY, FISHY SOUP FROM SCOTLAND, MADE WITH SMOKED HADDOCK

RICE, CHICKEN AND SHRIMP ARE STIR-FRIEND IN INDONESIA FOR NASI GORENG

AMERICAS HANDHELD CLASSIC, THE HAMBURGER, CAN BE SUBLIME

SINK YOUR TEETH INTO CEVICHE, ZESTY MARINATED FISH FROM PERU

IN VIETNAM ROLL DELICATE BO BIA IN RICE PAPER

CRISPY-SKINNED PEKING DUCK IS CHINAS CULINARY CALLING CARD

BERRIES, BREAD AND SUGAR MAKE ENGLANDS SUMMER PUDDING WORTH THE WAIT

CASSOULET FLAVOUR-PACKED MEAT AND BEANS FROM FRANCE

HANG OUT AT A HANGI BEACH BARBEQUE IN NEW ZEALAND

SWEAT OUT A FIERY CHONGQING HOT POT IN CHINA

RICE, FRESH VEEGTABLES AND A SPICY SAUCE FORM SOUTH KOREAS BIBIMBAP

CLAM CHOWDER, SEAFOOD SOUP FROM AMERICAS NORTHEAST SEABOARD

SLEEP IN A CASTLE

OH, WHAT A NIGHT! PLAY OUT ALL YOUR PALACE FANTASIES AND LAY YOUR HEAD ON THE PILLOWS OF KINGS AND QUEENS OF YORE.

You – *yes, little old you* – are sleeping where Robert the Bruce; Mary, Queen of Scots; Oliver Cromwell; Sir Walter Scott; even Queen Victoria slept. All these luminaries have walked within Dalhousie Castle's thick 13th-century walls in Scotland – and so can you.

The ancestral home of the Ramsay family became a hotel in 1972, as many such piles have had to in these less aristocratically friendly times. However, it still echoes with its illustrious past. The Grey Lady, the spirit of a 16th-century laird's mistress, reputedly haunts the stairs. Fixtures from the original drawbridge can be seen above the door and a Civil War–musket shot is still embedded in the outer walls.

You'll lay on a plush four-poster bed, in a room of 16th-century furnishings, exposed stone walls and a profusion of tartan drapery. There's a fire roaring in the drawing room, a restaurant in the dungeon, and a spa in the old storage vaults. Pose by suits of armour, watch falcons fly across the grounds and listen for a piper striking up Robbie Burns' Address to a Haggis. You'll feel like a fleeting part of the castle's story, more so than if you'd just made a day trip. You are living the kitsch-yet-awesome Scottish stereotype, in quite some style. ●

**Castle Hotel,
Schönburg, Germany**
Teetering on a hilltop beside the Rhine, parts of this bastion date back to the 10th century. It's as romantic as they come; all the rooms are bursting with character – number 22 has a particularly brilliant balcony.

Ashford Castle,
County Mayo, Ireland

This sprawling estate is frequently voted one of the best hotels in the country. As well as wow factor it offers plenty of lordly activities, from falconry and fishing to horse riding and clay pigeon shooting.

Château de Tennessus,
Poitou, France

Medieval, moated Tennessus is château perfection. It has original spiral staircases, arrow slits, hoardings, even a working drawbridge. B&B rooms (The Knight's Chamber, The Watch Tower...) start at just €105 a night.

Hostel Heemskerk,
the Netherlands

The 13th-century Slot Assumburg, easily accessible from Amsterdam, has big towers, venerable stone walls, its own moat – and beds for €23, making regal sleeps a possibility for even budget travellers.

A Day

1.
2.
3. CHUCK OUT THE CHECKLIST

Some places you pass through, others have an extra gravitational pull. Go for a week, end up staying for months. Or at least that is how it should b e. But in a world where we increasingly travel with timetables and checklists, the art of allowing ourselves to be seduced by somewhere, letting a destination derail us – and our schedules – is being lost.

And more's the pity, as these magnetic planetary spots are, often, the last places you imagined you'd end up pausing. And thus the world surprises you, as it should. Take Bali. It's heaving with tourists, tainted with the scars of religious extremism and suffering from a rebranding by way of the blockbuster Eat, Pray, Love. But... there's a reason that this mystical Indonesian island became the 'pray' part of the story. There really is something so soul-stilling about its orderly tiers of rice fields, temple-like mountains and brilliant-white, jungle-fringed beaches.

Do as artists and travellers have done for a century: arrive for those beaches and stay for the grace of the island's interior. The central town of Ubud has been drawing creative types since the 1930s, seducing Europeans with spiritual, decorative and figurative painting,

intricate batik and sculpture. In the face of mass tourism,
Bali has somehow preserved its rich Hindu culture with dignity and smiles. Temples rise over the crashing ocean like serene gods; handmade Hindu offerings line the street corners, more colourful, even, than the island's myriad endemic butterflies and sudden, Technicolor sunsets.

Bali is the place to master the art of doing nothing, to spend a while in gentle meditation and mindless contemplation.
For travellers who let themselves simply 'be', Bali induces a case of eat, love, stay. ●

Do as artists and travellers have done for a century: arrive for Bali's beaches and stay for the grace of the island's interior

FACE YOUR FEAR

GRAB IT! THAT THING YOU FEAR THE MOST – TAKE IT BY THE EARS AND LAUGH IN ITS FACE. THERE'S NOTHING MORE EXHILARATING.

T*he day starts at Triple B Ranch unapologetically.* You're woken by the thunder of a 40-strong herd of horses coming in from the bush for breakfast. If this isn't enough to rouse you, the accompanying neighing, whinnying and snorting will. It's time to get up, boot-up and buckle-up – the day starts here.

Eliminate ignorance and so too goes fear. And being taught to ride by a horse-whispering rancher is arguably the best way to overcome any equine nervousness. Novices and experienced riders alike are drawn to Triple B, a working ranch in the Waterberg Mountains, South Africa's borderlands with Botswana. A wilderness once beloved of Mandela, the Waterberg is home to big game, bigger mountain ranges and hardy herds of Anglo-Arabs, Thoroughbreds and Boerperds. Here, horses are 'tamed' using the round-pen techniques of Shane Dowinton, an expat Brit who applies his natural horsemanship to all species, maintaining there 'are no bad horses, just bad people'.

The day's activities include yoga-in-the-saddle and rounding-up cattle, allowing nervous riders to quickly forget their mount and concentrate on the task in hand. And then there's the game viewing. There's nothing like catching-up with a herd of giraffe to make you forget about your rising trot; staying in the saddle is a means to an end. Horseback safari is an electrifying experience, as you become one with the pack of wildebeest, hartebeest, zebra, impala, kudu, rhino and even hippo.

And at the end of the day, you'll kick back, boots off, with a beer. Storms crackle along mountain ridges, while electric-blue kingfishers flash through trees like forked lightening. If South Africa is, as locals say, God's Country, then Waterberg is His hilltop retreat. ●

Walk with wild things, Tanzania
Combat a fear of big beasties by putting yourself in the capable hands of the Maasai, on a walking tour through Tanzania. Learn how to forage for bush tucker, track big game and identify mammal calls. Immerse yourself in this ancient, pastoral culture, and learn how beautiful the coexistence of man and beast can be.

A head for heights, Italy
Follow in the footsteps of WWI soldiers, trooping across the Vie Ferrate (Iron Ways) of the Alps. This skyscraping series of mountainside cables, metal rungs, rope ladders and chain bridges allows access to some of the most heart-stopping views in Europe.

Public speaking, USA
Join Boom Chicago, one of the world's leading improv groups based in the Netherlands, to master acting techniques that will transform your public-speaking presence. Learn about body language, breaking down the wall between speaker and audience, and refine that awe-inspiring finale.

Fear of Flying
If there's no greater way to conquer a fear than to face it head-on, aviophobes should consider piloting a plane. Most introductory flying lessons include a 'walk around', where the pilot explains the basics of the instruments, plus the chance to take-off, cruise and sometimes land a dual-control plane.

A Day

PRIMAVERA FESTIVAL, BARCELONA   Alamy/Christian Bertrand

LET THE MUSIC MOVE YOU

IF LIVE MUSIC IS YOUR PASSION, THERE'S NO BETTER PLACE TO BINGE THAN A FESTIVAL IN SPAIN'S PARTY CITY, IN REMOTE CAPE VERDE OR THE WILDS OF WALES.

You *open one eye slowly, tentatively,* and see from your window that the sun is already high in the sky. Your ears hum with Disclosure's closing tracks from last night and you can still see the dancing lights from Arcade Fire's thrilling set. You stretch lazily, reach for coffee and hope that today will match up to your first day at Barcelona's first-rate festival, Primavera Sound.

You gather your mates and head out the door, deciding to skip the bus and take the beach promenade, sipping a beer as you stroll by the waves. The crowd is already building as you approach the Parc del Fòrum; the sea glints, and the atmosphere builds. You ease your way into the music-filled mayhem by swaying along to Sharon Van Etten, grab a few beers before heading to see SBTRKT, and then throw yourself into the mosh pit for The National. The crowd is immense, and you raise your arms into the air, letting yourself be carried by the momentum of the music.

The tunes keep coming and no-one looks set to stop. You dance in the Boiler Room dome til the sun starts to show, find your friends, and as the tens of thousands of revellers start to depart, you decide that the return walk with the sun rising is probably the perfect way to sober up.●

Boi Bumbá, Parintins, Brazil
Each June the river island town of Parintins plays host to Brazil's foremost folklore festival, which tells the tale of the death and resurrection of an ox. The story is relayed through the eyes of two competing samba schools – Caprichoso and Garantido – in a typically Brazilian riot of colour, music and lavish carnival.

Green Man Festival, Brecon Beacons, Wales

Set in the beautiful surroundings of Glanusk Park near Abergavenny, this four-day festival hosts over 1500 performers, has an excellent and eclectic musical programme, literature events, comedy and kids' entertainment. Green Man boasts the UK's only 24-hour festival licence, a spectacular site and bountiful distractions so you may never make it back to your tent.

Monterey Jazz Festival, USA

The world's longest-running jazz festival kicked off in 1958 with the simple plan of bringing together 'the best jazz people in the world...having a whole weekend of jazz'. The modern-day festival continues on the original site at the Monterey Fairgrounds, mixing leading live performances with workshops, panel discussions and global food and drink.

Salzburg Festival, Austria

Every summer Salzburg plays host to the world's premier celebration of opera and drama. Held over six weeks during July and August, the festival attracts visitors from around the world to see leading performers and groundbreaking collaborations.

A Day

THE MEAL OF A LIFETIME

FIVE HOURS, 12 COURSES, AND BRAGGING RIGHTS THAT WILL LAST A LIFETIME. BLOWING YOUR ANNUAL VACATION BUDGET ON ONE MEAL REALLY IS WORTH IT.

You know it's slightly bonkers to spend a month's salary on a single lunch. Maybe more than slightly. And you know it's crazy to spend eight hours flying each way for one meal. But then you somehow manage to finagle a table at Copenhagen's Noma – one of the world's best restaurants – and you don't think twice.

Now you're not just dressing for dinner, you're packing for it too. And your priority isn't just sharing those Instagram photos with jealous friends, it's to be surprised and delighted by this first-class culinary journey.

And so you show up at Noma slightly before noon, while the northern light is still slanted at the late-morning, industrious angle. But your mission is wholly pleasure. Eleven 'snacks' come out before you decide whether you want the 8- or 12-course tasting menu. You eat them all, and especially love the raw oyster in a cast-iron pot. And then you order the 12-course lunch, with wine pairings – you've come this far, how can you not go all the way now?

Your afternoon unfolds slowly, with course after course brought out and explained by one of René Redzepi's entourage of interns. You can ask them exactly how the juniper foam got that texture, and they know. Or you just talk about German metal bands – the heavy staffing in the kitchen means the cooks have time to socialise.

Lunch is really the way to do this. At Noma you can watch the day unfold, watch the light change over the harbour, the reflections on the buildings change their timbre, and be aware of all the hours you're giving over to pure pleasure. ●

FORAGED FOOD AT NOMA RESTAURANT, COPENHAGEN   Ditte Isager

1

El Celler de Can Roca, Girona, Spain
The restaurant that unseated Noma as number one on influential Restaurant magazine's definitive list. The three Roca brothers create culinary masterpieces that combine 'countryside and science'.

2

D.O.M., São Paulo, Brazil
Rock-star chef Alex Atala's palace of gastronomy, where he skillfully employs modernist cooking techniques on traditional Brazilian ingredients.

3

Alinea, Chicago, USA
Wünderkind Grant Achatz pushes theatrical boundaries with his 18-course tasting menus – a recent menu had dessert listed simply as 'balloon: helium, green apple'.

4

Dining Impossible, worldwide
Danish bon vivant and self-proclaimed ambassador of pleasure Kristian Brask Thomsen organizes three-day gastronomic benders for just 18 globetrotting guests at a time. Events are regularly held in Copenhagen, Barcelona, North America and other global destinations.

DRESS UP FOR A DAY

IF YOU'VE MORE COSTUMES IN YOUR CUPBOARD THAN A YOUNG LIBERACE, TRY ON A COUPLE OF OUR TOP PICKS FOR THE WORLD'S FANCIEST FANCY DRESS OPPORTUNITIES.

ELVIS EUROPEAN CHAMPIONSHIPS
BLACKPOOL, ENGLAND

The northern home of 'kiss me quick' hats, illuminated trams and donkey rides along a wind-blown beach gets a dose of Deep South in January, when the impersonator-heavy Elvis European Championships come to Blackpool's Norbreck Castle. Brush up on your hip rotations, dig out your pantsuit, and practise your 'uh-huh-uh-huh's.

COSPLAY PUBS
TOKYO, JAPAN

If dressing as a schoolgirl, a manga character or even Hello Kitty is your thing, hit downtown Tokyo for a spot of fancy dress in one of numerous cosplay (short for 'costume play') pubs, where the stars of manga, graphic novels, video games and anime cartoons and storybooks come to life in intricate, elaborately detailed fancy dress costumes.

JOMSVIKINGS
EUROPE

The world's largest Viking re-enactment society battles it out in various locations across Europe, offering the perfect opportunity to haul out your warrior regalia. The adventures of the group are based on the doings of the original Jomsvikings, a 10th-century Baltic military brotherhood. Novices can join the scene at festivals on the continent.

VILLAGE HALLOWEEN PARADE
NEW YORK CITY, USA

New York City's the place to be come 31 October, when the Village Halloween Parade arrives in a feast of dazzling fancy dress creation, with 50,000 costumed revellers and another 2 million turning out to watch. The pageant was conceived in the mid-'70s by a local puppeteer who lamented the decline in the city's Halloween celebrations.

DIA DE LOS MUERTES
PÁTZCUARO, MEXICO

If you find yourself down Mexico way on 2 November, Pátzcuaro provides the perfect place to experience the bright side of Dia de los Muertes (the Day of the Dead). Families gather to pray for deceased loved ones, building private altars and decorating graves with sugar skulls, flowers and the favourite foods of those who've 'passed over'.

HIKE TO THE MOON

IF YOU'RE CRAVING AN ALTERED PERSPECTIVE, ESCHEW THE SUN AND TURN YOUR DAY UPSIDE DOWN. SEEING THE WORLD BY THE LIGHT OF THE MOON OFFERS A RENEWED SENSE OF BOTH SERENITY AND EXCITEMENT.

There's something magical about moonlight. The way it bathes everything in a deep, golden glow, looms large then high and lights up the sky so brightly even the stars retreat. And when surrounded by nature, it feels especially profound, making full-moon hikes full of promise and joy. The best ones start late in the evening and high in the mountains, on a trail you know well enough to tackle in the dark hours.

Sandstone Peak in the Santa Monica Mountains makes for a perfect night hike. At around 11pm the glow should be bright enough to reveal the countryside's secrets. You may glimpse an owl peering from the treetops, and grazing deer tracking down a midnight snack. The trail is clear enough to follow through the sagebrush and emerges onto a moonscape plateau between two peaks. The tallest is Sandstone, overlooking the Pacific Ocean, the water white-gold with the moon's reflections. Find a flat rock and take in the scene. Stories are spun, laughter shared – perhaps someone will pass you a bottle of hooch – this moonlit adventure will linger long in the memory. ●

Rave
Choose your poison wisely – perhaps a bucket of Red-Bull-throttled rum punch? Grab a bunch of good friends and head to one of several beach bars on Ko Pha Ngan, Thailand, for one of the most famous full-moon parties in the world. Dance, laugh, and howl in the light of the moon, but just make sure you make it home by morning.

Paddle
Paddling takes on a sloshing, calming, quiet in the moonlight. Full-moon whitewater is commonly offered on class II and III river runs, which supercharges the serenity with a safe shot of adrenaline. If it's the ocean for you, know that tides can get wicked during full moons, so check the tidal tables and ask local experts. There's nothing more spectacular than stroking toward the golden patches of a melting moon.

Run
Global urban trend-setters have started to gather in large packs and take on runs through the nighttime streets of New York, LA, Seattle, and even towns in Estonia. You get to dodge the hottest part of day and exercise in spaces gloriously empty of their daily traffic.

Cycle
Whether you're biking solo on a beach path, heading into town with pals for a night out or taking part in a community night-ride like Critical Mass, moonlit cycles bring cool breezes, a real sense of freedom and a whole new way to see the landscape.

A Day

GET LOST & BECOME ONE

CLIMB INTO YOSEMITE OR DIVE BELOW THE OCEAN TO LOSE YOUR SENSE OF SELF.

How many valleys are there in the world? Not a couple of rolling hills leading down to a stream. Not even the kind of valley that sits beneath a couple of alpine mountains. But a flat expanse of land surrounded by granite walls that appear to have risen from the ground. A dramatic announcement that 'this place is not flat'.

You know, maybe there are many. But when you hear of one that does what Yosemite Valley can do – that sense of being subsumed by something infinitely greater and grander than your individual self – make a note of its location and go.

In the half-light of a May morning, the snow on Half Dome glows. Winter barely lets spring have its turn. Among the feelings that the valley inspires – the awe, the insignificance, the First World questions of existence – there is the sensation of revelling in greed. This is all yours.

The place is a shortcut to being humbled by nature. But what you can attain walking solo in the trails is a sense of oneness. True, you're not a billion years old, carved by a glacier, you haven't witnessed dinosaurs and you'll die soon enough while this place lives on and on and on. But all the same, it happens; your thoughts are metered by the beat of your boots on the granite, the resounding anthem draws you in. You are connected here, as an object, no more or less out of place than the stones, the stream, the squirrel or the bear. You start out solo and before you know it your self has disappeared. ●

YOSEMITE VALLEY, CALIFORNIA   Willie Huang

100

You Only Live Once

DIVING AT THE GREAT BARRIER REEF   Getty/Jeff Hunter

GET LOST & BECOME ONE

Great Barrier Reef, Australia

When you slip beneath the surface, time as you know it stops. It is another world. And the shock of colour underwater will take your breath away (but try and hold it in!). The sea turns into a confetti-factory explosion of marine life. Colours that shouldn't exist are paraded everywhere you look. Creatures –giant, tiny, fleeting – fall over themselves beneath you. Floating, goggles down, snorkel up, this sensory overload chamber is so numbingly amazing you disappear into it. Only the need for air brings you back.

Isle d'Ouessant, France

The island is hammered by the Atlantic waves. The land is bare and wind blown. Créac'h Lighthouse looms above you, a beacon on this most solitary of places. You walk the 8km to the other end of the island, by rocky bluffs above white water and sea foam, and past the occasional sheep, to the Stiff Lighthouse. If this were a country, its chief export would be light. At the island's town, Lampaul, you find the cemetery, a moody view to the past, unknown sailors resting with the roll calls of lost ships. You're taken by the romance of shipwrecks and angry seas, storms and rescue. You're alone and clinging to life, lit by the flashes of light cutting through the gloom. Waiting for salvation.

London Underground, England

Wait until it looks full, till it's almost overflowing. Then make your dash and squeeze your way into the carriage. Mind the gap as you go. The press is complete. You've never felt so close to so many people. What is everyone thinking? Why are they just staring like that? And then you realise that they're thinking the same thing. That in every head you see there's a similar chatter of questions and wishes. Your own face is no more animated than theirs, despite the torrent of thoughts running through your mind. All this worry, mirth and bemusement and your claim to being unique fades away, consumed by the crowd. As the train slows for the next station, you join the throng and prepare to exit, a little less sure of your own importance.

Death Valley, USA

You head out on the Methuselah Trail, grey and dry underfoot, making your way to the grove. Not a soul disturbs the journey. It's a challenging walk and you imagine life here; it seems all but impossible. But then you meet them, the twisted, gnarled bristlecones. These were growing at the same time the pyramids were being built. They are alive. Still alive. They are timeless. Their driftwood skins and crazed contortions are mesmerising. Time stands still for you. Just for a moment a tiny tiny moment.

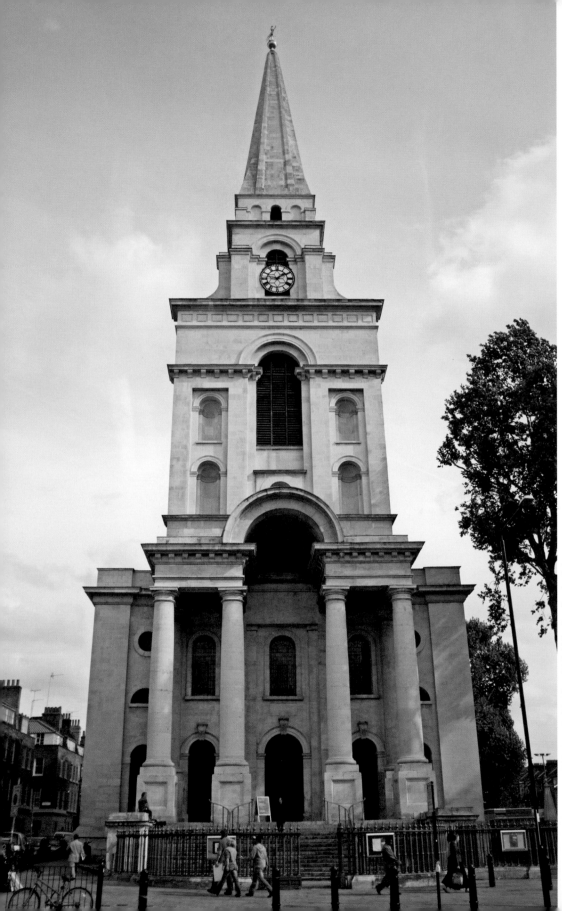

OPEN HOUSE

In any city, the urge to peek behind closed doors is almost overwhelming. Whether visitor or resident, there are places forbidden to all but a few – private houses, businesses, institutions. For the incurably curious, the Open House movement offers some respite. On one weekend a year, in an increasing number of cities around the world (London, Dublin, Melbourne, Rome, New York and Chicago) many of those usually closed doors are opened to the public. Guided tours by architects offer a tantalising glimpse of a city's secret layers.

NICHOLAS HAWKSMOOR'S CHRIST CHURCH IN LONODN   Getty/Stephen Robson

A Day

SIGNATURE DISH

I *was 18 and in Paris for the first time.* My father was treating me to a cooking class at the Ritz Escoffier. My imagination was lit up like the Eiffel Tower at night. What would we be learning to cook? Pheasants in chestnut sauce? Foie gras soufflé? A cream-puff tower? Imagine my surprise then, when I arrived in the Ritz's basement classroom and saw what we'd actually be making. Scrambled eggs. Yes, scrambled eggs, that cafeteria-chafing standard, that childhood mum's-too-tired-to-cook weeknight stand-by. A monkey could make scrambled eggs. A chicken could make scrambled eggs.

But as the teacher in his tall white toque began to talk, a hush fell over the classroom and we all focused intently as his slim, elegant hands cracked eggs into a copper bowl. The secret to this simplest of dishes, he said, was to cook the eggs at a very low heat, stirring constantly with a fork in a gentle circular motion to keep the curds soft and delicate. As you stir, slowly add small lumps of butter and drizzles of cream. Most importantly of all, don't rush things.

Finally, he scooped tiny servings of the eggs into paper cups and passed them around the classroom for us to taste. They were – and this is really the only word to describe them – perfect. Like buttery, savoury, daffodil-yellow clouds.

Now, whenever I want to impress a guest or make a loved one feel special, I'll cook them 'my' signature scrambled eggs. Sometimes with chives. Sometimes mushrooms. Sometimes plain.

The lesson is this: there's value in perfecting a simple dish, whether a meticulously prepared cup of Chinese pu-erh tea, a flawlessly crispy grilled cheese sandwich, or a sublime bowl of spaghetti with olive oil and garlic. Perfect it. Make it yours. Then make it for everyone. ●

There's value in perfecting a simple dish, whether a meticulously prepared cup of Chinese pu-erh tea or a sublime bowl of spaghetti

MEET THE MAKER

**WHETHER YOU LOVE WINE, ART, FASHION OR SPORT,
THE FINEST LOCAL PRODUCTS ARE MADE BY HAND.**

Julien Mareschal, the tall, jazz-playing winemaker at Domaine de la Borde in the Jura town of Pupillon is pouring you a taste of something special. It's *vin de paille*, a traditional blend of local grape varieties. The first grapes on the vine, he explains, are cut and put on boxes to dry for six months (*paille* means straw). The grapes shrivel as the sugars concentrate; then they're slowly pressed. The wine is aged in wood barrels for at least three years, which results in, you discover at Julien's winery, a sweet, green-gold dessert wine that is utterly unique to this understated region of powerful rivers, waterfalls and forested limestone mountains (which lent the name Jurassic to the world) to the east of central France.

Without talking to this young winemaker you would not have been introduced to *vin de paille*; nor would you have understood the Jura's place in winemaking – with land costing less than half of that in Bordeaux, Jura draws adventurous young winemakers. Julien goes on to tell you about another local speciality, *vin jaune*. The Jura might be overshadowed by its neighbour Burgundy but for one weekend of the year, the launch of the region's very own wine variety on the first weekend of February, when 80 winemakers and 40,000 wine lovers converge on the host town, the Jura is the belle of the ball. And when you leave, Julien offers one more tip – the local cheesemaker who produces the very best Comté cheese to accompany a glass of his wine. ●

❶ Woodblock prints
Kyoto, Japan
In the Japan of 200 years ago, the woodblock print brought art to the masses. The woodblock printing workshop of Takezasa-do in Kyoto, where the fourth and fifth generations of the Takenaka printing family work, is down an alleyway off busy Shijo Avenue.

❷ Woollen capes,
Madrid, Spain
Capas Seseña is the only place in Spain that still makes the heavy cloak known as the capa española, a garment traditionally reserved for formal occasions, such as bullfights or nights at the theatre. Pablo Picasso liked his so much he was buried in it.

❸ Craft beer,
London, England
South London's 'beer mile' runs beneath Bermondsey's railway arches. Inside the four microbreweries yo u're likely to be served by the brewer. All four produce pale ales and European styles such as saisons and dubbels.

❹ Skis, Colorado, USA
Telluride, a rootsy haven for snowhounds in southwest Colorado, is home to Wagner Custom, creators of handcrafted made-to-measure skis. Drop in to collect the finished skis and you'll also pick up some tips on the best runs in the steep San Juan Mountains.

A NIGHT AT THE MUSEUM

SLIPPERED FEET PAD DOWN CORRIDORS BURSTING WITH STORIES, AND EXHIBITS SPRING TO LIFE AS YOU OVERNIGHT IN A MUSEUM.

The grand, high-ceilinged halls are eerily quiet, echoing with only a few light snores – and several millennia of history and innovation. Tonight, you're not just bedding down with your kids and their classmates, you're lying with legends. Under this roof are Ramses and Shiva; Easter Island moai, and Moche warriors; Mayans, Aztecs and Alexander the Great; Hopewell peoples, Minoan warriors and Olmec gods. There is priceless Inca gold, Lachish reliefs and a two-million-year-old stone tool. Oh, Buddha's here too. It's quite a sleepover.

Many museums, galleries and zoos worldwide now offer overnight experiences, a chance to enter after the crowds have left and explore the exhibits in your own sleepy time. These special events usually offer behind-the-scenes opportunities:make your own movie at a media museum; watch laser shows at astronomy centres; play historical dress-up and craft replica artefacts; or watch animals get up to their nocturnal shenanigans on a zoo stay. Having a whole museum as your home is an inspiration, and an invitation to look beyond the usual glass casements. You might be dozing under the belly of a giant blue whale or amid 3000-year-old sculptures from Ancient Egypt.

Many events are themed: London's British Museum runs Viking, Ancient Lives and Ming overnighters; Calgary Zoo offers Penguin, Rainforest and Savannah options, on which you can snooze near different enclosures; and the California Academy of Sciences runs separate Penguins+Pajamas nights for families, and over-21s, so adults get in on the action too.

There are usually snacks and breakfast, as well as fun and games. There may not be a lot of actual sleep, but if you do manage to nod off, imagine the dreams... ●

Smithsonian, Washington DC, USA
This venerable institution – setting for 2009 movie Night at the Museum 2 – allows ankle-biters to sleep under Phoenix the whale in the Ocean Hall after an evening of activities.

Wellington Zoo, New Zealand
From 7pm to 9.30am the zoo is yours:
help feed and look after the animals,
bed down overlooking Monkey Island
and join in the morning chores, before
the doors reopen to the public.

Golden Hinde, London, England
Dress up as a Tudor sailor, become
part of the crew and learn how to
navigate and fire a cannon before
laying your head down on the gun
deck. In the morning a Tudor-style
breakfast awaits.

Vancouver Aquarium, Canada
Family Sleepovers get hands-on at the
marine lab before you drift off by one
of the aquarium's tanks. Hugs & Fishes
is for couples, complete with wine,
a Sea-fari of Passion (on which you
watch marine courtships) and a night
serenade from the tuneful belugas.

A Day

BACK TO NATURE

WILDLIFE-WATCHING IS NOT ONLY MEDITATIVE BUT IT CAN REAWAKEN SENSES DULLED BY CITY LIFE. TRAVEL TO SCOTLAND TO RECONNECT WITH THE WILD.

I*t's October on the windswept slopes of Scotland's glens* and the air is filled with the sound of rhythmic grunting. On the islands of the Inner Hebrides off the west coast of Scotland, that bellowing can mean only one thing: it's the red deer rut and the islands' stags are staking their claim to the prime territories and duelling with their rivals. While the rest of the island's residents are winding down for the winter, come autumn the islands' deer have only one thing on their mind – making the next generation, and they aren't too bothered who knows about it. These magnificent creatures – stags stand 130cm tall at the shoulder, with antlers that can be 1m in length and have 16 points – inhabit both the Isle of Jura and community-owned Isle of Rum. There are 900 red deer on Rum, most easily seen in the north around Kilmory, where they have been filmed for television shows. In addition to rut-watching, Rum's rangers can offer guided walks and wildlife-viewing, with options ranging from butterflies to eagles.

On larger, wilder Jura, the deer population outnumbers people. They're hard to miss, visiting the foreshore to feed on mineral-rich seaweed and taking over the north of the island for the rut, a spectacular setting for one of nature's great annual rituals. But you don't have to go to Jura to see and hear red stags rutting – in London's Richmond Park they bellow in the bracken from late September to the end of October. Such natural experiences, says writer Patrick Barkham, are a sort of peaceful exhilaration. ●

❶ Flamingos, France
The marshlands of the Camargue in southern France are the setting for one of nature's most choreographed courtships. In rhythmic, pink battalions flamingos strut across the Pont de Gau ornithological reserve, which is perhaps the best place to see this performance.

❷ Red-crowned cranes, Japan
Courting cranes dance for each other on Hokkaido in winter, bowing, jumping, strutting and tossing grass and sticks. To the Japanese the cranes symbolise luck and longevity.

❸ Howler monkeys, Costa Rica
Like deer, male howler monkeys are judged on the tenor and volume of their calls – which is why the forests of Manuel Antonio National Park on the west coast of Costa Rica are a cacophony of whoops and barks.

❹ Bower bird, Australia
The male Satin bower bird furnishes his bower (both a stage and nest) with blue objects, from flowers to bottle tops. Drop a flower of any other colour into his bower and he'll remove in an instant. Find the colour-coordinated couples at Lamington National Park in Queensland.

A Day 🕰

RAFTING ON KLARÄLVEN RIVER IN SWEDEN   Getty/Giuglio Gil

BUILD YOUR LIFE RAFT

INDULGE YOUR INNER HUCKLEBERRY FINN BY BUILDING AND FLOATING YOUR OWN RAFT IN SWEDEN AND BEYOND.

The *beaver looks worried* as you clumsily attempt to pull the raft over to the riverbank to moor up for the evening and set up camp. You're on the Klarälven River in Värmland, Sweden, on a wooden raft measuring 6m by 3m, which weighs twice as much as a family car, travels at 2mph and has the turning circle of a barge. No stranger to passing trade – this waterway has been a logging route for generations – perhaps it's your technique the beaver's wary of?

Everyone's a critic. Who cares what the beaver thinks anyway? You haven't worn shoes for the last three days, and you're happily discovering your inner Huckleberry Finn. Yesterday you caught a fish. And cooked and ate it. The kids took a bit of convincing when they realised you were building the raft yourself, out of just logs and rope, but it's held together so far. At the end of the eight-day expedition, you'll simply untie the ropes, let the logs loose, and there will be no sign you've ever been on the river. It's the ultimate eco trip. Zero emissions and maximum engagement with your natural surroundings. And what surroundings they are – pure, pristine Nordic wilderness. ●

Transylvanian river tramping

Your sudden shivering fit has nothing to do with the cold water of the Olt River. You've just realised you're exploring Dracula's backyard on a raft constructed from the same timber that Vlad the Impaler (who inspired the garlic-dodging legend) once used to spear his victims on. The first day of this paddling-and-hiking tour of Transylvania was spent building the raft, which you're now sailing from Augustin to Mateias, tackling several rapids en route. Tomorrow you'll paddle to Hoghiz, from where the Carpathians and the Count's castle beckon.

Borneo to be wild

Racing down rapidly moving rivers on bamboo rafts is a way of life in Malaysian Borneo, and various events in Sarawak encourage visitors to build their own craft and join in, while also experiencing the indigenous rainforest cultures of the region. You overnight in an Iban longhouse during two days of racing in April's Baleh-Kapit Safari River Expedition, while October's 10-hour Baram Whitewater Rafting Challenge passes through remote villages and introduces you to communities such as the Orang Ulu. Both events feature serious rapids.

Fool's gold in the Yukon

You're an experienced punk rafter – you have the boat-building skills required to lash the right sort of logs together with the correct kind of knots, and the river know-how to take on a wild waterway without having your hand held. The ultra-remote Yukon Territory, where Canada meets Alaska, is your kind of playground. Here you'll follow in the oar strokes of Jack London and the stampede of gold-chasing prospectors who landed in Skagway in the 1890s, climbed the Chilkoot Trail into the Klondike and built homemade rafts to traverse the Yukon River from Whitehorse to Dawson. Just beware the man-eating Five Finger Rapids.

Ride the Amazon

The shriek of a howler monkey pierces the Peruvian rainforest dawn as you launch your freshly constructed raft onto the planet's greatest river. This is it – 180km of the Amazon lie between you and the finish line in the jungle city of Iquitos. Will your log raft – built of balsawood, like Thor Heyerdahl's Kon-Tiki – survive the next three days? Will you live to tell the tale of the Amazon International Raft Race, the world's longest raft race? Can you beat the locals, who have won every race, bar one, since the event started in 1999?

BUILD YOUR LIFE RAFT

MAKE A DATE FOR DANCING

Where words aren't sufficient, get to know the locals on a dancefloor. Whether you're swinging to Cuban salsa in Havana or waltzing in Vienna, a night out dancing lifts the mood like nothing else. Learn some steps on pages 162-63.

DANCING THE SALSA IN HAVANA Mark Read

SLEEP IN AN ICE HOTEL

Every winter at Jukkasjärvi, 18km east of Kiruna, the amazing Ice Hotel is built from hundreds of tonnes of ice from the frozen river. This custom-built igloo has a chapel and a bar – where you drink from a glass made of ice . The 50 bedrooms are outfitted with reindeer skins and sleeping bags guaranteed to keep you warm; the hotel promises the rooms never get colder than -8ºC...

THE ICE HOTEL, SWEDEN   Getty/David Clapp

A Day

SAVVY WAYS TO SEE THE SUPER-SIGHTS

**IF YOU FIND YOUR BUCKETLIST MATCHES FAR TOO MANY OTHERS',
JUST TRY A LITTLE SIDESTEP. WITH A BIT OF FORESIGHT,
YOU CAN MAKE THE REALITY LIVE UP TO THE DREAM.**

Embarking on the iconic pilgrimage to France's Mont St-Michel in August is, quite frankly, asking for trouble. The incessant, nose-to-tail traffic blocking the final stretch is enough to make you want to dump the car and walk.

Do it! The easy hike across flat sheep pastures is idyllic. The contemplative crown of the mount teases on the horizon and, bar a handful of walkers at the initial roadside stile, you should find yourself alone. Mid-way across the grassy plain dotted white with sheep, break for lunch – a stinky round of gooey Camembert, a baguette and a bottle of local Normandy cider. Apart from having to dodge sheep dung to spread the picnic rug, this is the stuff of French dreams.

And why not defer hitting the concrete causeway linking the mount with the mainland because from then on, it is pure unadulterated August-crowd hell, confirming that savvy-traveller suspicion that the real beauty of Europe's tourism superstars often lies in the seductive mirage they proffer from afar. ●

Leaning Tower of Pisa, Italy
Dodge the unromantic scrum of overzealous souvenir sellers, boisterous school groups and photo-posing pandemonium on Piazza dei Miracoli. Amble instead through medieval backstreets east of the piazza to the Museo dell'Opera del Duomo and venerate a miraculous mirage of Italy's greatest icon from its back garden – a beautiful cloistered courtyard to boot.

St Peter's Basilica, Vatican City
There's no reason to endure the inevitable crowds here. Find yourself a room with a view – such as a two-bedroom apartment with a staggering, full-frontal from its 4th-floor perch of one of the most magnificent church domes in the world.

The Uffizi, Florence, Italy
Get in through the back door, literally. The Corridoio Vasariano – an elevated covered passageway built in 1565 for the Medici to meander between riverside Florentine palaces in appropriate secrecy – has priceless art works. It also happens to sneak into Florence's superstar Uffizi art museum in the Third Corridor, moments from High Renaissance maestros Michelangelo and Raphael.

St-Tropez, Provence, France
It was the sensual sweep of burnt-red rooftops and the Italian baroque bell tower seen from the sea that famously seduced the French pointillist painter, Paul Signac, when he sailed into the enigmatic fishing village of St-Tropez in 1892. And arriving by boat (from Ste-Maxime, Port Grimaud or St-Raphaël) remains the only way in high season to understand the sultry beauty of this pouting, Côte d'Azur sexpot.

A Day

THE NEED FOR SPEED

FLOOR IT! TEST YOUR MOTORING METTLE ON A NO-HOLDS-BARRED, HOLD-ONTO-YOUR-HATS DRIVE OF A LIFETIME.

You're about to enter 'Green Hell' – or, to use its more official title, the Nürburgring Nordschleife racetrack. There used to be a big tree and an altar dedicated to St Anthony by the start line, but it was removed in 1935. Shame: some holy protection could come in handy.

You rev your car's engine and you're off; 21km of sinuously snaking, brutally bucking, dipping, cresting, curvaceous tarmac lies ahead. With no speed limit.

This track, built in 1925 and dinted by 73 separate bends, is legendary. It was the most notorious Grand Prix track on the Formula 1 circuit – until Niki Lauda crashed here in 1976 and it was deemed too unsafe to race in modern Formula 1 cars. But its notoriety endures.

On certain days, the public is allowed to tackle the Nordschleife in their own cars – though it's highly recommended to do a few circuits as a passenger first. That way you can start to get the measure of this motor-racing monster, which twists mercilessly and drunkenly though the Eifel Forest. It's essentially a public road, requiring you to adhere to Article 3, Section 1 of the German Highway Code (you must be in full control of your vehicle, whatever speed you're going). But there's no actual restriction on that speed.

As you face section after punishing section – the Schwedenkreuz, Adenauer Forst, Metzgesfeld, Wippermann – your velocity is the very last thing on your mind. Staying on the road and out of the trees is your chief concern. But as you pass under that finishing gantry, feeling like Lewis Hamilton, you can't help but look down at your watch, note your lap time, and be overcome by the urge to do it all again – just a little bit quicker. ●

YOUR MIG-29 AWAITS   Getty/Anton Balakchiev

Bobsleigh, Lillehammer, Norway
Bomb down the 1710m-long Olympic bobsleigh run in one of Norway's oldest winter resorts. Climb into a four-man bob (with a pilot) to reach speeds of 120km/h and face the thrill of 5G.

 Cresta Run, Switzerland
This historic toboggan course was first carved from the Engadine Valley's ice in 1885. It twists, turns and plunges 157 vertical metres in 1.2km; the record is a terrifying 50.09 seconds.

 MiG flight, Nizhny Novgorod, Russia
Loved Top Gun? Then live it. The MiG-29 Flight Program at Russia's SOKOL airfield sees you take to the sky with a fighter pilot. Break the sound barrier, feel 9G, and complete acrobatic Immelman turns. Epic.

 Formula Rossa, Abu Dhabi
Theme parks are not just for kids. Ferrari World's Formula Rossa is the world's fastest rollercoaster, accelerating to 240km/h in under 5 seconds and chicaning like an F1 car. Safety goggles – and gumption – required.

 A Day

E N J O Y
T H E
S I L E N C E

The quietest place on earth is an anechoic chamber at the Orfield Laboratory in South Minneapolis. The silence inside this room, which is encased in thick concrete and 1m-wide fibreglass wedges, is disorienting. You'll need to sit down and most people can't bear more than 45 minutes. Is an anechoic chamber a practical antidote to the cacophony of our daily lives? No. Instead, try the beach on Benguerra island in the Indian ocean.

Wait until nightfall and then pad down to water's edge and wander along the sand. With just a couple of boutique lodges on the Mozambican island you've got a good chance of avoiding your fellow guests. Wait until you're out of earshot then lie back and feel yourself become absorbed by the warm sand and the stars above as you listen. What you'll notice is, far from the being silent, the island night is full of bird sounds, the soft wash of surf and even the squeak of sand beneath. ●

Olympic National Park, Washington, USA
Although it's accessed from Hwy 101, Olympic National Park remains one of the least peopled parks in mainland USA. Here, when mountain, forest and ocean meet, you can wander through some of the oldest forests in the country without seeing another soul. Reach the coast and the soundtrack will be the crashing Pacific surf on a wild shore.

Damaraland, Namibia
In northwest Namibia, where 42% of the country is protected, Damaraland is one of the last refuges of the black rhino. Few people live in this ancient landscape and because it's harder to see megafauna, safari parties head elsewhere. This means that you'll have the place to yourself – just you and the family of elephants noisily sucking up acacia pods like giant vacuum cleaners.

The Empty Quarter, Arabian Peninsula
Rub al-Khali – the 'abode of silence' – spans a fifth of the Arabian Peninsula, taking in Saudi Arabia, Oman, the United Arab Emirates and Yemen. Imagine a desert larger than France or Texas with dunes 250m tall; on some mornings, when they're cloaked in fog, any sounds are further deadened. The hard part is getting in – and out – on the soft, shifting sands.

Northumberland National Park, England
With one of the lowest population densities in England, the Northumberland National Park has more than 1000 sq km in which to get away from the hurly-burly. The north is dominated by the Cheviot Hills, once home to Bronze Age people. To the south is Hadrian's Wall.

RUB AL-KHALI, OMAN   Getty/Josef Friedhuber

17
independent countries
visited within 24 hours by record-breaking team of Yvo Kuhling, Liselott Martynenko Agerlid, Philomena O'Brien and Todd Hepworth in 2012.

290.22
kilometres
road distance run in 24 hours by Greek ultra marathoner Yiannis Kouros, known as Pheidippides' Successor, in 1998. He also has the track 24-hour record, which is 303.5km.

2
days
time William Allen spent driving around England's circular M25 in 1998, trying to find the turn-off for his daughter's house. (It's possible to do a full lap in one hour 40 minutes.)

13,804
kilometres
ground distance covered by Qantas' QF7 service from Sydney to Dallas, Fort Worth in 15 hours 25 minutes. Saudia's SV41 flight from Jeddah to Los Angeles takes longer (16 hours, 55 minutes), but covers less ground (13,409km).

22
centimetres
length a tapeworm can grow in your gut in a single day.

2.414
cups of coffee
drunk per day, per person in the Netherlands.

70
miles
additional daily distance an eastward sailing ship can make while crossing the Atlantic, versus one sailing westward, due to prevailing westerly winds.

20,000
calories consumed
per day by Sumo wrestlers, on a diet of Chanko-nabe.

2901.4
kilometres
furthest distance travelled by train in 24 hours, set in Japan by Americans Corey Pedersen and Mike Kim in 2008.

238
miles
distance travelled by Ben Friberg on a stand-up paddleboard (SUP) in 24 hours, along the Yukon River in Canada in 2012.

45
average number of climbers
each day on each of the six routes up Tanzania's Mount Kilimanjaro during 2011–12.

41
days
holiday time in Brazil, which has the most generous vacation allowance enshrined in national law.

JOIN THE TRIBE

In the most remote corners of the world, it's possible to meet and even stay with indigenous people. During summer in Mongolia, tented ger camps on the Gobi's steppes may be open to travellers. On Sarawak in Malaysia, the leader of the local Iban longhouse may offer you shelter from a storm. And then there are the Wigmen of Papua New Guinea's Huli tribe, who grow their hair into a perfectly domed style before it is cut off to become a ceremonial wig, which they're very happy to show off to guests.

MEET THE HULI TRIBE OF PAPUA NEW GUINEA   Guy Needham

FIND BURIED TREASURE

THERE'S A SECRET WORLD OF GOODIES BURIED BENEATH THE EARTH'S ROCKS AND WAVES. LOOKING FOR LOOT – FROM PIRATE BOOTY TO SECRET STASHES – IS AN ADVENTURE ALL ITS OWN.

S*urrounded on all sides by scorched earth* and pounded by the sweltering desert heat, Coober Pedy and its swag of opals lie sparkling in the middle of the South Australian Outback. The heat, dust, flies and harsh sunlight are somewhat of an assault and you immediately realise why most of the action in this town happens... underground. You revel in your cave hotel's cool embrace and marvel at how much the town has managed to squeeze into its subterranean world.

But what you're really looking for down here are gems. Named after the local aboriginal term 'kupa-piti' (meaning 'whitefella in a hole'), this far-flung town is also known as the opal capital of the world. You're itching to strike out and find some stones but there's a good deal to be gleaned at Tom's Working Opal Mine so you take a tour before heading out to 'noodle' – that's fossick to you and me – in the town's many mine dumps. With the sun high overhead, you sweat under a slather of sunscreen, painstakingly sifting through the dusty mullock heaps, until, there! You see a glint among the rocks – a tiny bit of opal! And then another! And you're soon tucking more and more of the tiny pieces into your bag.

Maybe you can't start planning retirement just yet but you can say that you've truly discovered your own buried treasure. ●

1
Wreck diving, Florida, USA
Thought to be home to more sunken treasure than any other state in the USA, Florida's blue waters may be hiding millions of dollars worth of loot. Check local legalities before you wriggle into your suit, and never dive alone in Florida's oft-treacherous waters: those wrecks are down there for a reason.

2
Arctic amethysts, Kola Peninsula, Russia
Far above the Arctic Circle, all that glitters is not ice: western Russia's extreme north sparkles with the purple slivers of the prized amethyst. The rugged Kola Peninsula is home to the windswept, Tersky Coast, an ideal hunting ground for this legendary gemstone.

3
Norman Island, British Virgin Islands
Peg-legs, planks and parrots – if there was a map showing the home of every pirate cliché known to fancy-dressers, Norman Island would be marked with an X. The inspiration behind Robert Louis Stevenson's Treasure Island, it's a haven for snorkellers and nature lovers, but also those convinced there are undiscovered doubloons hidden in its caves.

4
Roman coins, England
Either togas suffered from a lack of pockets or departing Romans hadn't time to stop at a currency exchange because the English countryside is aglitter with ancient coins. Wielding metal detectors, treasure hunters have been responsible for massive finds; in 2010 a chef uncovered a pot filled with 52,000 coins dated between AD253 and AD293.

A NIGHT TO REMEMBER

YOU MIGHT NOT REMEMBER THE FINER DETAILS BUT A GREAT
NIGHT OUT WITH FRIENDS ALWAYS ADDS UP TO MORE THAN
THE SUM OF ITS PARTS. GET THE GANG TOGETHER AND PLAN A
BACCHANALIAN BASH WHEREVER YOU ARE.
HERE ARE ITINERARIES FOR FIVE OF THE WORLD'S
NIGHTLIFE CAPITALS TO GET YOU STARTED.

Maps by **Wayne Murphy**

Times Square ○

Grand Central ▣

Penn Station ▣

HUDSON RIVER

⑤

MANHATTAN

③

②

QUEENS

EAST RIVER

WILLIAMSBURG

④

World Trade Center ○

Brooklyn Bridge ○

①

A night in
NEW YORK
USA

1. Dead Rabbit

Far from dead, this new kid on the cocktail block has wasted no time swagging awards. During the day, hit the sawdust-sprinkled taproom for specialty beers, historic punches and pop-inns (lightly hopped ale spiked with different flavours). Come evening, scurry upstairs to the cosy Parlour for 72 meticulously researched cocktails.
deadrabbitnyc.com

2. Balthazar

Still the king of bistros, bustling (OK, loud) Balthazar is never short of a discriminating mob. That's thanks to three winning details: its location in SoHo's shopping-spree heartland; the uplifting Paris-meets-NYC ambience; and, of course, the stellar something-for-everyone menu. Highlights include the outstanding raw bar, steak frites, salade Niçoise, as well as the roasted beet salad.
balthazarny.com

3. Angel's Share

Show up early and snag a seat at this hidden gem, behind a Japanese restaurant on the same floor. It's quiet and elegant with creative cocktails, but you can't stay if you don't have a table or a seat at the bar, and they tend to go fast.

4. Maison Premiere

You'll half-expect to see Dorothy Parker stagger into this old-timey place, which features an elegant bar, suspendered bartenders and a jazzy soundtrack to channel the French Quarter New Orleans vibe. The cocktails are serious: the epic list includes more than a dozen absinthe drinks, various juleps, an array of specialty cocktails.
maisonpremiere.com

5. Cielo

This long-running club boasts an attitude-free crowd and an excellent sound system. Join dance lovers on Deep Space Monday when DJ François K spins dub and underground beats. Other nights feature various DJs from Europe.
cieloclub.com

A Day

A night in
HONG KONG

1. Sevva
If there was a million-dollar view in Hong Kong, it'd be the one from the balcony of ultra-stylish Sevva – skyscrapers so close you can see their arteries of steel, with the harbour and Kowloon in the distance. At night it takes your breath away.
sevva.hk

2. Globe
Besides an impressive list of 150 imported beers, including 13 on tap, the Globe serves T8, the first cask-conditioned ale brewed in Hong Kong. Occupying an enviable 370 sq m, the bar has a huge dining area with long wooden tables and comfortable banquettes.
theglobe.com.hk

3. Tim's Kitchen
This restaurant is considered one of Hong Kong's best – as evidenced by the Michelin honour and the praises lavished by local gourmands. It serves masterfully executed Cantonese fare over two well-illuminated floors, with signature dishes such as crab claw poached with wintermelon. Reservations essential.
timskitchen.com.hk

4. Lung King Heen
The world's first Chinese restaurant to receive three stars from the Michelin people, still retains them. The Cantonese food, when combined with the harbour views and the impeccable service, provides a stellar dining experience. The signature steamed lobster and scallop dumplings sell out early.

5. Drop
Deluxe lounge action, excellent tunes and potent cocktails keep Drop strong on the scene. It's like walking into Wallpaper* magazine, but the vibe here is unpretentiously inclusive and the crowd reaches a fever pitch on big nights. The members-only policy after 10pm Thursday to Saturday keeps the dance floor capacity at a manageable 'packed like sardines' level.
drophk.com

1. Max und Moritz

The patina of yesteryear hangs over this ode-to-old-school brewpub named for the cheeky Wilhelm Busch cartoon characters. Since 1902 it has packed hungry diners and drinkers into its rustic tile-and-stucco ornamented rooms for sudsy home brews.
maxundmoritzberlin.de

2. Cafe Jacques

A favourite with off-duty chefs and local foodies, Jacques charms with flattering candlelight, warm decor and fantastic wine. It's the perfect date spot but you only have to be in love with good food to appreciate the French- and North African–inspired blackboard menu. Reservations recommended.

3. Hops & Barley

Conversation flows as freely as the unfiltered pilsner, malty dunkel (dark) fruity weizen (wheat) and potent cider produced at this congenial microbrewery inside a former butcher's shop. Fellow beer lovers range from skinny-jean hipsters to suits swilling postwork pints among ceramic-tiled walls and shiny copper vats.
hopsandbarley.eu

4. Freischwimmer

In summertime, few places are more idyllic than this rustic 1930s boathouse turned canal-side chill zone. The menu draws inspiration from all corners of the world. Also a great spot for Sunday brunch and late-night warm-up drinks before hitting the area's clubs.
freischwimmer-berlin.com

5. Berghain

Only world-class DJs heat up this hedonistic haven inside a labyrinthine former power plant. Upstairs, Panorama Bar pulsates with house and electro, while the factory floor below leans towards hard techno. Arrive after 5am.
berghain.de

A night in
BERLIN
Germany

A Day

A night in
BUENOS AIRES
Argentina

1. Manolo
Honest local cuisine – steaks, salads and a huge menu of Spanish pastas and meat-and-potatoes platters – keep this friendly, family-run corner joint alive and kicking. The budget-friendly prices pull in neighborhood families and groups of hungry boys after fútbol practice. Reserve for dinner.
restaurantmanolo. com.ar

2. Doppelgänger
This cool, emerald-hued corner bar specialises in vermouth cocktails. The atmosphere is calm and the lengthy menu is fascinating: start with the Journalist, a martini with a bitter orange twist, or channel Don Draper and go for the bar's bestseller – an old-fashioned.
doppelganger.com.ar

3. Cafe San Juan
Having studied in Paris and Barcelona, celebrity chef Leandro Cristóbal now runs this renowned San Telmo bistro. Start with tapas, then delve into the grilled octopus, molleja (sweetbreads) cannelloni and the amazing pork bondiola (deliciously tender after 9 hours' roasting).

4. Bar Sur
Historic Bar Sur is one of the city's most celebrated (and expensive) tango show venues; you'll pay handsomely to sip champagne at one of a dozen tables. Be prepared – the upscale dinner show is often participatory – so avoid it if you're not prepared to try a few tangled steps...
bar-sur.com.ar

5. Mitos Argentinos
This cosy old brick house in San Telmo has hosted rock groups for over a dozen years. It's not too big, with lots of tables, a perfectly sized stage and a small balcony above. Known for its tributes to 'rock nacional' bands.
mitosargentinos. com.ar

1. Bermondsey's Beer Mile

Begin your evening early with a Saturday afternoon stroll along the railway arches in South London that have become home to several craft breweries. Kernel Brewery is open until 2pm, Partizan until 5pm.

2. Tapas Brindisa

Brindisa attracts a well-heeled, foodie crowd who know good tapas when they taste it. No bookings are accepted, so come early if you want to bag an outside table on Borough Market days.
brindisa.com

3. Bistrot Bruno Loubet

Overlooking St John's Sq, this is an elegant hotel restaurant with much-lauded chef Bruno Loubet at the helm. High-quality ingredients are transformed into dishes full of gutsy flavour combinations. As you'd expect, there's a well-chosen wine list and the service is impeccable.
bistrotbrunoloubet.com

4. Book Club

This former Victorian warehouse has been transformed into an innovative temple to good times. Spacious and whitewashed with large windows upstairs and a basement bar below, it hosts a variety of offbeat events, such as spoken word, dance lessons and life drawing, as well as a program of DJ nights.
wearetbc.com

5. Fabric

This impressive superclub is still the first stop on the London scene for many international clubbers. The crowd is hip and well dressed without overkill, and the music – electro, techno, house, drum and bass and dubstep – is as superb as you'd expect from London's top-rated club.
fabriclondon.com

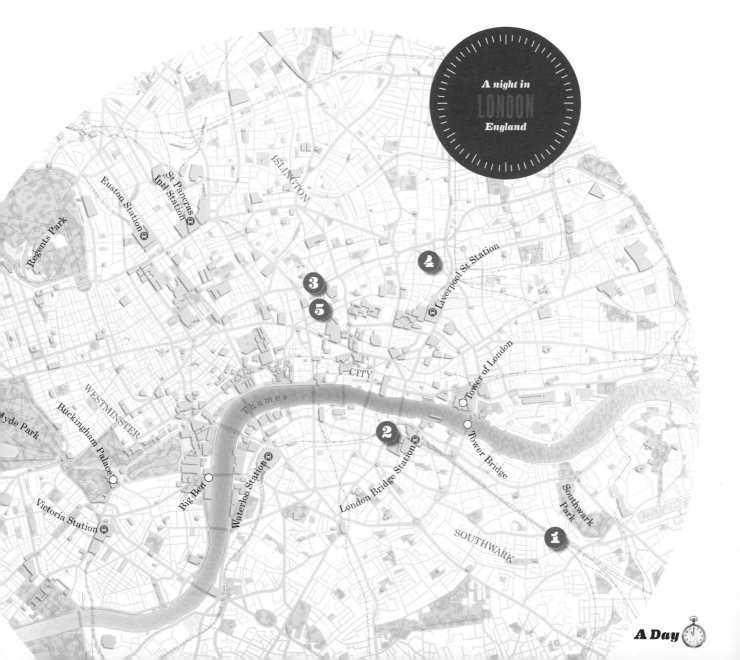

A night in LONDON England

A Day

SEE THE SUNSET

Put the camera down, there are enough snaps of sunsets in the world already. Instead, sit in stillness and just watch. Reflect on the day that is in the process of becoming yesterday, and what tomorrow will bring. Sunsets are a daily reminder of the passage of time. The average Westerner will see around 30,000, but every now and then, go somewhere spectacular, such as Arches National Park in Utah, and make one count.

A Day

SEEK SPIRITUAL ENLIGHTMENT

**ABSINTHE IN PARIS, GIN IN LONDON, WHISKY IN HOBART...
'THE ROAD OF EXCESS LEADS TO THE PALACE OF WISDOM', SOMETIMES.**

Hallucinations, fits, madness… all are ailments once said to be induced by drinking absinthe. The green, liquorice-flavoured liqueur had been banned in France since 1915, and was shrouded in mystery. But now the drink also known as the green fairy (*la fée vert* in French) is illegal no more. The heady drink exploded in popularity in France during the late 19th century, when artists and writers such as Van Gogh, Rimbaud and Wilde savoured its unusual taste, and the effects of drinking it – although most now accept that the influential French wine industry, threatened by the fashionable drink, was behind the ban.

You watch as the bartender begins the ritual, pouring a measure into a small glass, balancing a perforated spoon holding a sugar cube over the glass and then slowly adding water to the spoon, so sweetened water drips into the absinthe. Brewed from a concoction of natural herbs, true absinthe includes three crucial elements: anise, fennel and Artemisia absinthium (grand wormwood, used as a remedy since the time of the ancient Egyptians). Now you wait expectantly but receive only an agreeably – aniseed-flavoured buzz – perhaps more research is required. ●

1
Whisky, Tasmania
Some mistake, surely? Isn't the best whisky from Scotland? It turns out that Tasmania can also deliver some seriously impressive single malts, especially Sullivan's Cove distillery, just outside the state capital Hobart. It must be something to do with wind and rain.

2
Gin, London
London has come a long way since the debauched scenes of Gin Lane in the 18th century. Today, connoisseurs of the gin-and-tonic can tour a new wave of gin distilleries in the city, such as Sipsmith in west London, where you can admire Prudence and Patience, its twin copper stills.

3
Tequila, Mexico
Tequila's got a bad reputation for causing many a night out to take a wrong turn. But artisan producers, such as Casa Noble in the Highlands of Jalisco state, are restoring tequila to its rightful place as a drink to be sipped not slammed.
Tour Jalisco to taste some fine aged tequilas.

4
Sake, Akita, Japan
In the snowy north of Japan, Akita prefecture is the source of the country's best sake; experts say the cold prolongs the fermentation time. We say sample Akita's premium sake (best served cold) on a tour of the historic kuras or craft breweries and make up your own mind.

THE JACOBITE STEAMS OVER GLENFINNAN VIADUCT, SCOTLAND   Pete Seaward

GET STEAMED UP

**TAKE A TRIP BACK IN TIME WITH
A DAYTRIP ON A STEAM TRAIN.**

The Jacobite, Scotland's daily steam-hauled service has achieved a new kind of stardom as the *Hogwarts Express* in the Harry Potter films, in which it steams majestically across the Glenfinnan Viaduct. As you cross the snaking, single-track bridge there's a glimpse of Loch Shiel, and of the monument that marks the spot where Bonnie Prince Charlie first assembled his Jacobite army that nearly did so well for the Scots.

Even without a boyish interest in levers and furnaces, the history and landscape this train passes through is enough to ignite a passion for steam travel.

Beyond Glenfinnan, the train climbs through forests of ash, carpeted in a tartan of bluebells and bracken. The peaks are hung with the fraying rope of streams in spate and the lochs look like slices of sky fallen to the ground. Trailing clouds of steam, the *Jacobite* clatters through this mythical landscape, breathing hard. Then you round a corner and a door is thrown open to the sea. Suddenly, there's a view of islands out across the Sound of Arisaig, where Eigg, Rum and Muck crowd the horizon. Beyond Arisaig lie beaches, and water that's an otherworldly Caribbean blue. And then there's Mallaig, with the Isle of Skye in the distance, and you're standing on the rain-soaked platform at the end of your journey, a foot in the past and the present. ●

1

The Watercress Line, England
Watercress grown in Hampshire's water meadows was historically delivered to London's markets by steam train; part of the Mid-Hants railway, from Alresford to Alton, has been restored and sees steam trains return regularly to Hampshire's green countryside.

Durango & Silverton Narrow Gauge Railroad, USA

On this 70km restored railroad, a 1920s steam engine climbs 3000ft into Colorado's Rockies, over wood bridges and through forests, arriving at the historic mining town of Silverton. It's a breathtaking ride.

Puffing Billy, Victoria, Australia

Puffing Billy is just one of around 500 surviving (in various states of repair) steam engines in Australia. The much-loved, little green train puffs 24km daily from Belgrave to Gembrook in the Dandenong Ranges, just outside Melbourne.

Cass Scenic Railroad, USA

Short and sweet, this 18km heritage railway in West Virginia's forested mountains was built to service the logging town of Cass. Today it hauls sightseers up to Bald Knob station in open-air carriages; you'll need to wrap up warm.

TAXIS IN BANGKOK, THAILAND   Varsha Arora

TAKE A CAB

Nothing beats arriving in a strange new city – by day or night – and taking a taxi from the airport. This is your first sight of your destination. You're still decompressing from the flight, you're absorbing new sounds and smells and you're weighing up your driver. They're often emblematic of their city: forthright in London. Brusque in New York. Is yours a saviour or a shyster? And do you really want to see his cousin's hotel?

THE ESCAPE ARTIST

**COLIN EASTWOOD CYCLES ENGLAND'S
SOUTH DOWNS WAY IN A DAY – OR TWO**

A **lot of great ideas** are dreamed up in the pub. This one wasn't. It was something we'd talked about for years, maybe a decade. But marriages and kids came along, then I moved abroad. As is the way with these things, other 'stuff' happened and the plan took a backseat to what weekends are usually filled with. Time passed but one summer we could wait no longer: it was on.

The plan was this: on Saturday we'd jump on the early train out of London with our bicycles. An hour later we'd be in Winchester and at the start of the South Downs Way. We'd ride that 160km chalk ridge south towards its end in Eastbourne as far as we could until there was no longer enough light by which to see the ruts and fist-sized rocks of the track. Then we'd find a secluded corner of a wood, break out the bivouac bags, cook a stew over a campfire and settle down for a night under the stars. It was what adventurer Alastair Humphreys (see p307) calls a micro-adventure - a fleeting escape from the daily routine and a communion with nature and the hopefully clement elements.

In common with many of England's long-distance footpaths, such as the Ridgeway and the Icknield Way, people have been walking the South Downs for about six thousand years

> The sun arced over our heads and somewhere between the perpetual motion of the bicycle wheels and the spinning world, there seemed to be harmony

of the chalk ridge's sixty million year age. If you know where to look there's evidence of their presence: the climb up Old Winchester Hill, which we reached after a couple of hours of pedalling, passes an Iron Age fort and Bronze Age barrows. From the top of this bowl, as we stood under beech trees a vivid shade of green, the ground sloped steeply downwards, sprinkled with white sheep.

We pressed on past Butser Hill, the highest point on the South Downs, and flew along the farm tracks beyond. The sun arced over our heads and somewhere between the perpetual motion of the bicycle wheels and the spinning world beneath its tyres, there seemed to be harmony. In the golden afternoon light of late spring, low enough that it caught seeds floating in the hazy air, we passed a boy and his younger sister freewheeling the other way as we climbed yet another hill; I think he had a fishing rod strapped to his back. I remember thinking 'treasure days like this, you don't know how precious they are.'

We rode onward, always going up or down, tyres skittering over flints and chunks of chalk. At intervals along the route artist Andy Goldsworthy had carved giant chalk balls, as high as a man, in order that they could weather and shrink under the pressure of time and the elements.

As the sun dipped behind clouds on the horizon to our right, we could hear the soundtrack to the day shift; birds called to each other before roosting and a new nocturnal chorus started. Bats fluttered about our heads as we pulled out the bivvy bags and set up the stove.

We woke early to skylarks above us and a dull ache in our aging backs. But waking at dawn's limpid light had its own compensations; the world looked fresh, the sea in the distance sparkled. Fed and watered, we were ready for the day's ride to Brighton, via Devil's Dyke and the end of the Way in Eastbourne. But each mile we covered also brought us closer to the end of the escape from daily life. As we skirted the city of Brighton, the real world of timetables and traffic returned, and it took all the willpower we had not to turn around. ●

A Day

CLIMB A VOLCANO

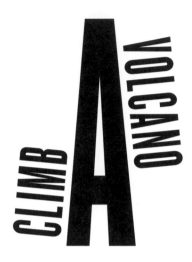

CLIMBING COTOPAXI, ECUADOR   Getty/Christian Kober

VOLCANOES IGNITE SOMETHING IN ALL OF US. TAKE A DAY TO CONNECT WITH THE DEEPEST REACHES OF OUR LITTLE PLANET.

One of the most accessible high-altitude volcano climbs is the ascent of South America's Cotopaxi, a 5897m-high peak that dominates Ecuador's central highlands with its glacier-draped cone, smoking fumerals and imposing stature.

Getting to the top starts in the dark. After a sleepless evening trying to acclimatise at 4800m, you leave the climber's refuge at midnight, stepping out in a headlamp glow across the bizarre moonscape of snow, shadow, rock and ravine. You'll don crampons and ice axe, and rope-up when you hit the glacier proper. From here, it's a six- to eight-hour mission past crevasses and hanging seracs toward the invisible summit.

By the time the sun starts to rise, you're nearly at the top, and a trance-inducing pace of step-breathe-rest, step-breathe-rest has taken over your body. A few more paces and you arrive: the top of the world. Stretching down below you, the volcano's shadow creeps across the high Andean plain. Quiet for now, the perfectly formed crater still smokes, and you pause to take a few more pictures before your descent. ●

Mt Fuji, Japan
Like many volcanoes around the world, Japan's 3776m Mt Fuji is sacred. Buddhists call it the 'Peak of the White Lotus'. Hundreds of people make it to the summit every day during the July and August climbing season, resting for the night in one of a dozen mountain huts. Find true solitude with a winter ascent.

 2

Kilauea, Hawaii, USA
Hawaii's Kilauea is arguably the most active volcano in the world; the current eruption has lasted since 1983. With a glorious lava lake at the summit caldera, a visit here, with views of flowing lava and billowing clouds of ash, is truly spectacular.

 3

Mt St Helens, USA
Part of the Pacific Rim of Fire, Mt St Helens' towering 2549m peak reigns over the lush and precipitous Cascade Mountains in Washington. Most famous for its ruthless explosion in 1980, killing scores of people and raining ash across the world, the beautiful peak can be climbed in a day.

 4

Kilimanjaro, Tanzania
The famous 'Snows of Kilimanjaro' are predicted by some to disappear in the next 20 years; now's the time to reach the 5895m summit – the highest in Africa – to ensure you see them. Along the way, you'll hike through pristine wilderness and journey with friendly porters and guides who make their livelihood from this natural wonder.

 A Day

Chapter
03

In which we take a week or two to drive the world's most
helicopter, spend an adventure-packed week on
Closer to home, a week is time enough to discover delights

EEK

exciting roads, spot the **Big Five** on safari, hail a
an island and swap houses with someone.
on your doorstep and learn dance steps to impress.

A Week

Chapter

03

GLASGOW TO OBAN, SCOTLAND
ASTON MARTIN DB5

Dramatic history meets beauty on this drive through Scotland's Highlands to the west coast town of Oban, where a dram of whisky awaits.

Start by leaving gritty Glasgow for the Loch Lomond and the Trossachs National Park, Scotland's first national park but long a favourite weekend getaway with its thickly forested hills and romantic lochs. The Trossach's are Rob Roy country: Robert MacGregor was the outlawed leader of the wildest of Scotland's clans and many Scots see his life as the symbol of the struggle of the common folk – detour east on the A85 to his grave in the small village of Balquhidder.

Get back on the road to Oban, a waterfront town on a delightful bay. Then continue up the coast towards Fort William if you wish to return to Glasgow via the A82 and Glen Coe, scene of the massacre of the MacDonald clan in the 17th century, and more recently driven by James Bond in the *Skyfall* film. **Start?** Glasgow **Finish?** Oban **How far?** 200km **When?** September for autumn hues. ●

GLEN COE, SCOTLAND   Getty/Jon Douglas

152

ROAD TRIPS

ROAD TRIPS RULE! DISCOVER THREE CLASSIC ROUTES
– AND THE PERFECT CAR IN WHICH TO DRIVE THEM.

GRAND STRADA DELLE DOLOMITI, ITALY

ALFA ROMEO GIULIA

Ranging across the South Tyrol, Alto Adige and Veneto, the Dolomites are one of the most beautiful mountain ranges in the world. Here, Austrian and Italian influences combine with the local Ladin culture. On this grand road trip your hosts may wear lederhosen, cure ham in their chimneys and use sleighs to travel from village to village.

To start, exit Bolzano on the SS241. As the route climbs towards Parco Naturale Fanes-Sennes-Braies, it passes the spectacular area of Alta Badia; throughout the day the play of shadow and light on the peaks of Pelmo, Civetta and Marmolada is breathtaking.

The high Fanes plateau, with its sculpted ridges and buttress towers of rock, has transfixed artists and poets for centuries; Wordsworth considered it a 'region of the heavens'. The trip ends at the Alpe di Siusi after a staggering 15km drive. There are few more beautiful juxtapositions than the green pastures and the Sciliar mountains.
Start? Bolzano **Finish?** Alpe di Siusi **How far?** 195km **When?** June for spring flowers. ●

BLUE RIDGE PARKWAY, USA
FORD MUSTANG

America's favourite byway curves through the leafy Appalachians, where it swoops up the East Coast's highest peak and stops by the nation's largest mansion.

The Blue Ridge Parkway stretches from Shenandoah National Park in Virginia to Great Smoky Mountains National Park in North Carolina. Construction of the road began in the Great Depression, harnessing the strength of out-of-work young men. In the Tar Heel State, the road carves a sinuous path through a rugged landscape of craggy peaks, crashing waterfalls, thick forests and charming mountain towns.

Start with a good night's sleep in Valle Crucis, a bucolic village west of Boone. At Grandfather Mountain, stop at the swinging bridge for views of the mountains.

Asheville, North Carolina, is the hippest town in these parts, with plenty of local microbrews to try, and the Blue Ridge Parkway Visitor Center nearby.

Start? Valle Crucis **Finish?** Waterrock Knob **How far?** 338km **When?** May to October. ●

A Week

STAY IN A TREEHOUSE

RELIVE YOUR CHILDHOOD IN A ROOM ABOVE THE FOREST FLOOR. SWEET DREAMS ARE MADE OF THIS.

Building a treehouse in childhood was one of those construction projects that, once embarked upon, always went over time and budget. The designer would have to account for fewer branches than anticated. There would need to be extra beams. More planks would have to be bought. And the result would often be lethally unsteady, plagued with splinters, and far from watertight.

But in Swedish Lapland, just outside the village of Harads, 60km south of the Arctic Circle, Britta and Kent Lindvall have done much of the hard work for you, creating the Treehotel. These are no ordinary treehouses; the facilities might be basic but the designs are brilliant. The architectural illusion of the Mirrorcube hides your room for the night among the trees. The Bird's Nest is inspired by a sea eagle's nest, and the UFO is simply out of this world.

These super-stylish and sustainable treehouses still have things in common with the childhood treehouse of your dreams. Sleeping suspended in the forest, you're still closer to the elements, the wind rushing through the branches, the rain pounding on the roof, soft flurries of snow in winter, warm late-night sunshine in the far northern summer, birds both seen and heard. For a few days a year, get back to nature and curl up in one of these treehouses. ●

THE MIRRCUBE TREEHOUSE IN SWEDEN   treehotel.se

THE BANGKOK TREEHOUSE, THAILAND   bangkoktreehouse.com

STAY IN A TREEHOUSE

Château dans les Arbes, France

As if a secluded hideaway in the trees wasn't enough of a childhood dream come true, at Châteaux dans les Arbes in the Dordogne, the leafy abodes are also miniature castles. Housed around the former moat of a ruined stronghold, the three creations are the handiwork of veteran treehouse-builder Rémi, who modelled them on nearby châteaux, complete with turrets and spires.

Free Spirit Spheres, Canada

The Free Spirit Spheres are suspended in the canopy by a web of ropes in the temperate rainforest of Vancouver Island. The smooth, wooden pods are designed to co-exist with their surroundings, and have minimum impact on the trees and wildlife. Creature comforts, including bathrooms and a sauna, are back on solid ground, while beyond the forest are the wineries and artisan eateries of the Cowichan Valley.

Chole Mjini, Tanzania

This cluster of seven treehouses is cradled by baobab trees on Chole, a tropical island east of the Tanzanian coast. Perched amongst vegetation and crumbling ruins, the thatched huts look like the creations of marooned voyagers, and staying in one feels about as removed from urban life as it's possible to be. Beyond the reach of electricity or even roads, they're perfectly placed for guests to appreciate the peace of the island.

Bangkok Treehouse, Thailand

Turbocharged Bangkok makes an unexpectedly tranquil location for a treehouse. In the city's southeast is Bang Krachao, a near-island carved by a loop of the Chao Phraya river. It's a place of mangrove, palm and fruit trees, threaded with waterways, semi-rural villages and centuries-old temples hidden in its midst. Presiding over the river are the dozen mid-air hideaways that comprise the eco-conscious Bangkok Treehouse.

LEARN TO DANCE

GET YOUR STEPS STRAIGHT IN FOUR OF THE DANCE CAPITALS OF THE WORLD AND TAKE A NEW SKILL HOME

Whether you're a smooth mover or the clumsy owner of two left feet, nothing can compare to getting to the roots of a dance in its home country. Forget dingy dance halls and robotic instructors, where else can you find an authentic atmosphere but where the people live and breathe the steps invented by their ancestors? You'll learn the history, appreciate the passion and culture and, with any luck, take your newfound expertise home with you – a secret skill you can tap into whenever you please, forever conjuring up memories of that special lesson in that special place. And no-one – no-one can ever tell you that you 'can't dance' when you know you've learnt from the very best in the world! Get set to impress by channelling your inner Astaire or Rogers, once you've swallowed your pride of course. The best bit will be surprising yourself, not just your friends back home.

Turn over for a tutorial in four dances...

LINDY HOP

NEW YORK CITY, USA

Evolving in the black communities of Harlem in the 1920s and '30s, the Lindy Hop was considered instrumental in breaking through the race barrier at the Savoy Ballroom, one of few racially integrated dance halls of the era. Considered a fusion of jazz, tap, breakaway and the Charleston, the Lindy Hop's most recognisable steps are the swing-out and the air step, where at least one of the dancing couple has both feet leaving the floor in time to the music. There's no denying its global resurgence in 'swing dancing' clubs but for real authenticity, go back to where it all began at the Harlem Swing Dance Society.

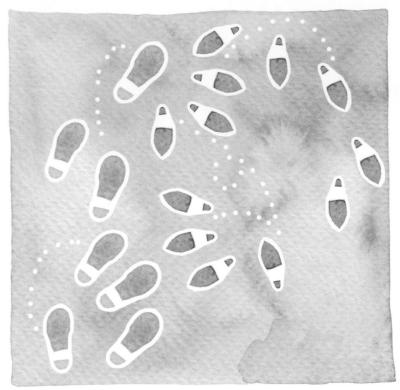

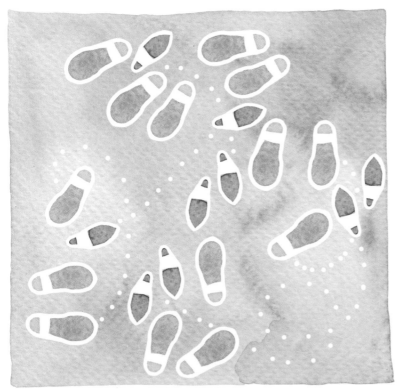

WALTZ

VIENNA, AUSTRIA

The waltz initially caused a stir for its 'dubious morals', given that it – gasp!— required a gentleman to put his arm around a lady and hold her close, unlike less intimate group dancing, previously the fashion in the 1780s. Originating as a folk dance in the Austrian suburbs, the Viennese waltz slightly anticipates the second beat, making it that bit faster than other waltzes.

And what better way to glide in ¾ time than by the Danube River to Johann Strauss' Blue Danube Waltz? In fact, ditch Auld Lang Syne and see in the New Year the romantic Austrian way, waltzing to Strauss; the Elmayer Dance School will also teach dance manners and etiquette!

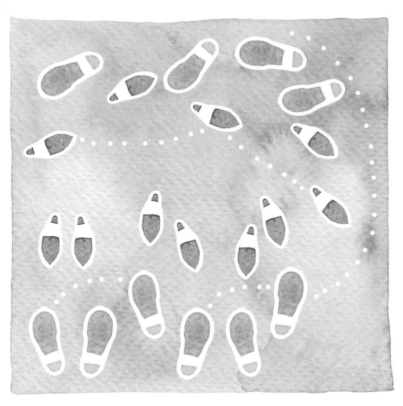

SALSA
HAVANA, CUBA

So you think you can salsa? Then you're in for a surprise in Havana, baby. Cuban salsa (also known as 'Casino') has its origins in sexual flirtation and is a lot more rotational than salsa dances taught elsewhere in the world.

Leave your gender equality at the door: male-dominated, Cuban salsa features a strong leader with a push-pull style – ideal for learners! Tradition requires males to be 'macho' and the women 'sexy' and the music needs to be 'felt' rather than necessarily following a beat. Don't be intimidated: it's all part of the cultural experience. Casa del Son in Old Havana is your safe place to start learning.

TANGO
BUENOS AIRES, ARGENTINA

The tango's history began in the bars and brothels of the city's colourful port area, La Boca. Here, immigrants from all over Europe mingled their own musical traditions with local rhythms like candombe, which arrived a century or so earlier on African slave ships. The rhythm and lyrics combined to symbolise the plaintive cry of the homesick immigrant, the jilted lover's bitter lament and the porteño's hymn to Buenos Aires. Away from the public displays and dinner shows there are milongas (tango dance halls) across the city, from cavernous ballrooms to intimate clubs. Try the Escuela Argentina de Tango for classes and BA Milongas for up-to-date listings.

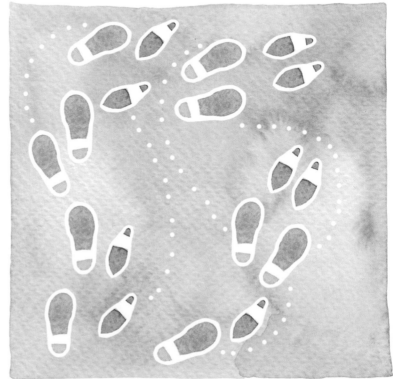

LEARN TO
DANCE

SEEK OUT SECRET PLACES

Not every amazing sight will find its way onto the cover of a guidebook. Indeed, some have been forgotten about completely. Websites such as Atlas Obscura are dedicated to rediscovering these alternative attractions. Even in cities there are mysterious places under and above ground. One fertile hunting ground is the former Soviet republics; check out the concrete war memorials built in the 1960s and 1970s in the former Yugoslavia. And what about this strange construction? It's the former Communist headquarters on Mt Buzludzha in Bulgaria, now abandoned.

STARA ZAGORA, BULGARIA   Matt Munro

DOORSTEP DISCOVERY

NICOLA WILLIAMS LEARNS TO LOVE WHAT'S LOCAL

As the last of the sun's rays blazed across the water before sinking behind the dark mountains beyond, the old-fashioned wooden schooner sliced through its pink reflection. Red sails tangoed in the soft summer breeze and we lazed in their shade, sipping the last of our champagne. And to think this was right on my doorstep, on the southern shore of Lake Geneva.

Several months prior, I'd taken a tumble, broken my back, and was trussed up in a brace for the best part of a year. Travel per se was not prohibited – but planes, trains and automobiles were. If I was to go anywhere, my internal compass required a dramatic reboot.

Monday
My culinary curiosity was the first to succumb. All too soon my ritual morning stroll wound up at the village boucherie where golden roast chickens tantalised on a spit outside, and the line snaked out the door on Sunday mornings. I grilled the butcher for his culinary secrets, smugly leaving with

several veal slices and his recipe for paupiettes de veau (veal roulades) simmered in local Savoie wine.

Tuesday
I walked to the neighbouring village to buy fish direct from the fisherman. I'd often watched his boat cross the lake from my kitchen window, a lonesome speck returning home from a pre-dawn voyage to empty out crayfish pots and nets swimming with silvery

Forget jetting off to Italy to hunt truffles... the sudden grassroots intimacy I was experiencing with my home was revelatory

perch and féra. But it took perseverance to find the unpaved lane leading to his house on the shore. The passion with which Madame, deftly filleting the catch, explained how to create the perfect oil, lemon and garlic marinade to douse over her legendary hand-cut carpaccio de féra was humbling and overwhelming.

Wednesday
I started devouring signs. I learnt that the Espace Litorelle, our village hall, which had caused such a rumpus at the time with its radically contemporary facade, was named after la litorelle (Littorella uniflora), a rare and protected aquatic plant with tiny cream flowers that has grown for centuries on Lake Geneva's shores.

Thursday
Indulging one's inner child is an essential part of travel – even on one's very own doorstep – hence the day I discovered the Chemin des Douaniers, an overgrown footpath that sneaked from the public beach into thick woods. Ten minutes stumbling over tree roots in the half-dark rewarded with brilliant blue sunshine, a Dolby Surround view of the open lake and a clear footpath that curled as far as the eye could see along the lake's pebbled shore. This secret lakeside path, a voyeur's peephole on the lavish villas bejewelling Lake Geneva, was pure gold.

Friday
As summer bit the dust and the rains came, I found myself tramping with the local farmer's wife through soggy oak and hornbeam woods in search of wild boletus, golden chanterelles and nutty tasting Trumpets of Death (not deadly, I quickly learnt). Forget jetting off to Italy to hunt truffles or to Japan to chase the sun, the sudden grass-roots intimacy I was experiencing with my home was revelatory.

Saturday
And so I came to sail La Licorne, a magnificent grand dame of a double-mast schooner that had worked the seas as a fishing vessel in the 1960s, perfectly capping off my local voyage of discovery. ●

RIDING IN THE ROCKY MOUNTAINS   Getty/Cavan Images

SADDLE UP FOR HORSE PACKING

GIDDY UP! PICK A STEED, SLIDE INTO THE SADDLE AND SPEND A WEEK IN SOME TOUGH TERRAIN THAT WILL HAVE YOU CONTEMPLATING YOUR EXISTENCE IN NO TIME.

Always *secretly wanted to be the Marlboro Man?* Your trip starts in Montana in a small town two hours' drive from anywhere. You overnight in a funky historic hotel, and wait for your guide – an honest-to-goodness cowboy organised by Off The Beaten Path in Bozeman – to collect you in his pick-up. He drives to the trailhead, where a horse trailer is waiting, and while you eat a ham sandwich made by his wife, he saddles-up the horses and packs the gear onto five mules.

And then you set out. The parking lot, such as it was, fades into the distance as the horses ascend the trail into the Beartooth Mountains. All is silent, save for the soft crunch of dry leaves under hooves; there's no expectation of conversation on a long, companionable ride. It's accepted – no, expected – that you'll use the time in the saddle to ponder thorny problems, contemplate your place in the world, let the larger-than-life vistas give you healthy perspective. Your phone won't vibrate, and you won't get a status update, except those from your horse when she's hungry or tired. You'll tune into her as she plods steadily into the wilds. Your back and thighs may get achy, you might feel a bit saddle-sore, and you've certainly earned the right to feel worn out. But you're looking forward to three more days of the same.

Hours later your guide announces it's time to make camp. You could sit your weary bones down on a rock with your book, your thoughts or just that mountain view while he does all the work. But hard, honest labour appeals to you, so you help with the chores: fetching water from the sparkling mountain lake, pitching the tents, feeding the horses, collecting firewood (OK, tinder in your case – there's no question who's doing the real work here). Then you share stories by the campfire, while he grills steaks and you gaze at the riot of stars overhead. ●

1

Fazenda Catuçaba, Brazil
This charming farmhouse-turned-boutique-hotel celebrates rural Brazil's equestrian culture, offering rides of varying lengths with charming guides.

168

Triple Creek Ranch, USA
Horse riding is a year-round activity at this Montana hideaway. Things ramp up each autumn, when the ranch hosts a women-only 100km trail ride (returning nightly to the comfortable ranch, rather than camping out) called Klicks for Chicks, and donates part of the profits to a local Parkinson's charity.

Equitours, worldwide
This outfitter has 40 years of experience organising horseback vacations for riders of all abilities in far-flung destinations. Guests might gallop with zebras in Kenya, ride with nomads in Mongolia, drive cattle in Wyoming or saunter through vineyards in France.

La Morada de Los Andes, Argentina to Chile
Every February this winery and luxury residential community in Mendoza hosts guests on a five-night Gourmet Andes Crossing through the mountains to Santiago. The riding is hard, but the wine flows freely.

A Week

NEW YORK

There are two places that are truly once-in-a-lifetime musts – and they couldn't be more different. You've got a week, do you spend it in the Big Apple, fast, loud, pulsing with creative energy?

Population *8.3 million*
Population density *10,725 / sq km*
Visitors *55 million*
Restaurants *24,000*
Most famous landmark *The Statue of Liberty*

THE HIGH LINE PARK ON THE LOWER WEST SIDE OF MANHATTAN   Matt Munro

NEW ZEALAND

Or do you visit the Land of the Long White Cloud, green, serene and pulsing with natural energy? Or – and this is the right answer – somehow do you vow to see both before you die?

Population *4.5 million*
Population density *16 / sq km*
Visitors *3 million*
Restaurants *c.7000*
Most famous landmark *The Big Sheep Shearer of te Kuiti*

CHOPPER

TAKE THE

IMAGINE SKIING THE BEST RUN OF YOUR LIFE. ON REPEAT. TEN TO 15 TIMES A DAY. FOR A WEEK. ONCE YOU'VE HELI-SKIED, NOTHING ELSE WILL COMPARE.

T*his is the kind of descent* most people experience once in a lifetime, and only then if perfect weather conditions hit, and they had the good sense to rise at the crack of dawn and make first place in the lift queue.

You're on EA's Last Frontier heli-trip to the Skeena Mountain Range in British Columbia, just 40 miles from the Alaskan border. The terrain at your disposal is 25 times the size of Les Trois Vallées (the largest ski resort in the world), and averages 25m of snow a year, compared to an approximate 5m in Alpine resorts.

In a group of just five, you tackle waist-deep dry cold powder, charging down mountains few people have ever seen, let alone skied. You marvel at the variety of terrain, encompassing steeps, wide-open bowls, seemingly endless glaciers and top-quality tree skiing. With each turn the snow's layer of surface hoar makes its crystals sparkle in the sun, and the experience feels that little bit more magical.

When you can't take any more and your legs start begging for mercy you treat them to a hot tub at the Bell 2 Lodge, home to atmospheric log-wood cabins with cosy fires and mellow vibes. ●

Heli-biking, Wanaka, New Zealand
Circle Mt Cook, New Zealand's highest mountain, and three giant lakes, taking in breathtaking views of snowy peaks before landing at 2200m for the start of the country's highest mountain-bike trail. You'll begin with dual single track undulating along the ridgeline, moving onto rolling hills for the lower section of your ride and finishing up at the region's oldest pub.

Heli-boarding, Kamchatka, Russia
Home to some of the best freeriding on the planet, Kamchatka boasts 29 active volcanoes, many of which you can snowboard down, ending up at the Pacific Ocean. McNab Snowboarding offers heli-trips here for fit and experienced backcountry boarders. McNab, who guides, holds the US Medal of Valor for rescuing a stranded climber – so you're in safe hands.

Heli-hiking, Pir Panjal Range, the Himalayas
If you want to hike some awesome, untrodden Himalayan terrain and arrive in high spirits rather than with serious journey ennui, try a Himalayan Heli Adventure in the Pir Panjal Range. Aside from quick access to the most pristine rocky meadows with high mountain backdrops, the heli-ride itself is truly stunning.

Heli-kayaking, Bear Glacier, Alaska
Swoop in above the icebergs and spectacular glacial landscape of the Kenai Fjords National Park, then leave your chopper and kayak right up to Bear Glacier. The trip provides a totally different perspective on this region, plus the chance to get a close-up view of whales, seals, sea lions and puffins.

SUPER SAFARIS

WITNESS THE MAJESTY OF MOTHER NATURE'S GREATEST CREATURES IN AFRICA'S FIVE FINEST PARKS.

With each stroke of the paddle you are stirring a river where giants lurk. And as you glide slowly along the still surface of the Zambezi in your canoe, you quickly get the feeling you are being watched... Eyes pop up here and there, vanishing beneath the surface as swiftly as they appear. You listen to your guide and stick to the shallows, which keeps the onlookers at a distance, something you're grateful for given these eyes belong to creatures who weigh over 1500kg and sport canines that are half a metre long. Hippos are much like icebergs – what looms below is far more impressive than what is visible above the water, and most importantly, you never want to crash into one.

The mighty river's banks in Zambia's Lower Zambezi National Park are no less dramatic – vervet monkeys screech from branches to warn of prowling leopards, hulking elephants tower over sandbanks, and 5m-long Nile crocodiles bask in the sun with their mouths agape and their glistening teeth on display. You might even follow a lion pride from just a few metres away and look each of them in the eye as they stop to slake their thirst.

Yet, despite all the natural theatrics and sense of danger, there are such feelings of peace and absolute wonder. That is what makes a safari so very special. You aren't just seeing the world's most iconic species of wildlife in astoundingly beautiful surroundings, you're witnessing them living their unique lives on their terms. You're a guest in a world that is not yours. And it's never possible to forget that. ●

A Week

You Only Live Once

A LEOPARD IN THE SERENGETI NATIONAL PARK   Fiona McAnally

1
Serengeti National Park, Tanzania
The Serengeti, which covers 14,763 sq km and is contiguous with Masai Mara National Reserve in Kenya, is Tanzania's most famous park. Wildebeest (and the leopards that ambush them) of which there are over one million, are among the most prominent residents roaming its vast plains and their annual migration is the Serengeti's biggest drawcard.

2
Etosha National Park, Namibia
Covering an area of more than 20,000 sq km, Etosha National Park is one of the world's great wildlife-watching venues. Its name, which means Great White Place of Dry Water is inspired by a vast flat, saline desert that is converted by rains into a shallow lagoon teeming with animals for a few days a year. The surrounding land-scape is home to 114 mammal species and 340 bird species.

3
Kruger National Park, South Africa
In South Africa's must-see wildlife destination, enougb elephants to populate a city wander around, giraffes nibble on acacia trees, hippos wallow in rivers, leopards prowl through the night and a multitude of birds sing, fly and roost. The park has an extensive network of roads but if you prefer to keep it rough there are also 4WD tracks and walking trails. The far north of the Kruger is the wilder side.

4
Moremi Game Reserve, Botswana
Moremi is the only part of the Okavango Delta that is set aside for the preservation of wildlife. It's a massive oasis, now home to the Big Five (lion, leopard, buffalo, elephant and rhino) and one of the largest populations of African wild dogs. Wildlife concentrations are mind-boggling during the dry season but Moremi is also one of Botswana's most exclusive places to expect to pay for the privilege.

SUPER SAFARIS

50 WAYS TO UNPLUG

By Patrick Kinsella

PLAY A GAME OF CARDS IN A NEW YORK SPEAKEASY

JOIN IN WITH A GAME OF BOULES IN A VILLAGE IN CENTRAL FRANCE

SPEND AN AFTERNOON LAZILY KAYAKING ALONG THE CROATIAN COAST

WATCH THE WEATHER ROLL IN AT VANCOUVER ISLAND

SKIM A STONE ON ONE OF THE GREAT LAKES OF NORTH AMERICA

HAVE A GAME OF STREET FOOTBALL IN LA BOCA, BUENOS AIRES, ARGENTINA

EXPERIENCE AN IMPROMPTU MUSIC SESSION IN A PUB ON THE WEST COAST OF IRELAND

DO SOME GUERRILLA KNITTING IN CALIFORNIA

BUILD A HANGI IN NEW ZEALAND

GO SKI TOURING IN LEBANON

LISTEN TO A VINYL RECORD IN AQUARIUS RECORDS, SAN FRANCISCO

TUCK INTO SOME LEGENDARY BANANA BREAD ON A LAKE MALAWI BEACH

RENT A BIKE AND CYCLE ALONG A CANAL IN AMSTERDAM

WALK A DOG (OR YOUR FRIEND'S DOG)

CYCLE AROUND THE ANCIENT WALLS OF LUCCA IN TUSCANY, ITALY

EXPERIENCE A GAME OF NON-PROFESSIONAL AUSTRALIAN RULES FOOTBALL IN THE NORTHERN TERRITORY

BUY A SECOND-HAND BOOK ON CHARING CROSS ROAD, LONDON

SNOOZE ON UPPEVELLI BEACH, SRI LANKA

VISIT A VINEYARD IN MOLDOVA

VISIT THE OLDEST ORGANISMS ON EARTH, THE STROMATOLITES IN SHARK BAY, AUSTRALIA

CAMP OUT IN A SAFARI TENT IN THE OKAVANGO DELTA, BOTSWANA

GO NIGHT SWIMMING AMONG BIOLUMINESCENT PLANKTON IN MAYA BAY, THAILAND

RIDE A HORSE ALONG THE BEACH IN MONTEGO BAY, JAMAICA

SEE SUNRISE OVER CAPE TOWN FROM THE TOP OF TABLE MOUNTAIN

QUAFF A LOCALLY BREWED BEER IN BRUGES, BELGIUM

WATCH SOME COW WRESTLING IN VALAIS, SWITZERLAND

PUT DOWN THE IPAD AND PLAY AN AL FRESCO GAME OF CHESS IN ST PETERSBURG

SOUR IN PERU

WALK AROUND THE WALLS OF DERRY IN NORTHERN IRELAND

STAND NEXT TO THE DIPLODOCUS SKELETON IN LONDON'S NATURAL HISTORY MUSEUM

ATTEND A TEA CEREMONY IN JAPAN

IMMERSE YOURSELF IN AN ONSEN IN RURAL JAPAN

SHARE A GOURD OF MATE IN BARRA DE VALIZAS, URUGUAY

DOZE IN AN APRICOT ORCHARD IN THE ATLAS MOUNTAINS OF MOROCCO

OBSERVE A FAMILY OF GRIZZLY BEARS IN KLUANE NATIONAL PARK, YUKON, CANADA

PACK A PICNIC FOR THE BEACH

FIND A FOSSIL ON CHESIL BEACH, DORSET, ENGLAND

SEE THE OTHER SIDE OF LAS VEGAS AND GO MOUNTAIN BIKING ON THE NEARBY TRAILS

DRINK A PISCO

GET A WET SHAVE IN THE MARKET BARBERS IN SALALAH, OMAN

WATCH A GAME OF VILLAGE RUGBY ON THE YASAWA ISLANDS, FIJI

GO BACK IN TIME AT NEOLITHIC SITES ON ORKNEY, SCOTLAND

WALK THROUGH A WADI IN OMAN AND SLEEP OUT IN THE OPEN UNDER THE DESERT STARS

EXPLORE THE CATACOMBS IN PARIS

DO A SESSION OF LAUGHTER YOGA IN BANGALORE, INDIA

TRY FREE SOLOING (ROCK CLIMBING OVER WATER) IN HALONG BAY, VIETNAM

TAKE A BOAT TO FINGAL'S CAVE IN SCOTLAND

LOUNGE AROUND IN A THERMAL POOL UNDER THE MIDNIGHT SUN IN ICELAND

EAT A DINOSAUR-SIZED STEAK IN MENDOZA, ARGENTINA

VISIT A GAELTACHT AREA OF IRELAND AND TRY ORDERING A PINT IN IRISH

HIT THE BOOKS AT THE BIBLIOTHÈQUE NATIONALE DE FRANCE

A COMPETITOR AT THE WORLD BEARD & MOUSTACHE CHAMPIONHSIP   Alamy/EPA

BECOME A WORLD CHAMPION

WE'VE EACH GOT A UNIQUE GIFT. AND WHERE THERE'S TALENT, THERE'S A TOURNAMENT. TRY YOUR HAND AT AN ARCANE EVENT AND YOU NEVER KNOW WHAT MAD SKILLS YOU MIGHT UNLEASH.

The buzz of anticipation simmers through freezing Sōbetsu, Hokkaido. You and your six snow-hungry friends are sizing up the 150 teams that make up the competition at this seriously upgraded version of a snowball fight, held annually in northern Japan.

The Showa-Shinzan International Yukigassen (Japanese for 'snow fight') is an icy take on 'capture the flag', with teams of seven players, 90 machine-made snowballs and one mission: to get the opponents' flag or tally points through body hits.

You don helmets, gloves and ready your team flag – and the whistle blows. Blizzards of snowballs rain down but you swing yourself this way, then that, narrowly missing them all. You crouch, crawl, duck, dive and lurch for cover before making a final break for the flag. Success!

But that was just the prelim – your real fight to be champs starts now. ●

World Beard & Moustache Championship, worldwide

This superhip, globetrotting event, created in Germany in 1990, will be held in Portland, Oregon (of course) in 2014, and Leogang, Austria the following year. Contestants frequently put as much effort into their outfits (Edwardian suits etc) as the hairy creations on their faces. Nothing beats the unpredictability and wonder of a conceptualised freestyle moustache.

Best Baggers Contest, USA

Grocery bagging is a serious business, with the best baggers able to scientifically fill every cubic inch. Every year, regional competitions culminate with a national Best Baggers Contest, hosted by the National Grocers Association. If you take care to properly distribute the weight, and complete your bagging with lightning speed while maintaining a friendly attitude, you can be number one.

Wife Carrying, Finland

This proud Finnish tradition involves a man negotiating a 253.5m obstacle course while carrying his wife (or the closest he can get), usually upside-down, with her legs wrapped around the man's neck. It's held in July and is governed by the decree that 'everyone must have fun'.

World Stone Skimming Championship, Easdale Island, Scotland

This Scottish tradition involves standing at the shorelines of an old slate-mining island, picking a stone out of a bucket and sliding it across the surface – if it skips at least three times, you're eligible. But it's distance travelled rather than the number of skips that takes the prize in this event.

A Week

MISSISSIPPI BLUES PERFORMANCE

**GARTH CARTWRIGHT GETS THE BLUES
IN THE DEEP SOUTH**

Strip back any form of contemporary music and you'll find something that owes a debt of gratitude to the blues. A journey to its birthplace paints an eye-opening historical portrait and is an inspirational pilgrimage for fans of the genre.

Travelling through the Mississippi Delta, you'll spot funky little roadside shacks, often built out of scrap materials and defying all conventional building codes (and don't even think about health and safety). These are the legendary juke joints, the last remaining vestiges of the place where the blues took shape. Once providing a place for African-American sharecroppers to relax after a hard week's labour, juke joints were rowdy places – juke is a West African word meaning 'disorderly' – filled with music and dancing,

U2 and The Rolling Stones have been known to drop in on an after-hours juke, while Robert Plant has, on occasion, got up and sang

and a welcome escape from a crushing existence.

Although now much reduced in number, juke joints are still crowded with locals at weekends, both in urban and rural areas; here they seek out the blues – live, DJed or simply on the jukebox. Juke joints remain the closest a blues fan can get to hearing the music, raw and local.

Paying homage to the likes of Robert Johnson, Muddy Waters and Howling Wolf, blues pilgrims originally tended to be white American music fanatics who risked imprisonment by entering the jukes – until the end of segregation in the late 1960s it was illegal for whites and blacks to socialise together. As blues won a broader international audience, due to the success of British rock bands, Stevie Ray Vaughan and BB King, pilgrims from all across the world began riding Highway 61, which runs through the Mississippi Delta and pulses with blues history. U2 and The Rolling Stones have been known to drop in on an after-hours juke, while Robert Plant has, on occasion, got up and sang.

Mississippi now has a whole host of activities for blues pilgrims. Blues Trail Markers across the state show where famous artists lived, worked, prayed, recorded and died. Clarksdale, 90 minutes' drive south of Memphis, is a mecca for fans; Bessie Smith tragically died here, while Ike Turner and Sam Cooke are famous sons of the run-down cotton town. It's home to the Delta Blues Museum, as well as Cat Head, a fabulous shop specialising in blues and folk art. Ground Zero Blues Club, a live-music bar and restaurant part-owned by Morgan Freeman, is well worth seeking out. Amongst a variety of accommodation there are re-conditioned sharecropper shacks for those who want to experience how the blues singers lived, albeit with 21st-century comforts. And in April the town explodes with the annual Juke Joint Festival, where revellers gorge on beer, barbecue and, of course, plenty of the blues. ●

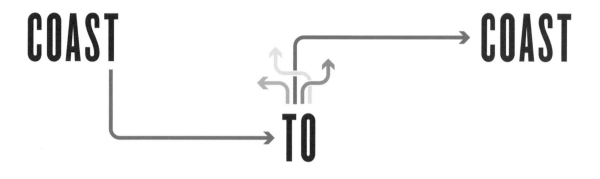

COAST TO COAST

FROM SEA TO SHINING SEA: THERE'S MORE THAN ONE WAY TO CROSS A COUNTRY. RIDE A BIKE ACROSS ENGLAND, A HORSE ACROSS COSTA RICA OR HIKE IRELAND.

Just one more hill... If someone tells you that on the Sea to Sea (C2C) cycle route across northern England, you should be suspicious. For the route crosses some of the more rugged stretches of the country, huffing and puffing its way over the Pennines, England's spine, via the northern Lake District National Park.

For a physical challenge, cycling across a country is as easy or hard as you make it. It's around 550km across Italy, which could easily stretch into a week's ride via idyllic Umbrian and Tuscan towns, fuelled by delicious homemade pasta and Chianti. Then there's the USA, with Adventure Cycling's shortest mapped route being its 4800km Southern Tier tour through California, Arizona, Texas, Louisiana and Florida. This will take more than a week.

But as you pedal up Whinlatter Pass in England's Lake District, before stopping at the 4500-year-old Castlerigg stone circle near Keswick, you may be thankful that this route across England's northern neck is just 225km. Most of the 12,000 cyclists who attempt it annually do so from west to east, hoping for a following wind to push them over the Pennines. And then it's downhill all the way to Newcastle or Sunderland. Mostly. ●

You Only Live Once

HORSE-RIDING IN COSTA RICA   Getty/Brian Bailey

COAST TO COAST

Ireland by foot
There are almost 10,000 pubs scattered across Ireland and by halfway of your cross-country walk from Dublin to Portmagee on the Atlantic coast, it feels as though you've been inside most of them. Ireland is a country that refuses to be rushed, so take your time on this 622km trail, which stitches together waymarked trails through Wicklow, South Leinster, East Munster, Blackwater and Kerry.

Costa Rica on horseback
On each day of this sea-to-ocean odyssey you've faced totally new terrain with your criollo steed, from soft Caribbean sand at the outset to the lushness of the rainforest. The highlands of this astonishingly diverse country will provide the main challenge, as you cross the back of Central America and descend to the Pacific coast.

Ski across Spitsbergen, Norway
Few people have done a self-sufficient, coast-to-coast traverse of the largest island in the archipelago of Svalbard, skiing across glaciers and spending each star-spangled night in a mountain tent on the ice. During the four-day west-to-east expedition from the Barents Sea to the Greenland Sea you'll feel like an arctic explorer.

Australia's Savannah Way by 4WD
Leaving steamy Cairns and rising through the rainforests to the Tablelands that tower above the Wet Tropics, a long and rough road lies in wait. Driving in the hoofsteps of the old drovers, you've got 3700km to negotiate before reaching Broome in the gorgeous Kimberley. It's incredibly remote driving; mind the saltwater crocs.

SHOOT A VIDEO

With the advent of compact and high-quality video cameras there's no reason not to strap on a GoPro and tell the story of your trip from your own point of view. Just remember to cut and edit before you share; nobody wants to see the wobbly out-takes.

HUNT A MONSTER

THEY SEEK HIM HERE! THEY SEEK HIM THERE! TRACK DRACULA IN TRANSYLVANIA, YETIS IN THE HIMALAYA AND LARGE LAKE-DWELLING MONSTERS IN SCOTLAND.

Sprawling along the edge of the snowy Carpathians, Europe's last truly wild mountain range, Transylvania is a land that is rich in myths and legends. A region of Romania since 1918 but historically an independent province, Transylvania's history has been shaped by the people that have passed through over the centuries: Saxons, Ottomans, Hungarians, Jews, Serbs and Roma Gypsies. With them came stories collected on their travels: tales of goblins and giants, fairy queens and woodland nymphs, unearthly phantoms, man-eating ogres and predatory ghouls.

Venture out on a moonlit night and you might encounter the *pricolici*, the devilish werewolves said to be the restless spirits of violent men. And then there are the legends of the *strigoi*, or vampires, which fired the imagination of an Irish writer by the name of Bram Stoker, and inspired him to write his Gothic bestseller, *Dracula*, in 1897...

Dracula is everywhere in Transylvania. Every town claims a tenuous link with his real-life counterpart Vlad Țepeș, the warlord who ruled the kingdom of Wallachia intermittently between 1448 and 1476, and who had a predilection for impaling his enemies on stakes. Few places sell their Dracula connections harder than Bran Castle in the Carpathian foothills, about 30km south of the well-preserved medieval town of Brașov. But disentangling truth from tales is more difficult; Vlad's actual castle was 200km north – and many of the more bloodthirsty myths about him were propaganda. ●

Yeti, Himalaya
Of all the giant ape-man legends, the yeti is the most enduring and documented. This is perhaps because it occupies one of the most remote corners of the world, in the foothills of Nepal and Tibet, where it conveniently leaves an occasional footprint.

Nessie, Scotland
Deep, dark and narrow, Loch Ness stretches for 37km between Inverness and Fort Augustus. Its bitterly cold waters have been extensively explored in search of Nessie, the elusive Loch Ness monster first 'sighted' in 1933.

Bunyip, Australia
In a land delineated by Aboriginal mythology, tales of the Bunyip are some of the more nightmarish. The beast – consistent descriptions are hard to find – inhabits swamps and rivers. When otherworldy screams are heard in the Outback at night, the Bunyip is blamed.

Bigfoot, USA
Star of many a blurry Super-8 video, Bigfoot resides in the beautiful forests of the Pacific Northwest. It established itself in popular folklore in the 1950s, round about the time that the regions wild woods were being explored by increasing numbers of hikers.

A Week

US$100

weekly budget

of Graham Hughes, who used buses, taxis, trains to visit 201 countries in the world over 1426 days, finishing in November 2012.

13.7

shots

of liquor South Koreans drink per week on average, mostly in the form of soju, a fermented rice spirit.

6

weeks

duration of a 1600km record-setting rickshaw ride around Britain by Tim Moss in 2010.

19 & 2

weeks and days

time it took Sean Conway to swim the length of Britain, 900 miles from Land's End to John O'Groats in 2013.

8 & 1

weeks and day

duration of a 2,246.21km roller ski trip taken by Cesar Baena in 2012, starting from Stockholm, Sweden and finishing in Holmenkollen, Norway.

224

minutes

average time people in France spend shopping every week.

20&2

weeks and days

length of time Geoff Smith spent buried underground in a 7ft wooden box in the garden of the Railway Inn, Mansfield, in 1999.

560,000

number of tourists

who flock to the old section of Venice (population: 57,960), each week during high season.

4,4&12

weeks, days and hours

the longest time it has taken a team to finish the Iditarod dog-sledding race in Anchorage to Nome in Alaska.

US$6181

cost of going glamping

for a week at Sanctuary Swala in Tarangire National Park, Tanzania, in high season.

9

weeks

average time it will take to walk New Zealand's new country-spanning trail, the 3000km Te Araroa (The Long Pathway).

8&5

weeks and day

length of the longest snowmobile journey, a 19,575km trip completed by Robert G. Davis from the US state of Maine into Canada in 2008.

MEND A BROKEN HEART

WHAT BECOMES OF THE BROKEN-HEARTED? PICK UP THE PIECES WITH THESE TRAVEL IDEAS FOR LIFE AFTER THE EX FACTOR.

Life goes on. And it is the little steps that move you forward, quite literally, on the Camino de Santiago. You're on the world's most famous pilgrimage trail, stretching almost 800km through the wilds of northern Spain. Every day eases the heartache and brings new horizons. You can't help but live by your senses as you traverse a 2000m mountain pass in the Pyrenees, battle driving rain on the wave-thrashed Atlantic coast, or hobble to the next *refugio*, blisters throbbing, as day fades to dusk. Forced to let go of the past and embrace the here and now, you become you once again.

Out here on the wide-open trail, there is time to think and space to breathe but no place to hide. Moments of quiet introspection aside, the camino is where friendships are forged and experiences shared – just as they have been for the past 1000 years. Walking side by side with new companions in the shadow of snowcapped peaks, through the undulating vineyards of Rioja and the mist-draped hills of Navarra is refreshing – liberating even. The constant rhythm of footfall on rock is cathartic. The spirit of camaraderie is life-affirming.

Yes, you have been to hell and back in your relationship, but after several weeks on the trail, the fog of depression begins to clear and your spirits soar as you take in the high barren plains of the *meseta* (tableland) and Galicia's ever-changing palette of greens. Like countless pilgrims before you, you rest your weary bones against the ancient pillars of Santiago de Compostela's cathedral, the final resting place of St James the Apostle. Sweet relief floods every fibre of your being; as one journey ends, another begins. ●

A Week

NEON-LIT NIGHTLIFE IN NASHVILLE   Myles New

MEND A BROKEN HEART

Sing the blues

It's only natural to grieve for lost love, but if you're gonna do it, do it right, yeah? Where better to wallow in the blues than in its rightful home. Follow the Blues Brothers to the dimly lit joints of Chicago or drown your sorrows while dreaming of new tomorrows in Nashville's neon-lit honky-tonks. The ultimate road trip to Bluesville is Highway 61 through Tennessee and Mississippi. It sure beats listening to Van the Man on your iPod.

Spread your wings

There's nothing like learning a skill to give you a new focus and lift your spirits, be it a week-long photography course in Morocco, a perfume-making workshop in France or a painting break with like-minded souls in Italy. Always wanted to learn to paraglide or hike the Inca Trail? Now is the time. Physical activity is a great stressbuster and confidence booster, and there's no place like the great outdoors for letting things go.

Trip of a lifetime

You're footloose and fancy-free again, and the world really is your oyster. Expense be damned – book that once-in-a-lifetime ticket to Antarctica or the Australian Outback that will give you the vast horizons you need to clear your head. Or perhaps you've always wanted to see the sun rise over the Mongolian steppe on the epic Trans-Siberian. There's never been a better time.

Give back a little

Why not turn a negative into a positive? Doing something worthwhile can provide a much-needed switch of focus. A voluntary conservation project in the Ecuadorian jungle, helping orphaned street kids from Mombasa's slums or a deployment with a disaster relief charity will present you with physical and emotional challenges that thrust you into the here and now, leaving you no time to dwell on the past.

AUTUMN LEAVES

WHEN AUTUMN LEAVES START TO FALL, TAKE A WEEK TO TOUR THE BRIEF FLURRY OF COLOUR. HERE ARE FIVE OF THE FINEST LOCATIONS AND THE LEAVES TO LOOK OUT FOR.

MAPLE
NARA, JAPAN

Autumn in Japan is every bit as stunning as the short-lived *haname* cherry blossom season in spring. *Kouyou*, or autumn leaves, can be seen across the country, starting in the northern island of Hokkaidō and spreading quickly south from the end of September. The ancient capital of Nara, a short train ride from Kyoto, makes a wonderful viewing spot. Its vast park is awash with colour, with sensational views of red, gold and yellow leaves along the paths up to Tamukeyama shrine in its northeast corner.

BEECH
FOREST OF DEAN, ENGLAND

This ancient woodland in Gloucestershire was once used as a royal hunting ground; its trees were also used to make Tudor warships. Today, it's the perfect spot for the more prosaic sport of 'leaf peeping'. The mix of oak, beech and sweet chestnut provides a rusty riot of yellow and gold. The Forest of Dean can be easily covered on foot or bike. Just keep an eye out for the wild boar that have called this place home since 2006.

ASPEN
COLORADO, USA

It's all about the aspens in Colorado, a tree so ethereally beautiful they named a town and a beer after it. The aspens glow golden in the autumn sun over Kebler Pass, a gravel road out of Crested Butte that passes through Gunnison National Forest in southwest Colorado. September is the best month.

RED OAK
AGAWA CANYON, CANADA

Hop on board the Agawa Canyon Tour Train in autumn and you'll be treated to some of the most beautiful fall foliage on the planet. The ride sets off from Sault Ste Marie on the Canada–USA border, covering 183 km of unspoilt country that looks at its best as the days begin to close in. The views here inspired Tom Thomson and the Group of Seven, Canada's most prominent landscape artists, throughout the early 20th century. You'll need to be quick though, as the leaves peak for a brief period around the end of September and beginning of October.

ASH
WHITE MOUNTAINS, USA

New England is synonymous with 'fall' and picking one must-see spot isn't easy. But New Hampshire's White Mountains are surely one of the best places to see autumn at its most colourful, not just in New England, but the world. Hike through the hills at the start of October and you'll be treated to brilliant red maple leaves. Or drive to Silver Cascade Falls in Carroll County to see the trees glow next to the 76m waterfall.

HONEYMOON OF A LIFETIME

MAKE YOUR FIRST HONEYMOON ONE TO REMEMBER WITH THESE FIVE ROMANTIC IDEAS.

S *nowflakes fall like delicate confetti* in a forest silhouetted against a night sky streaked with stars. You walk together through the hush of a frozen landscape, pausing to gaze in wonder at the Milky Way. Close to the Arctic Circle in northern Norway, the sub-zero temperatures bring you closer to the elements and to each other. Then the magic begins: you stop dead in your tracks, spellbound by the majestic Northern Lights. These swirling bolts of electric green and undulating rays of purple-pink are like being at an enormous disco for Norse Gods – there's nowhere better for your first dance.

It's a myth that a honeymoon has to be somewhere hot. Not when you can spend days kayaking in quiet exhilaration across fjords of molten silver, rimmed by dark mountains. Paddling to islets where it is just the two of you and the vast wilderness, mingling with migratory whales and dolphins, sea eagles wheeling overhead in a bruised sky.

You bounce across Saltstraumen, the world's strongest tidal current, in a rigid-inflatable boat; catch salmon in a river that runs swift and clear, and take a husky-driven sleigh together at twilight. The nights draw in quickly and you gather by an open fire to listen to melodic *yoik* (rhythmic poems) in the cosy shadow of a Sami *lavvu* (tent). The icing on the cake is a stay in the ice-carved bridal suite at Alta's Sorrisniva Igloo Hotel, complete with a four-poster draped in reindeer skins.

Just like with rings, there's no one-size-fits-all when it comes to romance. ●

THE AURORA BOEALIS IN TROMSØ NORTHERN NORWAY   Getty/Antony Spencer

196

A MARRAKECH RIAD Getty/Paul Harris

HONEYMOON OF A LIFETIME

It takes two
You're pedalling past the vineyards of the Danube on a tandem bike. You're kayaking in unison along New Zealand's pristine Abel Tasman coastline. You're helping each other traverse the toughest stretches of the Tour du Mont Blanc, where snow-tipped mountains ripple into France, Italy and Switzerland. Or maybe you're learning to make pasta together in Italy. If flopping on the beach is a no-no, a honeymoon that involves shared interests could be just the ticket.

City break
Paris will never lose its touch as the city of amour, but alternatives abound. The hurly-burly of Marrakech's medina soon fades when you step into a rose-petal-strewn riad or onto a roof terrace, open to a star-studded sky. Rome is eternally romantic, but oft-overlooked Italian cities like medieval Lucca, nestled among Tuscan vines, hills and olive groves, have a fresh-faced loveliness all of their own.

Ultimate adventure
Riding high on the buzz of tying the knot, you might want to up the adventure and make that trip of a lifetime you've always talked about. Camel trekking across the Sahara and camping out under the night sky, checking out the grizzlies and geysers in Yellowstone National Park, going on a gorilla safari in Uganda, or gliding over Cappadocia in a hot-air balloon as the golden warmth of sunrise spreads over its fairy chimneys.

Island in the sun
So you want the glossy magazine dream of sunsets, infinity pools, and sugar-white beaches? Go for the castaway experience in Polynesia; the coral atolls and blue waters of the Maldives or the crashing waves and Piton mountains of St Lucia. Paradise doesn't have to cost a mint; from Greece to Thailand and Italy to Indonesia, there are gorgeous beaches with a relaxed vibe and a more affordable price tag.

ISLANDS OF ADVENTURE

FORGET FLOPPING ON THE SAND; THESE ISLANDS ARE DESIGNED FOR AN ACTION-PACKED WEEK OF ESCAPADES IN MOUNTAINS, JUNGLES, VOLCANOES AND CROCODILE-INFESTED WATERWAYS.

Maps by **Wayne Murphy**

1. O'ahu, North Shore
Surfing on the North Shore is not for the faint-hearted or inexperienced; giant swells slam into O'ahu from the deep ocean. As a place to see masters of their craft, though, it's unequalled.

2. Na Pali Coast, Kauai
Sea kayaks are the best way to access the Na Pali Coast Wilderness Park, which is permitted from May to September, though it's not an excursion for beginners.

3. Mauna Kea, the Big Island
Star gaze at the Onizuka Center for International Astronomy on top of the dormant volcano of Mauna Kea. Telescopes are available until 10pm.

4. Kilauea, the Big Island
Hike in the Hawaii Volcanoes National Park; the Crater Rim Trail around the edge of Kilauea, a dormant voclano, features rainforest, desert and volcanic vents.

5. Moloka'i Island
Chill out on Molokai, the low-key island with the most native Hawaiians and no high-rise resorts. Take jungle drives or tropical forest walks.

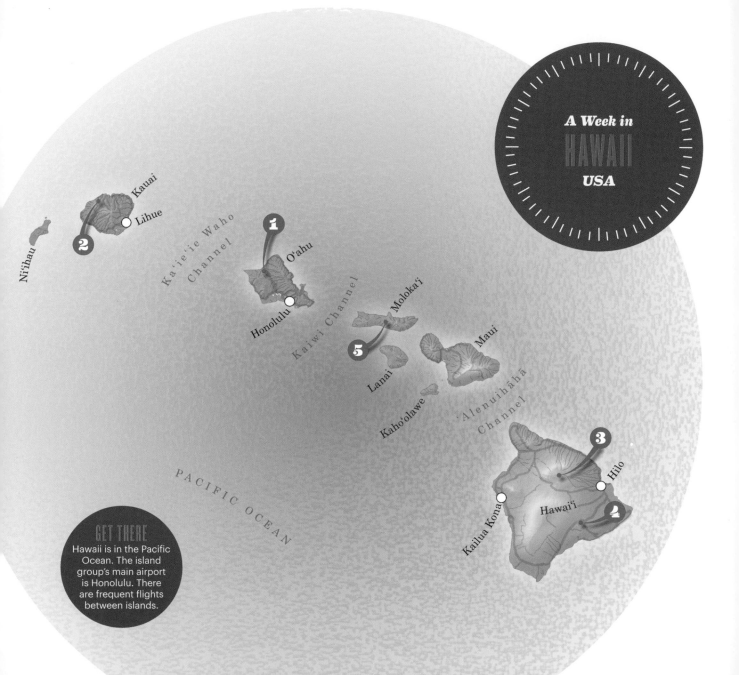

A Week in HAWAII USA

Kauai
Lihue

Ka'ie'ie Waho Channel

Ni'ihau

1
O'ahu

Honolulu

Kaiwi Channel

Moloka'i

5
Lanai

Maui

Kaho'olawe

'Alenuihāhā Channel

PACIFIC OCEAN

3
Hilo

Hawai'i

Kailua Kona

4

GET THERE
Hawaii is in the Pacific Ocean. The island group's main airport is Honolulu. There are frequent flights between islands.

Cap de Formentor

Balearic Sea

Balearic Sea

•Alcúdia

5

Badia d'Alcúdia

2

Serra de Tramuntana

•Inca

1

onera

•Manacor

Calvià •

• Palma de Mallorca

✈ Aeroport de Palma

3

Badia de Palma

•Llucmajor

4

MEDITERRANEAN SEA

Cap de ses Salines

Illa de Cabrera

GET THERE
Mallorca is one of the Balearic Islands. Palma's airport receives frequent flights. Mallorca can also be reached by ferry from mainland Spain.

A Week in
MALLORCA
Spain

1. Sa Gubia
Rock climb at this huge rock amphitheatre west of Bunyola. It's Mallorca's top sport climbing spot and the Spanish limestone is superb.

2. Sóller
Cycle from Sóller north or south into the heart of the Tramuntana range for some of the best bike-riding routes in Europe. It's easy to put together hilly loops though the mountains; spring and autumn are the prime seasons.

3. Santa Ponsa
Sail out of the smart and sheltered harbour of Santa Ponsa to join one of Europe's most popular yachting scenes. Charters and courses are available.

4. Parc Natural Mondragó
Kick back on these secluded beaches near Santanyí after your exertions. They all require a short hike down stony paths.

5. Parc Natural de s'Albufera
Bird-watch at these wetlands on the north coast, with more than 200 species, residents and visitors, to spot.

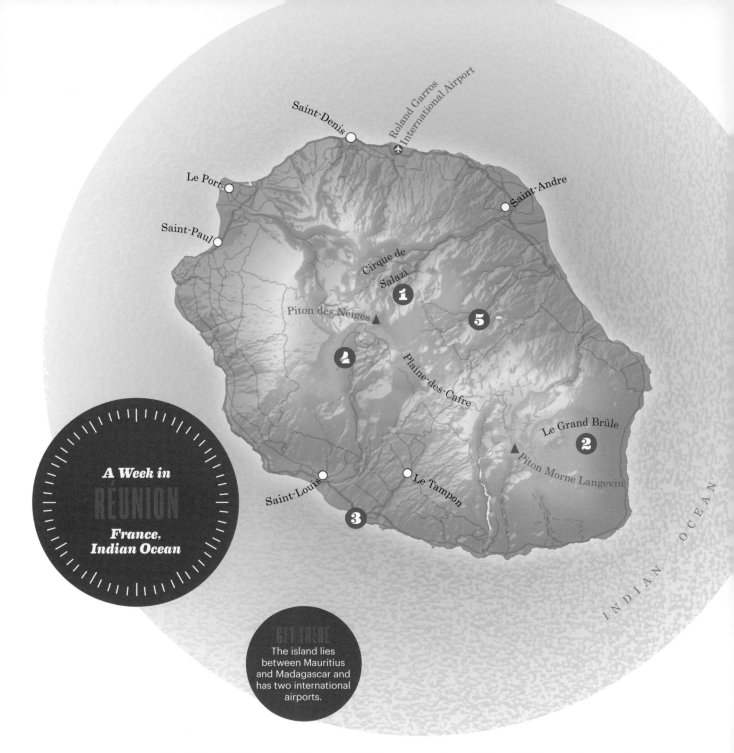

A Week in
RÉUNION
*France,
Indian Ocean*

GET THERE
The island lies
between Mauritius
and Madagascar and
has two international
airports.

Saint-Denis

Roland Garros
International Airport

Le Port

Saint-André

Saint-Paul

*Cirque de
Salazi*

1

Piton des Neiges ▲

5

4

Plaine-des-Cafre

Le Grand Brûle

2

▲ *Piton Morne Langevin*

Saint-Louis

Le Tampon

3

I N D I A N   O C E A N

1. Hell-Bourg
Go Creole in this pretty
village on the island's
east coast. Savour a
cold beer in a shanty bar
among Creole musicians.

2. Piton de la Fournaise
Climb this active volcano
if it's not too lively. The
5hr trek up the loose,
sun-scorched slopes is
challenging but looking
down into the crater and
across the Indian Ocean
is worth the effort.

3. St Pierre
Party in Réunion's third-
largest town, in the
island's southwest, which
pulses with an hedonistic
energy after dark.

4. Cirque de Cilaos
Hike in the spectacular
setting of a steep,
volcanic crest. There's
a variety of canyoning
trips in these snaggle-
toothed peaks where
you'll be climbing,
abseiling and simply
sliding down the slopes.

5. Grand Étang
Horse ride around the
largest lake on Réunion.
It's a low-impact way
to soak up the drop-
dead gorgeous scenery.
Horseback trips into the
interior can last a few
hours or several days.

1. *Whitehaven beach*
Beach comb on what is considered one of the greatest beaches in the world, thanks to its talcum-powder fine sand.

2. *Blue Pearl Bay, Hayman Island*
Scuba dive at Hayman Island, one of the 74 islands in the Whitsunday archipelago and a top diving destination.

3. *Proserpine River*
Spot saltwater crocs – and other Aussie critters – in these estuaries on a crocodile safari departing from Airlie Beach.

4. *Airlie Beach*
Learn to sail a yacht or start a bareboating trip at Airlie Beach, home of the Whitsunday Sailing Club. Sailing is the heart and soul of the Whitsundays.

5. *Shute Harbour*
Set out in sea kayaks from Shute Harbour to paddle your way through glassy waters from bay to bay, watching out for whales, dolphins and turtles.

A Week in the
WHITSUNDAYS
Australia

Hayman Island

Hook Island

North Molle Island

South Molle Island

Pioneer Bay

Cid Harbour

Whitsunday Island

Haslewood Island

Cannonvale

Whitsunday Airport

Turtle Bay

Long Island

Whitsunday Passage

Hamilton Island

Pentecost Island

Proserpine

Lindeman Island

Repulse Bay

Shaw Island

GET THERE
The Whitsundays are off the Queensland coast. Flights connect Hamilton Island with main cities.

Repulse Islands

BE BLOWN AWAY BY BIRDS

ARMED WITH CAMERA AND BINOCULARS, SEEK OUT THE CAPTIVATINGLY CURIOUS, THE BOLD, AND THE BEAUTIFUL OF THE BIRD WORLD. TIME IT RIGHT AND YOU'LL SEE FEATHERED SHOWS YOU'LL NEVER FORGET.

The grit and grind of Papua New Guinea's capital, Port Moresby, slowly recede as you bump along Sogeri Rd and exalt in a taste of the lush countryside, the sun lazily rising. This isolated archipelago may be a more challenging destination than most, but you're here for the unrivalled natural habitat and enviable array of birdlife. You turn off and head into the rugged Varirata National Park. As soon as you enter, birds call out their greetings and you catch a glimpse of a flycatcher, while a lorikeet flaps through the branches above you and off into the blue sky. You dive further into the park and along a slightly treacherous trail, before spotting the stars of this show – the Raggiana birds of paradise.

You hold your breath as these feathered fornicators begin their unabashed displays of avian affection. Plumes are swept, heart-stopping colours flashed and *amore* professed through a series of leaps, bounds and the spreading of wings, like the opening of ornamental fans.

With the sun now high overhead, you do your best not to crash back through the undergrowth. Taking a moment to pause, you quietly gasp as you spot a dwarf cassowary, its horny casque protruding as it stalks out of the rainforest, heading, it seems, directly for you with its gnarly toes and shimmering black plumage.

You hike on for spectacular views of the surrounding countryside and the Port Moresby area, vowing to return tomorrow for more glimpses of the exotic and the little-seen of the bird world. ●

RUFOUS-TAILED HUMMINGBIRD, ECUADOR   Jonathan Gregroy

BE BLOWN AWAY BY BIRDS

1 Ecuador

Home to over 1500 species, Ecuador has a huge diversity of birdlife. The rainbow-coloured beaks of treetop-dwelling toucans are often best spotted from boats on the river, where you'll also catch blue and yellow macaws, whose clumsy antics and raucous music provide plenty of entertainment.

2 Danube Delta, Romania

This network of channels, lagoons, reed islands, woods and pastures on the Black Sea coast is a natural wonderland, offering an up-close view of thousands of pelicans, herons, ibis, ducks, warblers and white-tailed eagles. Areas of the wetlands are only accessible by kayak or rowboat, from where you can watch the wildlife a mere arm's length away.

3 Kruger National Park, South Africa

Better known for the 'big five' of wild animals, Kruger is also the place to spot South Africa's 'big-six' birds – the southern ground hornbill, Pel's fishing-owl, lappet-faced vulture, saddle-billed stork, martial eagle and the kori bustard. Just as thrilling are the ostriches streaking across the savannah.

4 Queensland, Australia

Australia's isolation has evolved some unusual birds. The kookaburra sounds like it's laughing, while the lyrebird sounds like any noise it chooses to mimic. Then there's the flightless emu – the world's second largest bird after the ostrich; and an array of brilliantly coloured parrots. One place you're sure to encounter them all is Currumbin Wildlife Sanctuary in Queensland, where flocks of friendly lorikeets are a hallmark attraction.

A CLAPBOARD HOUSE IN SAN FRANCISCO, USA   Getty/Andrew McKinney

HOUSE SWAP

Whether you'd like to stay in a clapboard house in San Francisco, a cosy stone cottage in England's Cotswolds or an airy French apartment in Paris, specialist home-swap agencies will be able to hook you up with someone who owns one. The advantage of home-swapping, aside from the low cost (typically you pay for travel and living expenses) is that you have an immediate introduction to a neighbourhood and the opportunity to live like a local, if only for a week or two. The downside? You'll have to clean two houses...

A Week

Seeing

is

believing

EMILY MATCHAR FINDS TRUTH IS
STRANGER THAN FICTION

So many of the things that capture our childhood imaginations – unicorns, fairies, Santa Claus – sadly don't exist in the real world. But some things we assume to be mythical are in fact quite real.

Remember Glo Friends? Those glow-in-the-dark toys that lived together in the magical forest kingdom of Glo Land. Well Glo Land might not actually exist, but glow-worms really do. In New Zealand (a magical place in its own right) the Waitomo Glowworm Caves feature a large population of Arachnocampa luminosa, which radiate an eerie blue light. Ride a boat through the subterranean grotto, where these curious insects cling to the ceiling, twinkling like strange stars.

Pink dolphins might sounds like they belong firmly in a world of make-believe, but the bubble-gum-hued marine mammals are just as real as the more prosaic grey variety. In the Hong Kong fishing village of Tai O, locals will take you on small boat trips in search of the pink-tinted Chinese white dolphins, which have become increasingly rare in recent years. A surer bet is a visit to the Cambodian town of Kratie, where pink dolphins still frolic in the river.

If you believe hobbits don't exist outside Middle Earth, we understand. But allow us to present Homo floresiensis, nicknamed 'the hobbit', an extinct species of hominid whose bones were discovered in Indonesia in 2003. The hobbit was about 1m tall, and may have lived up until only 12,000 years ago.

Certain cities have always had the ring of the mythical about them. Take Troy. You probably read about it at school in The Iliad, not realising it was real. To be fair, neither did most historians, until archaeologists located its ruins in the Anatolia region of present-day Turkey in the 1870s. Visit the site to gaze upon the walls of the ruined acropolis that played such a huge part in civilization's founding.

These are just a few examples of the 'mythical' in real life. But the real fun is finding out for yourself. Believe in Atlantis? Visit Bimini in the Bahamas or the Greek island of Santorini, both hypothesized locations of the legendary sunken city. Think Bigfoot might be real? Camp out in the Pacific Northwest with your night-vision goggles and report back. As they say, sometimes truth is stranger than fiction. ●

Certain cities have always had the ring of the mythical about them. Take Troy. You probably read about it at school in *The Iliad,* not realising it was real.

MARVELLOUS MONASTERIES

GO BACK TO BASICS AND EXPERIENCE THE SERENITY OF AN AMAZING MONASTERY; SOME YOU CAN STAY IN AND OTHERS WILL EVEN SELL YOU BEER.

Bhutan's famous Taktshang Goemba, or Tiger's Nest, monastery was built at the place where Guru Rinpoche – one of the country's favourite religious figures – is said to have arrived on the back of a consort he'd transformed into a flying tigress. Legend tells that he went on to subdue a local demon before spending three months here meditating in a cave.

There are no flying tigers for you, just a stroll up the well-made path from a car park a couple of hours below, or a two-day hike across the craggy spines of the surrounding mountains that follows part of a smuggler's trail that continues to Tibet. The trail passes through cloud forests draped with tendrils of moss, over ridges where trees have been contorted sideways by the prevailing winds and eagles drift far above. At night you'll shelter in tents established by the Uma Paro hotel on a high plateau before setting off for the monastery at first light.

Ahead is the Tiger's Nest, a shimmering monument with golden pinnacles to its rooftops set over stark, whitewashed walls that somehow cling to the cliff face. From the path where pilgrims gather to look on in awe, ropes bearing prayer flags in a rainbow of colours are strung over a deep gorge towards the monastery. It's a sight that will stay with you forever – and the Tiger's Nest isn't the only monastery where you don't have to be a devotee to share in their unique atmosphere. ●

St Sixtus Abbey, Belgium
Here, silent monks of the Trappist order brew Westvleteren 12, a revered beer available in limited quantities only at the abbey itself by prior appointment. That doesn't dissuade beer-loving pilgrims from visiting Belgium's six Trappist breweries.

Santuari de Sant Salvador, Mallorca
On the Spanish island of Mallorca around a dozen monasteries offer accommodation. One of the most sublime, the Santuari de Sant Salvador, sits on a hill outside the southeastern town of Felanitx. It's comfortable, the food is good and you're far from Mallorca's crowds.

Kopan Monastery, Nepal
Kopan, on the outskirts of Kathmandu, is one of the best places in the Himalaya to learn the basics of meditation and Tibetan Buddhism. The seven-day or 10-day courses are usually given by foreign teachers. A popular one-month course is held in November.

San Giorgio Maggiore, Italy
Venice is not known for its tranquillity but that's exactly what you'll find at this 16th-century Benedictine monastery on a secluded island. Accommodation is spartan but how many hotels have Tintorettos? From the bell tower there are beautiful views of St Mark's Basilica.

BHUTAN'S TIGER'S NEST MONASTERY   Jonathan Gregroy

THE WALES COAST PATH AT ST BRIDE'S BAY   Pete Seaward

WALK THIS WAY

**BREAK LONG-DISTANCE WALKS INTO BITE-SIZE PIECES
TO MAKE THEM A WEEK-LONG ENDEAVOUR.**

Where the land runs out is a wild place, where the cliffs are the prows of ships, enduring the battering tides. This is where Wales meets the Celtic Sea and, since 2012, hikers have been able to witness this alchemical transition from solid to liquid along the 1400km-long Wales Coast Path, the first trail to follow a country's entire coastline.

But there's no rule that says you have to walk the whole path in one go. Instead, savour sections at a time and return to forge another link in the chain. Many of the best sections take in the Gower's beautiful beaches, Pembrokeshire's multicoloured cliffs and limestone arches, the remote edges of the Llŷn Peninsula and the ancient vistas of Anglesey.

For a taste, take a ramble along the dramatic Marloes Peninsula in the far southwest of Pembrokeshire just across St Bride's Bay from the diminutive city of St Davids. The Coast Path skirts the yawn of St Bride's Bay in a long curve that runs between fields and the coves, cliffs and beaches, all the way from St David's Head in the north to Skomer Island in the south. So begins one of the most beautiful walks in all Wales; on a clear day, you'll see the whole western tip of Wales.

For the most remote section of the Pembrokeshire coast, continue north to Strumble Head and the path to Cardigan – and don't skip the special section of path on Pen Anglas headland that is designed to be walked barefoot, with soft peat underfoot. ●

A Week

A MOUNTAIN HUT IN THE PYRENEES   Lottie Davies

WALK THIS WAY

Appalachian Trail, USA

The nation's longest footpath is over 3000km long, crosses six national parks and slices through 14 states from Georgia to Maine. Deep woods, alpine peaks, cow-dotted farms, and foraging bears are all part of the landscape. It's estimated that two to three million people trek a portion of the trail every year. Fewer than 600 hikers persevere all the way through, taking around six months; but if Bill Bryson can do it, so can you.

Via Dinarica, The Balkans

Three contrasting routes form the newly established Via Dinarica, which splices together historic trails through the Dinaric Alps from Albania to Slovenia. You can go via the coast, hike over the mountains (the 965km-long White Trail) or through forested foothills (for cyclists). It's an ambitious undertaking: the trail passes through Kosovo, Montenegro, Bosnia & Hercegovina, Serbia before arriving at Slovenia's highest peak.

The Lycian Way, Turkey

Southern Turkey's coast is outlined by the 530km-long Lycian Way, which follows Greek and Roman roads and aqueducts and traditional herders' trails along cliffs, around coves and through forests of pine and cedar. Lots of the local villages are set up for travellers so it's easy to piece together short hops between them at the outset from Fethiye; it becomes more remote the further you go.

Pyrenean Haute Route, Spain & France

This is a walking route between two seas and two countries. It weaves across the high-altitude border between France and Spain, climbing and descending (and climbing again) the steep and sometimes exposed slopes of the Pyrenees; there will be snow on some of the peaks well into summer. But plenty of hospitable villages mean that this 800km trail can be divided into week-long portions.

INDULGE IN ART

Certain cities, even museums, demand more of your time than a rushed afternoon with the hordes. Florence's Uffizi museum, for example, has work by Caravaggio and Leonardo de Vinci hanging in its 16th-century halls. In Madrid's Prado you'll find Bosch, Velásquez and Goya. New York's Metropolitan Museum of Art has an all-encompassing collection ranging from Jackson Pollock to medieval armour. Arrive early on a midweek morning, or just before closing time to appreciate specific works with fewer people in the way; and return to see others at another time.

THE DUOMO, BASILICA DI SANTA MARIA DEL FIORE, FLORENCE,   Justin Foulkes

A Week

NOW OR NEVER

DON'T DELAY! SEE A TIGER OR A RHINO, A RARE FLOWER OR EVEN A GLACIER BEFORE THEY EXIST ONLY IN PHOTOGRAPHS.

Did those grasses just move? And is that a long stripy tail? There's a hush in the jeep as you and the rest of the early-morning tiger-spotters wait to see what if anything emerges from the edge of the forest. Then the owner of an unmistakeable pair of white-furred ears and an enormously long back rises and slinks away into the shadows, vanishing in the bars of light and darkness. Now you see him, now you don't. The group exhales.

You're in Bandhavgarh National Park in Madhya Pradesh, India and what you've just glimpsed is a Bengal tiger, the most numerous of all the tiger species. But when you know that there are just 3000 tigers of all species surviving in the wild across the Asian subcontinent, your elation at having seen one of nature's most majestic creatures will be tempered by sorrow. Bandhavgarh NP is one of the places in India where you are most likely to see a tiger (Pench National Park, also in Madhya Pradesh, is another). But every day India's handful of remaining tigers are at risk from poachers. Elsewhere the situation is worse; there are just 500 Sumatran tigers left.

Tiger-spotting tours are one way of raising awareness and funds for conservation efforts but with demand from China for tiger parts, it's hard to see how they'll thrive again. As Joni Mitchell sang, 'you don't know what you've got 'til it's gone'. ●

1
Glacier National Park, USA
Of course, Montana's Glacier National Park isn't going anywhere. But its name might need to be changed. Projections suggest that many of the park's glaciers will disappear over the next 20 years, as are many glaciers in the Himalaya and the Andes. It's a slow process that will impact many of the park's species.

2
Black rhino, Namibia
Of all the animals critically endangered by poaching for body parts, the black rhino is perhaps the most vulnerable. They're short-sighted, easy to track and have a very slow breeding cycle. There are fewer than 5000 left, with Namibia being the species' last, carefully protected stronghold.

3
Land art, worldwide
Transitory by its nature, land art uses the natural world as a canvas for artworks such as Andy Goldsworthy's sculptures, Robert Smithson's earthworks, which are affected by time and the elements, or Walter de Maria's Lightning Field in New Mexico, which is an array of 400 steel poles over 1.5 sq km.

4
The ghost orchid, Wales
Orchids, the more elusive the better, would drive plant-hunters to the far corners of the earth. One of the most fleeting sights is the pink bloom of the leafless ghost orchid, which spends most of its life underground. The National Museum of Wales in Cardiff has an extremely precious collection of these flowers.

A Week

REAL LIFE STORY

**FEW EXPERIENCES BRING A BOOK TO LIFE
AS READING IT IN THE PLACE IT IS SET.**

'*In those grand stone buildings* they could bankrupt or hang you as they pleased. They had a courthouse and prison and hospital plus four banks and two breweries and 15 hotels.' So writes Peter Carey, describing the Australian town of Beechworth in the voice of the outlaw Ned Kelly. The book is Carey's award-winning novel *True History of the Kelly Gang*, which follows the fortunes of the lanky 19th-century bushranger as he grows up in the frontier land of Victoria and gets to know every ridge and creek before his demise in Melbourne Gaol at the end of a hangman's rope in 1880.

Beechworth is still a vibrant country town; the prison is being converted into apartments and there's just the one brewery now but it's a good one, serving homemade pizza and beer at weekends. You can sit outside, turning the pages and recognising the places: at Beechworth's Imperial Hotel Kelly boxes Isaiah 'Wild' Wright, he follows the Ovens river south of Beechworth and has his first showdown with police at Stringybark Creek – 'On the ridges the mountain ash gleamed like saints against the massing clouds but down here the crows and currawongs was gloomy their cries dark with murder.' But it's not only the book that is illuminated by its setting; Carey's words help this beautiful corner of Australia live on in the imagination; as Kelly's mentor, Harry Power, says 'If you know the country ... then you will be a wild colonial boy forever.' ●

The Snow Leopard, the Himalayas
In a remote corner of the Tibetan plateau northwest of Dhaulagiri called Dolpo, Peter Matthiessen seeks to come to terms with nothing less than life and death as he hikes the sheep tracks of these Himalayan ridges and ravines.

A River Runs Through It, USA
Norman Maclean's short story, set in the 1930s, is about family and love and art and the passing of time itself. The cold, fast-flowing Blackfoot River in western Montana is the backdrop for this soulful American classic.

Ulysses, Ireland
James Joyce's Ulysses, published in 1922, is set during the passage of a single day in Dublin (16 June, 1904) and that day now sees an annual reenactment of scenes from the epic novel in landmarks across the city, known as Bloomsday, after Joyce's hero, Leopold Bloom.

The Beach, Thailand
From the backpacker holding bay of Bangkok's Khao San Road to the eponymous beach paradise, via Ko Samui and Ko Pha-Ngan, Alex Garland's mid-1990s novel remains a compelling picture of Thailand.

A Week

MAKE UP YOUR OWN MIND

One of the great lessons of travel is that situations evolve, and people and places change. Borders can open as well as close. And sometimes there are difficult decisions to make, such as whether to travel to countries such as Myanmar. The only answer is be informed, to travel responsibly and to make up your own mind.

SHWEDAGON PAGODA, YANGON, MYANMAR   Matt Munro

Chapter
04

AMC

In which, over a month or more, we venture to the Amazon, travel from

ONTH.

one end of a country to the other, train for a marathon
and celebrate the seasons. On the water we learn to surf and paddle.
We also find time to volunteer and participate in a tradition.
And to escape it all, we travel solo and build a log cabin in the wilds.

A Month

Chapter
04

STOWAWAY ON A SHIP

NOT ALL CRUISES ARE ABOUT AQUA-AEROBICS AND CABARET. HITCH A RIDE ON A CONTAINER SHIP AND YOU'LL SEE PARTS OF THE WORLD FEW HAVE LAID EYES ON.

Standing on the deck of the MV ISA, watching the chalky coastline of southern England sliding past the tanker's starboard bow, you wonder where this leviathan of a boat is really heading. You're aboard one of the world's last true tramp ships – a vessel whose final destination is unknown, even to its crew, a raggle-taggle bunch who you'll be breaking bread with at the captain's table for the next 30 evenings at least.

You're one of two passengers who joined the boat just before departure from the Dutch port of IJmuiden, but you know as much about where you're going as the sailors who steer her. One thing is sure – you will cross the Atlantic twice. The outbound voyage will take you west from Land's End, across the open ocean until the ship passes between Nova Scotia and Newfoundland and into the embrace of the Gulf of St Lawrence. From here you'll sail along the St Lawrence River, past Québec and Montreal and into the Great Lakes. After skirting the shores of New York State and crossing the inland seas of lakes Ontario, Erie and Huron, you'll finally arrive at Thunder Bay on the banks of Lake Superior, where the tanker will be loaded with a precious cargo of grain from the prairies.

And it is this load that will determine where you end up after making the return trip across the Atlantic. Depending on who flashes the most cash, you might end up in Morocco, or Turkey, Italy, Spain, Norway, Poland or even Russia. For now, though, you're happy to stroll the length of two football pitches along the deck, daydreaming of the adventure to come. ●

A Month

You Only Live Once

STOWAWAY ON A SHIP

  1

Big-Apple bobbing

This is how to arrive in the US – sailing past Ellis Island and the Statue of Liberty right into the core of the Big Apple. Maris Freighter Cruises take eight landlubbers on each trip the Hanjin San Diego makes from Europe to the US. You board in the Mediterranean port of La Spezia in Italy, and travel via Genoa, Fos sur Mer (France), Barcelona, Valencia and Algeciras in Spain, before spending 10 days crossing the North Atlantic to arrive in New York.

 2

Panama hat-trick

Just three passengers get to hop a ride on the Hamburg Süd-operated freighter that leaves Philadelphia and goes to Cartagena, on Colombia's Caribbean coast, before passing through the Panama Canal. From Balboa, you'll experience the agoraphobia-inducing enormity of the South Pacific Ocean before next making landfall in Auckland, New Zealand, some 28 days into the cruise. Next stops are Sydney and then Melbourne, Australia.

 3

Hunting the Snark

A tropical freighter-cruise can be had on the Aranui, a mixed-purpose passenger and cargo ship that works the waters of the Pacific Ocean between Tahiti and the Marquesas Islands. The Aranui accommodates 200 people and offers more comfort than your standard freighter, with air-conditioning and a swimming pool, where you sip cocktails as the boat bounces between the islands of the Marquesas, in the wake of Jack London's Snark.

 4

Suez me

Sailing out of Southampton in Britain, CMA CGM Cargo Cruises offer limited bunks on its EPIC (Europe Pakistan India Consortium) boats, which head down the coasts of France and Spain, before rounding the Rock of Gibraltar and entering the Mediterranean. At the eastern end of the Med, you pass through the Suez Canal and call at ports in the United Arab Emirates before crossing the Arabian Sea to either India or Pakistan.

PLAY MORE!

It's a happy talent to know how to play,' *Ralph Waldo Emerson*

Play reduces stress, makes us smarter, helps us solve problems and reinforces bonds. So, wherever you may be, at least once a month ensure that you go fly a kite, climb a tree or make a snow angel.

A Month

BUILD A CABIN OF YOUR OWN

WE ALL NEED A LITTLE BREATHING SPACE. HEAD TO THE WOODS OF MINNESOTA TO LEARN HOW TO BUILD A RETREAT OF YOUR OWN.

*Few people can have read **Walden*** by Henry David Thoreau, who built and lived in a 10 x 15ft cabin in Concord, Massachusetts in 1845, and not contemplated the idea half-seriously: a cabin of one's own in a sunlit glade somewhere far from the asphalt world. (In fact, Thoreau's hut was on the edge of town on land owned by his friend Ralph Waldo Emerson and he was never more than a short walk from a hot bath, or a cold one in Walden Pond.) Thoreau made it look easy; his cabin's frame went up in May and it was ready to be inhabited in July. For more than two years Thoreau came and went from the woods - as he writes 'I wished to live deliberately, to front only the essentials of life'.

For your first log cabin you'd be best advised to gain some professional tuition. The Great Lakes School of Log-Building and Stonemasonry in Minnesota, 2500km west of Massachusetts, has almost 40 years of experience in teaching first-timers how to keep their walls straight and their roofs watertight. You'll learn how to select and prepare logs, level a site, install windows and a door, make a roof truss and use sharp tools safely – don't forget to bring your own Gransfors-Bruks axe. To test your new skills and kick back on your own hand-built porch like a frontiersman or woman you'll need about six months, power tools, a plot of land – and a lot of logs. ●

Friggebod, Sweden
Since 1979, Sweden's building code has permitted the construction of buildings of less than 90 sq ft without a permit. These bijoux boxes are called friggebods and typically found on family-owned plots in the wilds, overlooking lakes. Some are available to rent but you're better calling on any Swedish connections you have.

Bach, New Zealand
You don't have to go far in New Zealand to escape the crowds and the traditional Kiwi holiday home, known as a 'bach' (pronounced batch), is often near a favourite (secret) beach or a trout-fishing river. Many have a hand-built, hand-me-down look but there are plenty of modern designs available to rent through agencies.

Shepherd's hut, France & Spain
Traditional shepherds in the Pyrenees didn't have an easy job, spending weeks alone in the mountains, warding off bears and wolves. But when the weather turned nasty they had cosy stone refuges to retreat into. Known as an orri in the eastern Pyrenees, many still stand and offer shelter to hikers who venture off the beaten track.

Bothy, Scotland
Pull on your hiking boots and grab your Gore-Tex to seek out the Scottish interpretation of a mountain hut – the bothy. The Mountain Bothy Association maintains around 100 shelters in the most popular parts of the Highlands but there are many more located in less frequented glens, which are carefully guarded secrets. As the MBA says, you need to be proficient in using a map and compass.

ON THE PORCH OF A HANDMADE LOG CABIN   Michael Heffernan

Stevenson Trail, France
The 252km Stevenson Trail (or GR70) runs from Monastier-sur-Gazeille to St Jean de Gard, following the path paced by Scottish writer Robert Louis Stevenson and his donkey Modestine in 1878. The countryside of the Auvergne, Cevennes and Languedoc-Roussillon is still magical; taking a mule is optional.

Great Railway Bazaar, Asia
In 1975 writer Paul Theroux travelled by train from London to Tokyo and back, a chug that included some epic rails: the Orient Express, Frontier Mail, Khyber Pass Local, Trans-Siberian. He revisited the route in 2008; some tracks are no longer accessible and some areas have opened up, but the journey remains a classic.

Priscilla, Australia
The most flamboyant tyre tracks to follow are those of Priscilla, Queen of the Desert. In the eponymous movie, this shiny tour bus transports three drag queens from Sydney to Alice Springs via red, raw and not-entirely-enlightened Outback Australia. Must-stops include Broken Hill, Coober Pedy and plunging King's Canyon.

FOLLOW IN FAMOUS FOOTSTEPS

YOU COULD BEAT A NEW PATH, BUT THERE'S MORE ALLURE IN THE PURSUIT OF POETS AND ADVENTURERS. RETRACE A GRAND TOUR TO EXPERIENCE THESE FAMOUS JOURNEYS.

You're setting off from Buenos Aires on a wheezy motorbike – just as Ernesto 'Che' Guevara and his friend Alberto Granado did, in 1952. These are eminent dust trails to follow: it was on this 9-month ride around South America that the charismatic revolutionary learned about his continent and formed many of his beliefs. As you purr southwards across the pampas, warm air buffeting your face, the thrum of the engine beneath, you start to sense how such a journey could change a person. The freedom! The adventure! And, simply, a damn fine ride.

Indeed, the route is epic – from BA, Che crossed Argentina, and then traversed Chile, Peru, Ecuador, Colombia, Venezuela and Panama. His ride linked the sparkling Patagonian lakes and the Inca wonder of Machu Picchu, the communities of the Amazon rainforest and thriving cities such as Lima and Bogotá.

Che did a lot of thinking on his journey – and you find yourself doing the same. On the bike, though moving at speed, you feel a part of the world, in tune with its weather and winds, more able to stop quickly at that Indian village, roadside fruit stall, Andean lookout. And you have the time and clarity to ruminate on all that you see. At night, with a pen in one hand, and a battered copy of Che's *The Motorcycle Diaries* at your side, you may well start to write your own magnum opus. ●

Patrick Leigh Fermor's Europe
In 1933, aged just 18, Patrick Leigh Fermor set off to walk from the Hook of Holland to Constantinople, variously staying with shepherds and nobles on his way across the continent. His books about the journey – A Time of Gifts and Between the Woods and the Water – provide inspirational guides.

CATCH THE SLEEPER TRAIN

SLOW DOWN AND TAKE THE INDIAN PACIFIC ACROSS AUSTRALIA, ONE OF THE WORLD'S GREAT TRANSCONTINENTAL TRAIN JOURNEYS.

The first European to cross the Nullarbor Plain, was Edward John Eyre in 1841. He described it as 'the sort of place one gets into in bad dreams'. On board the *Indian Pacific* train from Sydney to Perth, via the disconcertingly flat Nullarbor, your dreams will hopefully be happier than Eyre's as you're lulled to sleep by the rhythmic chugging of the train on its three-night journey westward.

After embarking in Sydney's grand sandstone Central Station, the *Indian Pacific* forges a leisurely path over the Blue Mountains, past ancient ochre gorges and rock formations, before descending into the fertile Murray-Darling Basin. You're on the way to Adelaide, South Australia's cultural capital where you can hop off the *Indian Pacific* and explore the wine regions of the Barossa Valley and the Adelaide Hills before rejoining the train for next two-thirds of the trip: the Nullarbor.

Few experiences put Australia's mind-numbing scale into perspective – although the *Indian Pacific* is by no means a fast train, for hour after hour, and all through the night, it trundles through a stunning empty landscape. You'll spot hawks circling above, perhaps kangaroos, but mostly there's just the Outback and your own thoughts. ●

California Zephyr, USA

The Zephyr lives up to its evocative name. Running daily between Chicago and San Francisco, two of the most vibrant cities in the US, this sleeper train crosses the Rockies, slices through hostile deserts and finds a way over the Sierra Nevadas during its 3900km journey. Like the nation's pioneers, travel westward for the best sunset views. The train takes 51 hours but why not stop for a while in Colorado and Utah?

234

 The Trans-Siberian, Russia, Mongolia & China
This is the warmly wrapped grandaddy of sleeper trains: a journey on the Trans-Siberian can take in Moscow's Red Square, Beijing's Forbidden City, the Great Wall, icy Lake Baikal and Mongolia's panoramic steppes, depending on the route you select. Most who ride the train hop on and off wherever they fancy along the 9000km route. What better way to arrive in Ulaanbaatar?

 The Blue Train, South Africa
For 27 hours the endless African veldt rolls effortlessly past your window as your travel in luxury from Pretoria to Cape Town. Yes, the Blue Train is not your average sleeper service; no tired sandwiches and threadbare recliners here: the 84 passengers enjoy the attention of a butler, gold fixtures in the ensuite bathrooms and a wildlife documentary unspooling outside.

 Milan to Palermo, Italy
Trenitalia's sleeper service from Milan to Palermo, the No.785 service, was recently threatened with closure. This would have been a tragedy; this night route from northern Italy to Sicily is one of the world's classics. Part party-train, part sightseeing tour of Italy's spine, you leave Milan at supper time and arrive in Palermo late the following afternoon.

A Month

你還記得那種什麼都不能理解的感覺嗎？當話語只是噪音，只能憑音調聽出是肯定還是反對；當文字像是鬼畫符，無法明白筆劃的含義；當人們的動作看上去似乎很開心，卻茫然不知緣由。想象一下那種感覺。漠然——是的。無助——也許。但你連自己不知道的是什麼都不知道！

不必害怕這種感覺，解決之道一直都在。你需要去旅行。

首先，列出一串書面語中不使用羅馬字母的國家。然後開始甄選：你要找的是幾乎完全沒有英文或羅馬文字的國家（或地區），比如中國，韓國，俄羅斯，埃塞俄比亞。不要呆在大城市，但也不需要走太遠，離首都一小時車程的地方就很好。然後，就⋯⋯漫步。

走得離你的住處越遠越好。搭一輛巴士。在人群中跌跌撞撞。保持微笑。生命只有一次，但一瞬間你就能變回孩子⋯⋯

**BEN HANDICOTT CROSSES THE
LANGUAGE BARRIER IN CHINA**

It's *New Year's Eve*, you're in a regional city in China. The roads are busy with cars the way department stores are with people at the sales. There's little movement though, just a great deal of noise. You shuffle along the street, a path of neon and people, so many people. Amid the throng, you move as a tide, inevitable and unstoppable. Vendors selling balloons or steamed buns push through, attracting the hungry and annoying the many.

In two hours of shunting along like this, you don't say a word. And you don't understand a word. Everyone is intent on making their way to wherever. No-one gives you a second look. Words fly meaninglessly around you, banners and signs are majestically unreadable. Everything is more or less familiar – people, streets, business, eating, laughter – but the overwhelming sense of confusion, of exclusion, leaves you with no touchstone at all. There's a mild

sense of panic. You can't ask anybody a question. You can't read anything except the occasional brand name on a billboard.

The crowd stirs; something has been communicated. There's a lull and people stop moving. Then a flash and as you look up, a clap like thunder. A booming salvo of fireworks. A noise of equal strength rises from the city as people cheer, then the fireworks retort. Clouds of smoke grow and confetti drifts above you. An hour of strobing light – gold, red and green lacework against the night, and the constant barrage of explosions; it's numbing. And then it stops and the elation of the crowd turns to fatigue. Beneath the orange glow of street lights, through the filtering smoke, colour is leeched from the banners and neon signs; all the brightness turn to sepia and as the crowds disperse, you head back the way you came, and no-one says a word. ●

 Can you remember not understanding anything? When words spoken were just noises, tones of approval (or not); written language just scribbles? Imagine that feeling. Unconcerned – surely. Helpless – maybe, but you don't know what you don't know!

Would it hurt to really tune out, to rediscover a sense of unconcern? Travel can give you this gift.

Make a list of countries that don't use roman script. And then refine it – you want countries (or parts of them) where English is not likely to be spoken at all, such as China. Don't stay in the main cities. You won't need to travel far – an hour from the capital will do it. Then just... wander.

Go as far as you can from your base. Catch a bus. Stumble through transactions. Smile. You might only live once but you can be a child again in a flash. ●

A Month

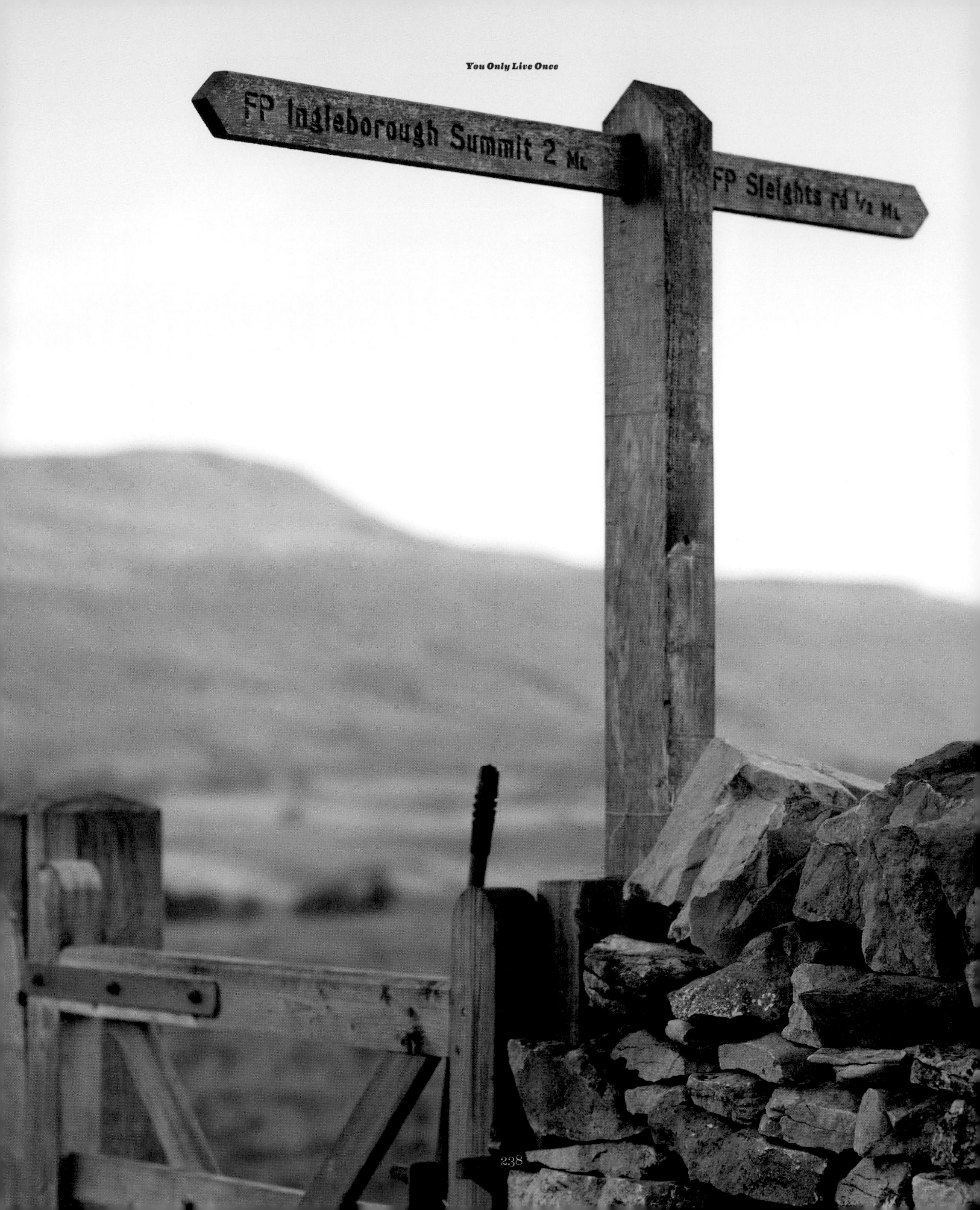
FP Ingleborough Summit 2 ML
FP Sleights rd 1/2 ML

GO END TO END

STARTING FROM ONE CORNER AND MAKING YOUR WAY TO THE OPPOSITE GUARANTEES A SENSE OF MENTAL, PHYSICAL AND CARTOGRAPHIC SATISFACTION.

Y*ou could have taken the short route* – but where's the fun in that? Land's End in Cornwall to John O'Groats, in furthest northeast Scotland, is only 970km as the crow flies, or about 1400km by road. But as you're linking Great Britain's mainland extremes on foot, you didn't really fancy walking alongside the M5 motorway.

No, a more interesting top-to-toe journey, a more satisfying way to tackle this challenge, is away from the tarmac. By stringing together national trails, public footpaths and country lanes you have crossed some of the country's most beautiful spots: the wild coast to Exmoor, bits of the Cotswold Way, up the spine of the Pennines, along the Union Canal, through the Great Glen. Despite the fact that roughly 64 million people cluster on this crowded island, it's surprisingly easy to get away from most of them if you chose your route well.

And you've done just that. There are myriad options, but your hike has taken you via the best of British, from smugglers' coves to honey-stone villages, from peaks to lakes, dales to lochs, Wainwrights to Munros. Your limbs feel strong, your mind as free as that golden eagle whirling over the hills.

As you near that final sign that announces Scotland's wind-whipped end of the road, your blistered feet have been pounding for the best part of three months. You've covered around 2000km; you are spent yet have never felt more alive. As is essential, you pose by the post with the other tourists – who've had the cheek to get here by coach! Disappointment starts to bubble – as pilgrimage spots go, John O'Groats is a damp squib, dampened further by all these bus-lazy people. But then you remember that quote – was it TS Eliot? Buddha? Bob Marley?? – 'it's not the arrival that matters, but the joy of the journey'. ●

MOTORBIKING IN HANOI, VIETNAM   Getty/Rieger Bertrand

 1

Vietnam by Motorbike
The Ho Chi Minh Trail, used to distribute supplies to the Vietcong during the Vietnam War, has been named 'one of the great achievements of military engineering of the 20th century'. Tackle its 1600km from Hanoi to near Saigon via neighbouring Laos by motorbike, for the ultimate Vietnamese end-to-end experience.

 2

Te Araroa, New Zealand
Opened in 2011, this 3000km hiking trail links Cape Reinga, at the north of the North Island, to Bluff, at the south of the South. Allow 120 days to do the total hike.

 3

The Pan-American Highway
There's around 48,000km of road (and one small blip) between northern Alaska and Argentina's Tierra del Fuego. In short, this is the mother of all road trips; bar a detour to negotiate Panama's Darién Gap, you can drive the entire length of the Americas.

 4

Tour d'Afrique, Cairo to Cape Town
Spend four months cycling through 10 countries to traverse a whole continent. You could do it solo, but more fun is the annual Tour d'Afrique, an epic race for riders of all abilities.

COMPLETE A MARATHON

A CHALLENGE THAT TAKES MONTHS TO TRAIN FOR IS OVER IN A FEW MERCIFULLY SHORT HOURS. MAKE YOUR MARATHON MORE INTERESTING BY TAKING ON THESE FIVE FAR-FROM-ROUTINE RUNNING RACES.

Y*ou don't know whether to high-five,* be sick, collapse or cheer. Big Ben looms ahead, but if it donged you wouldn't hear it over the roaring crowd, or the throbbing in your head. You're LESS THAN A MILE from completing the London Marathon. You're elated! But largely, physically, mentally broken.

And yet, you hobble on. Because, despite the agony, you know you're part of something huge. Humanity has swollen to more than the sum of its parts: the very best of people is on display, spectators and runners both. You round the Mall, see the finish, feel every sinew scream – but on you run. And you know you'll never be quite the same again.

ANY marathon changes you. But select one of these tough scenic races for the ultimate travel challenge. ●

COMPLETE A
MARATHON

① ANTARCTIC ICE MARATHON
ANTARCTICA

The race: Sub-zero temperatures, katabatic winds, slippy terrain, altitude-thinned air – as if 26.2 miles wasn't testing enough! But running in such pristine wilderness, where the only sound is the crunch of your own (weary) feet, is a privilege indeed.

The stats

Coordinates: *79°47'S, 82°53'W (Union Glacier Camp)*
When: *November*
Participants: *40*
Profile: *Largely flat, but run at altitude (700m)*
Temperature: *-20°C*
Fee: *€10,500 (US$14,000)*
Distance to South Pole: *1000km*
Average wind speed: *10-25 knots*
Daylight: *24hrs*
Probable calories burned: *10,000*
Kit list: *Thermal top, fleece, outer windproof shell, long johns, windproof trousers, gloves, mittens, two pairs of woollen socks, neoprene toe covers, balaclava, facemask, hat, neck gaiter, goggles*

② BIG SUR MARATHON
CALIFORNIA, USA

The race: The 26.2 miles from Big Sur Village to Carmel are prone to landslides, peasoupers and ocean-brewed storms. But they also follow Hwy 1, one of the world's most dramatic drives. Hard work, yes, but drop-dead gorgeous.

The stats

Coordinates: *36°6'N, 121°37'W (Big Sur)*
When: *April*
Participants: *4500*
Profile: *Hilly, total ascent 300m, 13 hills in last 13 miles*
Temperature: *10-15°C*
Fee: *US$150*
Porta Potties used: *385*
Pre-race pasta party comprises: *250lbs of pasta; 50 gallons of marinara sauce*
Proportion of waste material recycled or composted: *over 91%*
Economic impact of event: *$18 million*
Water supplied: *1675 gallons at start and finish; 7575 gallons on course*

③ THE GREAT WALL MARATHON
CHINA

The race: Most of this route lies alongside China's beefy barricade, negotiating rice fields and remote villages in the Huangyaguan region. The section on the Wall itself is only 3.5km long but completed twice and malevolently memorable: 5164 punishingly steep steps.

The stats

Coordinates: *40°2'N, 117°23'E (Jixian)*
When: *May*
Participants: *2000*
Profile: *Hilly, with 5164 steps*
Temperature: *20-25°C*
Fee: *US$1250 (6-night trip)*
Gradient: *up to 10%*
High-fives given to local children: *100+*
Oldest runner: *75*
Bottles of water carried on foot to the Wall on race morning: *15,000*
Year inaugurated: *1999*
Hiatus: *cancelled in 2003 due to SARS epidemic*

JUNGFRAU MARATHON
SWITZERLAND

The race: Though it doesn't actually go up the 3454m Jungfrau, this route from Interlaken (560m) to Kleine Scheidegg (2060m) is still a beautiful brute. It turns really vertiginous at the 25km mark, when 500m of ascent squeeze into five zigzagging kilometres, and carries on up from there. Breathtaking in every sense.

The Stats

Coordinates: *46°41'N 7°51'E*
(Interlaken)
When: *September*
Participants: *4000*
Profile: *Extremely uphill – total ascent 1830m: max altitude 2205m*
Temperature: *10-20°C*
Fee: *CHF140 (US$170)*
Elevation gain: *1823m*
Course record: *2.49:01*
(Jonathan Wyatt, New Zealand)
Time distance takes by train:
1.15:00 (Interlaken-Kleine Scheidegg)
Best fuel: *rösti (fried grated potatoes), birchermüesli, Rivella (milk-whey soft drink)*

5
LEWA MARATHON
KENYA

The race: Race the world's best long-distance runners AND the wildlife. This dust-track animal-infested 26.2-er crosses Lewa Conservancy, home to rhino, elephant, giraffe and buffalo. All good reasons to keep on moving...

The stats

Coordinates: *0°12'N, 37°25'E*
(Lewa Wildlife Conservancy)
When: *June*
Participants: *1000*
Profile: *Undulating, run at altitude (1700m)*
Temperature: *20-30°C*
Fee: *US$1,500 charitable donation*
Money raised for charity since inception: *US$3,800,000*
Animals potentially seen: *rhino, lion, leopard, buffalo, elephant, zebra, giraffe, oryx, ostrich and many more*
Security: *Armed rangers, Supercub light aircraft, surveillance helicopters*
Chance of winning: *0%*
(past competitors include world-record-holding Kenyan elites)

FROM 0–26.2 MILES...
...IN FOUR MONTHS.

Marathon attempts are won or lost in the months before the big day. If you've arrived at the week before your first marathon without having trained, you may have bitten off more than you can chew. For the modestly active person, however, four months of training will be enough to get you across the finish line (though you won't be troubling the Kenyans at the front).

BASIC TRAINING SCHEDULE

Weeks 1 to 4
Three rest days per week, not consecutively.

Two days per week with an easy jog, increasing from 20 mins to 50 minutes.

One day per week long run increasing from 40 to 70 minutes.

One day per week gentle recovery run for 30 minutes.

Weeks 5 to 8
Three rest days per week, not consecutively.

One day per week steady run for 40-60 minutes

One day per week speed running for 40 minutes

One day per week long run increasing from 80 minutes to ten miles.

One day per week gentle recovery run for 40 minutes.

Weeks 9 to 12
Three rest days per week, not consecutively.

One day per week steady run for 40-60 minutes

One day per week speed running for 50 minutes

One day per week long run increasing from 10 miles to 13 miles or a half-marathon race

One day per week gentle recovery run for 40 minutes.

Weeks 13 to 16
Three rest days per week, not consecutively

One day per week steady run for 40-60 minutes*

One day per week speed running for 50 minutes*

One day per week long run decreasing from 20 miles to 8 miles*

One day per week gentle recovery run for 40 minutes.

*in the week before the race taper your training and do only 2 x 30 easy runs and a 20 min jog

RAISING RIPPERS

IT'S NEVER TOO EARLY TO START ON THE SNOW. GET YOUR KIDS ON THE SLOPES AND YOU'LL BE RESPONSIBLE FOR THE NEXT GENERATION OF TOP-NOTCH BOARDERS.

You pause, look around at your friends, and suddenly ponder how long you've all been snowboarding. You're nudging close to (whisper it!) middle age, and far from being the spring-chickens who took to their boards with youthful fearlessness aged 18.

There's nothing for it, you're going to have to pass on a love of sliding sideways to your kids. You head to Morzine, where Rude Chalets runs Mini Shred Snowboard Weeks for four- to eight-year-olds in the second half of each snow season, when the weather is more likely to be warm and the snow soft and slushy.

The bright, crisp morning brings 1½ hours of tuition with an instructor. There's no more than two in a group – ratios those at French ski schools can only dream of! The kids love it – learning taking a backseat to an atmosphere of play in a winter wonderland.

The little 'uns are strapped to super-stable snowboards, making it virtually impossible to catch an edge, and pulled on a towing lead, like naughty puppies, while they get used to the sensation of riding.

And when you're not on the slopes, Morzine keeps you all happy. A relatively flat valley town that's easy to get around with buggies, there are indoor swimming pools for bad-weather days, a toy train and merry-go-round, and a slew of tourist-board-organised kids' activities. ●

1
Woodward at Copper Mountain, Colorado, USA
If your kids want to shine in the snow park as much as on the piste they should sign up for Freestyle Lessons with Woodward at Copper Mountain. The first half of the day is indoors amid the trampolines and foam pits of the Copper Barn, and in the afternoon they get to put their new gymnastic skills to the test on the award-winning snow parks, where some kickers have air bags to build up the progress slowly.

2
Hakuba Heroes, Japan
Hakuba gets crazy amounts of soft, fluffy snow that makes learning more fun, and is great for building snowmen. It's also warmer than many of the country's other resorts. Hakuba Heroes run group snowboard classes for kids over seven; it can also organise day trips to see the famous snow monkeys in Nagano or snow-mobiling missions for older children.

3
The Star Wars Experience, Sierra-at-Tahoe, California, USA
Children – or should that be Younglings or Padawans – as young as three can learn to snowboard with the help of Jedi Master Yoda and his mind tricks of movement, navigation and control at Sierra-at-Tahoe's snowboard school. The Star Wars Experience includes interactive visuals from the film, and custom wood-carvings of Chewbacca, RD-D2 and C-3PO.

4
Whistler Adventure Camp, Canada
If you send your child to a Whistler Adventure Camp don't be alarmed if their instructors appear to be a witch, wizard, or any number of animal cartoon characters – it's all part of the themed snowboard lessons, making learning as fun as possible. Après-ski ice cream is another tactic, and there's a Family Adventure Zone with horse riding, a maze, a luge and bungee trampolining.

A Month

VOLUNTEER!

LOOKING FOR A MORE MEANINGFUL TRAVEL EXPERIENCE? VOLUNTEERING WILL INTRODUCE YOU TO LOCAL COMMUNITIES AND BUILD YOUR SKILLS.

'*Time is money.*' How often have you heard that said? Perhaps it came to mind as you spent yet another late night in the office trying to meet a deadline; or perhaps you work in a profession where your time is billed in blocks of 15 minutes. Maybe you've just retired, having worked hard for years in return for an annual salary. Whatever your circumstances, you probably consider your time a precious commodity. So, why give your time for free?

Ask Paul Piaia: 'As I travelled to more and more developing countries I began to appreciate how lucky we are in the West. But as a backpacker travelling through places, there was never enough time to do more than just sightsee. I found out about an Australian medical NGO called Australian Aid International, which strives to make healthcare available in some of the most remote regions of the world. In October of 2005, an earthquake measuring 7.6 on the Richter scale hit northern Pakistan, resulting in three and a half million people being made homeless. AAI were looking for determined individuals to provide logistical support; we were either choppered in or trekked for hours to reach villages cut off by the quake.'

Volunteering is a two-way interaction; people like Paul Piaia share their expertise, or just their time, and in return receive a sense of satisfaction through being exposed to situations far beyond the daily grind. ●

1

VSO (Voluntary Service Overseas)
VSO, an international development charity working to alleviate poverty, is the largest independent volunteer agency in the world. VSO sends skilled volunteers who pass on their expertise to local people. It accepts applicants between 20 and 75 from a variety of professional backgrounds. Postings are usually for two years, although shorter placements do exist.

2

Peace Corps
Founded in 1961, the organisation is a federal agency of the US Government, and has sent 200,000 people on 27-month development, relief and humanitarian assignments around the world. Even though there was a whiff of Cold War politics behind its founding, these days the Peace Corps' focus is on providing long-term volunteers to needy regions. Any US citizen over 18 can apply.

3

Greenpeace
Started as a campaigning organisation in Vancouver, Greenpeace is now an international organisation with offices around the globe. Its mission has remained unchanged: to use non-violent, creative protest to expose global environmental problems. All offices offer plenty of volunteering opportunities, from stuffing envelopes to survival training.

4

Willing Workers on Organic Farms (WWOOF)
Well respected and long standing, WWOOF organisations match organic farms with volunteers. Placements usually involve helping out with the farm work but can also include working in an outdoor centre. The programme largely appeals to 'townies' looking for a rural experience and those interested in organic practices.

A Month

PLAY WITH GUITAR GODS

IF YOU'RE GOING TO PLAY IT, PLAY IT RIGHT. LEARN HOW TO STRUM WITH THE BEST OF THEM IN MEMPHIS ON A CLASSIC GIBSON GUITAR YOU'LL TREASURE FOREVER.

Some things in life have to be earned. You wouldn't play 'Mary Had a Little Lamb' on a Stradivarius, or 'Old MacDonald' on a Gibson Les Paul. Buying a top-of-the-line guitar is a rite of passage, earned by years of bedroom practice and endless repetitions of the riff from 'Mannish Boy'. Only when you've properly mastered all your pentatonics, arpeggios and modes is it time to put away childish strings and raid the college fund for the guitar of your dreams.

Sure, you could buy off the shelf from a local guitar store, but for that once-in-a-lifetime purchase, why not get your Gibson at source, direct from the factory in Memphis, Tennessee? You won't save a dime, but you will have the thrill of testing out your perfect axe just a block from the Beale Street bars where BB King played his first stage shows in the soulful heyday of the blues.

Kick off with a tour of the Memphis factory, where all of Gibson's hollow-body guitars – including the BB King tribute Lucille model – are painstakingly assembled by a team of master luthiers. Then, before you part with your hard-earned bucks, take in a Memphis blues show to see how the masters put a Gibson through its paces; for the real deal, head to Wild Bill's on Vollentine, the last of the old Memphis juke joints.

Having shelled out for the dream guitar, it might be worth stopping off at the junction of Highway 61 and Highway 49 in Clarksdale, 75 miles south of Memphis, where Robert Johnson allegedly sold his soul to the devil for mastery of the blues. Depending on how your own trade goes, you could be ready to join the Memphis Blues Society jam, held every second Sunday at the Blues Hall on Beale Street. ●

You Only Live Once

 1

Seeking a sitar
Buying a sitar is not a purchase, it's a journey. The best concert sitars are made to measure by master makers in Delhi, Kolkata and Benares, and learning to play this multistringed marvel takes almost spiritual devotion. Take your first step on the road under the guidance of a sitar master at the Academy of Indian Classical Music in Benares.

 2

Game for a gamelan?
OK, so it's not the most portable instrument, but the sound of the gamelan will transport you instantly to the jungles of Indonesia. The Mekar Bhuana Conservancy in Denpasar is devoted to the preservation of Balinese music, with one-on-one training and workshops using antique gamelan sets – perfect prep for buying your own.

 3

Rock your roots in Ireland
Nothing will help unlock a Celtic soul quite like learning the bodhrán (frame drum) and joining an impromptu Irish music jam, preferably with a freshly pulled pint to hand. Pick up the basics at the Helen McLoughlin Bodhrán School in Wexford, then seek out pub jam sessions at Tig Coili or The Crane in Galway.

 4

Bang your own drum, Senegal
West Africa was the birthplace of the rhythms that morphed into rock and roll, so this could be the perfect place to discover your inner groove. Sign up for drumming classes in Senegal and Ghana and the first lesson could see you heading into the forest for wood to carve into your own *djembe* (goblet drum).

A GIANT AMMONITE IN WHITBY, ENGLAND   Andrew Montgomery

FIND FOSSILS

Some 200 years ago, in the shale cliffs near Lyme Regis, on England's south coast, the teenage Mary Anning uncovered a 5m-long skeleton of an ichthyosaur, a species that last lived 90 million years ago. She was the first person to find an entire skeleton (which is now in the British Museum). There are many places around the world, from the dinosaur fields of Canada and the US, to China and Australia, where fossils, these remarkable links with long-gone ages, can be found. And, no, not all the good stuff has been unearthed yet: in 2014, a bachelor party stumbled upon a 10 million-year-old skull of a stegomastodon at Elephant Butte Lake State Park in New Mexico.

A Month

PADDLING IN THE SEA OF CORTEZ, BAJA CALIFORNIA, MEXICO   Getty/Steve Bly

LEARN TO PADDLE

A CRASH COURSE ON KAYAKING IN THE SEA OF CORTEZ
WILL EQUIP YOU FOR SALTWATER SORTIES ANYWHERE.

The wind is getting stronger and the waves higher. Brisk little squalls charge across the surface of the sea; in a boat, this would be fun but in a sea kayak you're not so much on the water as in the water – and this is your second day of sea kayaking ever. Thankfully, you've practised 'wet exits' – the knack of banging on the hull of an upturned kayak then pulling off the sprayskirt to swim out of the cockpit – but, all the same, you're relieved when you surf the warm Pacific waves to the beach where you will camp for the night.

But you're also exhilarated. For this is the first day of a four-day trip up the west coast of Espiritu Santo island just off Baja California in the Sea of Cortez, and travelling by sea kayak means that you're immersed in the environment (if not the ocean). Your guide has explained how and why the safest technique for waves approaching from the side, as they were earlier, is to dig in for a stroke on the oncoming face of the waves because that tilts your body into the waves and resists its inclination to roll the kayak. Then, as the crest passes under (or over) the craft, swing in for a second stroke into the receding backside of the wave, so you're not leaning down the wave. Even in inexperienced hands, however, a sea kayak can handle a lot. And stringing a series of perfect strokes together brings the same joy as surfing.

The Sea of Cortez, the narrow but menacingly deep channel of water between the 1600km-long Baja peninsula and mainland Mexico, was described by Jacques Cousteau as 'the world's aquarium'. It's one of the most diverse marine areas in the world, containing 31 marine mammal species (one third of the world's whale and dolphin species), 500 species of fish and more than 200 bird species. Kayaking allows you to be part of their world without making an impact. ●

You Only Live Once

KAYAKERS OFF JERSEY IN THE CHANNEL ISLANDS   Michael Heffernan

Kaikoura
New Zealand
Arguably the world capital of wildlife-spotting by kayak, at Kaikoura's kayak school you're likely to be distracted by seals, Dusky and Hector's dolphins and even migrating whales. If you're very lucky, a pod of resident orcas might check out your progress.

Channel Islands,
British Isles
These slabs of granite, sliced from the French mainland and scattered artfully into the sea, are full of mild adventures and small discoveries. With exquisite coastlines and sheltered coves, they'll keep kayakers entertained for days. There are two large islands, Guernsey and Jersey, and three smaller islets, including car-free Sark.

Dalmatian
Coast Croatia
Hop from one turquoise-fringed island to the next along Croatia's Dalmatian Coast; the Adriatic is generally warmer and calmer than the Atlantic plus there's the advantage of starting and ending your trip in historic Dubrovnik.

Stockholm Archipelago
Sweden
Stockholm's archipelago, which consists of 25,000 islands, is a remarkable and relaxing place. A good base for sea kayaking is the southerly island of Uto, where your only company on the water will be seals.

TRAVEL SOLO

'To awaken quite alone in a strange town is one of the most pleasant sensations in the world. You are surrounded by adventure.'
Freya Stark

There are many benefits to travelling solo from time to time. You will gain in confidence, become comfortable dining at a table for one, and be free to make new friends and wear a string of garlic whenever you please.

MEETING THE LOCALS IN SERBIA   Matt Munro

A Month ◗

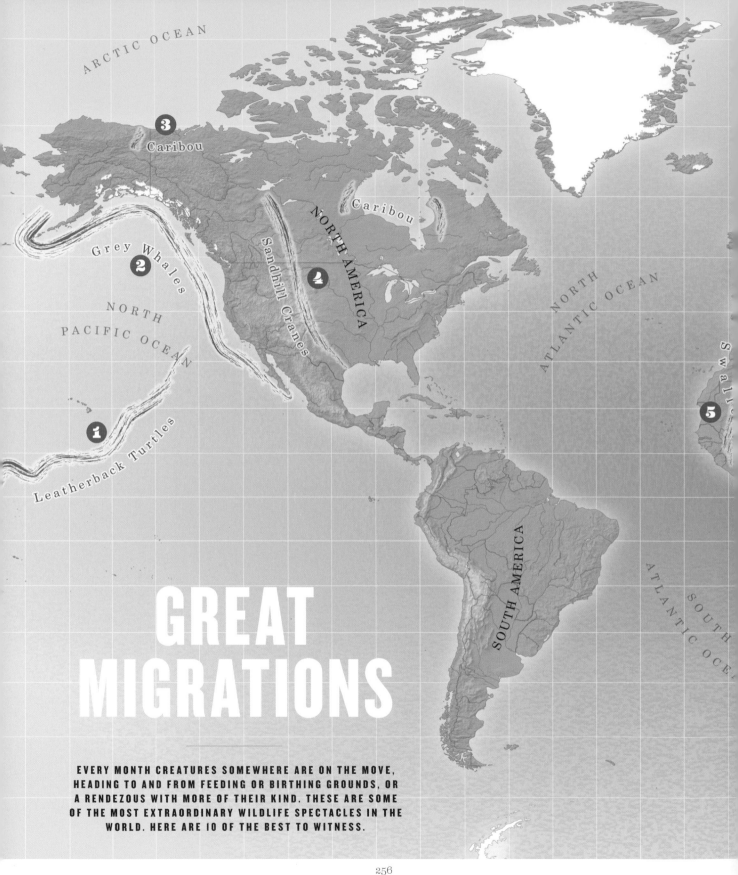

ARCTIC OCEAN

③ Caribou

Caribou

NORTH AMERICA

Grey Whales
②

Sandhill Cranes

④

NORTH
PACIFIC OCEAN

NORTH
ATLANTIC OCEAN

Swallow
⑤

①

Leatherback Turtles

SOUTH AMERICA

SOUTH
ATLANTIC OCEAN

GREAT MIGRATIONS

EVERY MONTH CREATURES SOMEWHERE ARE ON THE MOVE,
HEADING TO AND FROM FEEDING OR BIRTHING GROUNDS, OR
A RENDEZOUS WITH MORE OF THEIR KIND. THESE ARE SOME
OF THE MOST EXTRAORDINARY WILDLIFE SPECTACLES IN THE
WORLD. HERE ARE 10 OF THE BEST TO WITNESS.

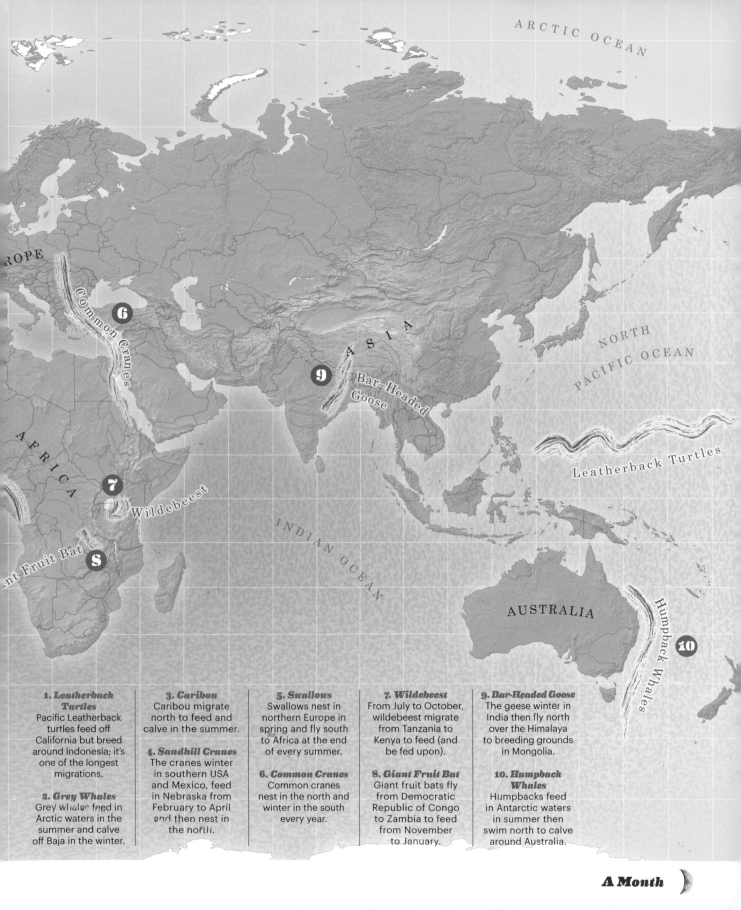

ARCTIC OCEAN

NORTH
PACIFIC OCEAN

ASIA

Bar–Headed
Goose

Common Cranes

⑥

⑨

ROPE

AFRICA

⑦

Wildebeest

nt Fruit Bat

⑧

INDIAN OCEAN

Leatherback Turtles

AUSTRALIA

Humpback Whales

⑩

1. Leatherback Turtles
Pacific Leatherback turtles feed off California but breed around Indonesia; it's one of the longest migrations.

2. Grey Whales
Grey whales feed in Arctic waters in the summer and calve off Baja in the winter.

3. Caribou
Caribou migrate north to feed and calve in the summer.

4. Sandhill Cranes
The cranes winter in southern USA and Mexico, feed in Nebraska from February to April and then nest in the north.

5. Swallows
Swallows nest in northern Europe in spring and fly south to Africa at the end of every summer.

6. Common Cranes
Common cranes nest in the north and winter in the south every year.

7. Wildebeest
From July to October, wildebeest migrate from Tanzania to Kenya to feed (and be fed upon).

8. Giant Fruit Bat
Giant fruit bats fly from Democratic Republic of Congo to Zambia to feed from November to January.

9. Bar-Headed Goose
The geese winter in India then fly north over the Himalaya to breeding grounds in Mongolia.

10. Humpback Whales
Humpbacks feed in Antarctic waters in summer then swim north to calve around Australia.

SURFING THE LONG BREAK AT PUERTO ESCONDIDO, MEXICO   Getty/Michele Falzone

ENDLESS SUMMER

LIVE THE DREAM: LEARN TO SURF IN MEXICO AND CATCH WAVES, DAY AFTER ENDLESS DAY.

Sure, *you showed up at the beach* without a clue about board wax, goofy stance or riptides. It didn't matter. Because after a few days of surf lessons in Puerto Escondido, Mexico, you were doing it—catching waves. Sure, you weren't showing off on the big tubes of the 'Mexican Pipeline,' the famous wave at Zicatela Beach that draws pro surfers from around the globe. You were riding the small and perfect curls nearby, the ones that shot you to the shore in a foaming rush of water and made you crave the next ride like nothing else.

That first day, your instructor pushed you hard. Every time you fell off the board, he made you get right back on. The next day, he didn't have to tell you what to do. You wanted to get on again. The waves seemed limited and the time was now. Every day, surfing felt more intuitive. During week two in the Mexican village, your instincts kicked in and your brain turned off. You felt the swells and communed with the vastness of the ocean.

It wasn't just the surfing that was feeling right. You were always relaxed and hungry, which led to eating plenty of sublime ceviche and taking naps in hammocks. There was the occasional nighttime beach bonfire and yoga class. Every evening, you spent the golden hour on the beach, basking in the glow you'd created by nailing a new sport in just two weeks. ●

Glitz & glam
Sure, French royals have made Biarritz a famously posh destination for centuries. But it's the surfers who currently dominate the scene, especially during July's annual surf competition. You seamlessly slip into the stream by taking surf and French lessons rolled into one, which makes for sweet afternoons of forgetting the pain of the subjunctive as you glide toward shore in perfect balance. Toast your accomplishments with a glass of champagne.

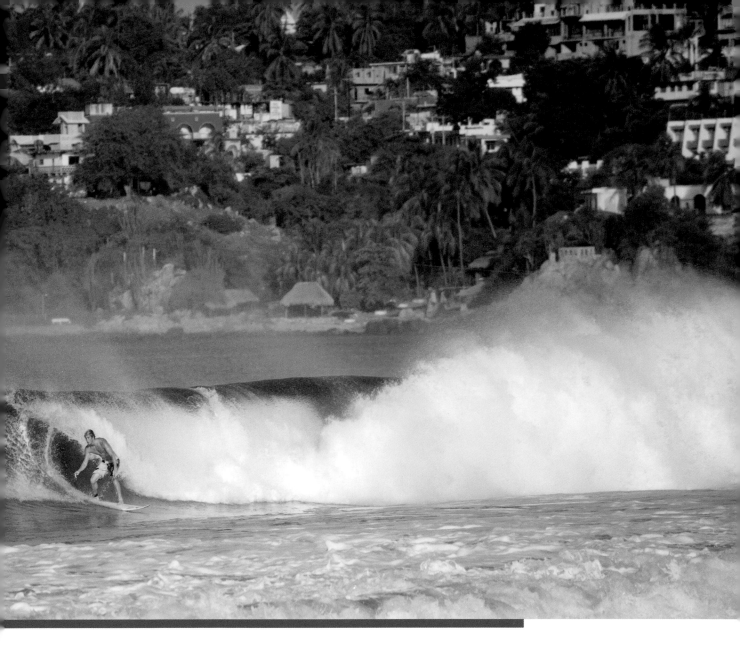

Into the wild
North of Brisbane on the Sunshine Coast, Noosa Beach reigns as one of Australia's premier surf spots. As part of the National Park, the beaches here feel wild. You may even spot a native koala hanging about in the trees as you carry your board to the break. You'll never forget learning to catch the smooth, glossy waves in the ridiculously turquoise waters.

Tropical paradise
You're the kind of newbie surfer who wants to learn within sight of palm fronds – in the tropics. But you like the quiet side of the tropics, a place with surf schools, but where the jungle creeps through every crack. That's why you learn to ride the waves of the crescent-shaped Playa Guiones in Nosara, Costa Rica. There you commune with likeminded surfers from around the world, who totally get your vibe.

Big appetites
When you catch a wave in San Sebastian, Spain, you can catch a glimpse of the town's low skyline, a reminder that you're well within the reach of civilization. The Basque town is a serious surf destination, but one that focuses equally on food and nightlife. Enjoy the predictable waves and soft sandy beach during the day, and then head to the city's best pintxo restaurants after the sun sets.

3

months

time it takes to make the perfect 1000-year-old egg (also known as century eggs), much-loved in Asia.

9.67

million

digital train tickets sold by Indian Railways per month.

10

months

time spent by Britons Paul Archer, Johno Ellison and Leigh Purnell, driving a London Black Cab for 32,000 miles across 41 countries – the world's longest taxi journey.

1,115,680

number of people

who pass through Beijing Capital International Airport in China per month.

9083.33

tonnes

of dulce de leche made in Argentina per month.

316,667

bikes sold

per month in Germany in 2013, compared to 245,833 cars.

3.8

days

amount of time the average Australian spends a month online.

30

months

time it took Briton Joff Summerfield to complete a 22,000-mile cycling circumnavigation of the world on a penny-farthing.

1,127,480

passports

number of US passports issued per month in 2013.

1250

new species of flora and fauna

discovered per month on average.

22

months

combined amount of time Russian cosmonaut Valeri Polyakov has spent in space, including one stay of 437 days 18 hours in 1994–95 on Mir.

196.42

hours

the average employee works in South Korea per month.

LESSONS IN LIVING LIGHTLY

We break camp early: the sun has yet to burn the mist off the treetops. Our campfire is still smouldering despite the insistent humidity that's already made wet rags of my shirt. Segundo, my guide from the local Huitoto tribe, deftly helps me unhook my hammock and mosquito net from the trees, scuffs out the fire, and we step wordlessly out onto a jungle path towards the river. I glance back through the trees to where we'd spent the night, rain tip-tapping on our hammocks' awnings, and Segundo's voice conjuring Huitoto legends of snakes, floods and vengeful gods. Our home for the night in the Colombian Amazon, larger than life under the blanket of darkness, is now untraceable.

Segundo strides out under the dripping forest canopy. I trot sweatily behind. Besides the hammocks he carries nothing. Around his waist, a hip pouch contains not much more than his mambe (coca powder) and tobacco. My knapsack of essentials comprises a sarong, a couple of T-shirts, token mozzie spray (the bites continue regardless), some toiletries (rarely used unless near a river), a sleeping bag, water and a camera. Most of my belongings had been dumped in a lock-up in Leticia, the closest Amazon hub town. Mobile phone? There's no reception. Rain mac?

What's the point, perspiration will drench you first. Wallet? Banks and shops are far away.

The very first time I trekked and camped in the Amazon, some 15 years previously, it felt as if heading for incarceration. Bound for the densely forested banks of Peru's Tambopata, seven hours up-river from the nearest town, I had handed over keys, phone and wallet to a lock-up, and with them, a significant sense of self. But what I found, in fact, was that this led to liberation rather than confinement. Without these fidgety fixtures of modern identity, I was free to just be.

Then, as now, my hosts equipped me with all I needed. I am directed to trees that produce water, twigs that double as

> I am directed to trees that produce water, twigs that double as toothbrushes; a directory of flora with mystical and medical attributes

toothbrushes, a directory of flora with mystical and medical attributes. Within a 3 sq m tract of forest, with the right knowledge, you could treat everything from cuts and abrasions to diarrhoea, arthritis and impotence. What you need here is not technical kit and clothing but know-how. Segundo navigates swiftly through seemingly impenetrable walls of rainforest like a man with an inner GPS, delivering us, suddenly, to a chacra – one of the Amazon's small, subsistence farms. It's as if he has just produced a rabbit from a huge, shrub-filled hat.

This formidable knowledge, however, is delivered with an equal dose of humility. Before each journey between chacras, Segundo discreetly kneels, inhales mambe and blows tobacco smoke low across the ground – a ritual of respect or superstition depending on your perspective. Like most Amazon tribespeople, he believes the forest to be very much alive, a physical and spiritual entity governed by Old Testament–like gods who must be appeased. Become cavalier at your peril; the trees here may take their revenge. Strangler figs and mangroves form gothic cages around you, 'walking' palms block your path, and vines seethe around your ankles, sprouting back minutes after your machete's slash. Everyone, it seems, has a hair-raising tale of a friend missing all night on a route they walked daily.

But this morning, all are present and correct in the maloca, the traditional palm-thatch longhouse at the centre of this chacra. Abuelo, the community's elder is going about morning chores, frying eggs and corn for breakfast, shadowed by the resident pack of skeletal pups. Tending to crops here must be like pruning a bramble patch with nail clippers, and yet the chacra thrives with corn, yam, pineapple and banana. Natural pest control comes by way of the weaver birds and caciques that prey on insects, nesting in one or two strategically planted trees.

Here is a wild world made manageable – not tamed but tacitly understood. I settle down between the vast roots of a kapok tree and watch one of the boys deftly weaving palm leaves for the maloca's roof, efficient against the rains for years to come. It's an age-old process, simple yet skilled and completely sustainable – a metaphor for a life lived lightly. ●

KEEP IT TRAD

SPRING, SUMMER, WINTER OR AUTUMN, WHATEVER THE MONTH THERE
WILL BE A TRADITIONAL RITUAL SOMEWHERE AROUND THE WORLD – SOME
STRANGER THAN OTHERS – WITH WHICH YOU CAN JOIN IN.

When the locals in a Stockholm bar invited you to come and celebrate Midsommarfirande with them, you were thrilled – how better to experience Sweden's Midsummer Festival than by getting out of the city and seeing how it's traditionally done?

But a few nerves began to jangle when they started telling you the stories – about washing a smörgåsbord of raw herring varieties down with silly sounding amounts of brännvin – and showing you videos of last year's shindig on their smartphones.

That maypole really did look a touch risqué from that angle. And what kind of jig were those people doing? Oh, that's right, the famous frog dance. Of course. Still, there looked to be plenty of hilarity and high spirits. More than you've ever seen before, now you think about it, here in this friendly but slightly tightly buckled country.

Midsommarfirande is a celebration of the summer solstice – a happy time this far north, when the sun-starved Swedes savour every bit of daylight they can get their skin under. In a modern interpretation of a tradition that goes back to pagan times, many evacuate urban areas and seek out al fresco parties, as fresh-air festivities kick off all across the countryside, on islands and yachts, and in lakeside cabins.

Overdosing on vitamin D, gravadlax, smoked salmon, and *nubbe* (Swedish snaps), people let their hair down, don garlands of flowers and indulge in some solar-powered flirting.

And then there's the *Små Grodorna* of course – the frog song – the moves to which you've been practising in mirror like Kermit going gangnam style. What do those words mean again? 'Little frogs are funny to look at / They don't have ears or tails'. Maybe something gets lost in translation, but there's no denying it – this place is hopping. ●

DANCING AROUND A MIDSUMMER MAYPOLE IN SWEDEN   Matt Munro

You Only Live Once

 KEEP IT TRAD

Sourtoe cocktails in the snow, Canada

'Bottoms up!' yells Captain Dick, who pours the 'special' measures in Dawson City's Downtown Hotel. You grit your teeth, and drink. The 80-proof whisky burns your throat, but the alcohol content of the Sourtoe Cocktail isn't what worries you. The real challenge is letting the dead person's toe touch your lips, as tradition demands in this curious corner of the planet, where 'strange things done 'neath the midnight sun', as the Yukon's bard Robert Service observed.
To earn themselves bragging rights, drinkers have been sipping Sourtoes – drinks with a preserved human toe floating in them – since 1973.

Penis envy in spring, Japan

Carving a penis from a giant radish – of course, what else would you be doing on the first Sunday in April? If you're anywhere near the Kanayama Shrine in Kawasaki, Japan, you're bound to be doing something relating to the male member, as is traditional during the Shinto Kanamara Matsuri. The occasion is marked by thousands of people – families included – who walk around eating various phallic food items, buying penis-shaped candles and generally celebrating gentlemen's genitals.

Barefoot climbing in summer, Ireland

The Irish summer's finally arrived and now you're sweating, even 700m above the Atlantic, on the flanks of Croagh Patrick in the wild-west county of Mayo. The sharp scree near the summit of Ireland's holiest mountain is tricky enough in walking boots, but the people ahead of you are battling it barefoot – no wonder there are injuries every year. This is Domhnach na Cruaiche, or Reek Sunday. Reek is the locals' name for the peak, not the aroma of pilgrim's feet as they dispense with footwear to follow a 1500-year-old tradition. In 441, St Patrick apparently spent 40 days fasting on this mountain, but the climbing ritual goes back further, to pagan times when the Celts celebrated the harvest festival of Lughnasadh.

Blazing barrels in autumn, England

Your eyelashes curl in the heat as a man sprints past, carrying a barrel billowing with furious fire at head height. You're in Ottery St Mary, a sleepy English hamlet that explodes into fiery action every 5 November, as locals observe a 400-year-old tradition. The exact origins of Ottery's Flaming Tar Barrels are lost in the smoke of time, but it harks back to the 1605 Gunpowder Plot. The Devon village's pubs sponsor tar-lined barrels, which are ceremoniously set on fire and hoisted onto the shoulders of participants, who then run up and down the increasingly busy streets – the object being to keep the barrel burning for as long as possible. As the evening wears on, the crowd swells, the cider drinking gets faster and the competition heats up.

TAILOR MADE

When the explorer David Livingstone finally met Henry Stanley on the shores of Lake Tanganyika, Livingstone was wearing a suit tailored by Gieves of Savile Row, London, and Stanley one by Henry Poole, also of Savile Row. A well-cut suit is clearly not just for dandies. But it is an investment in time as well as money; expect a waiting time of a couple of months. Unless you're in India, Hong Kong or Singapore, where the turnaround time is far more speedy.

A SEAMSTRESS IN SPAIN   Mark Read

SARAH BAXTER TRAVELS OUT OF SEASON

Indiana Jones – with an umbrella.** That's the aesthetic. The scene is pure Raiders; you may as well be wearing a sable fedora and belt whip, such is the cinematic jumble of exotic ruins encroached by jungle, such is the sense of adventure. But it ain't half wet.

The rain is falling with military fury. It's not droplets; this is ammunition-made-aqua, a soggying salvo of water-bullets firing from a gunmetal sky. It's the sort of storm that could maim, rain so forceful it leaves a mark on the skin, a sting on the cheek.

But this onslaught is awesome. Watching Mother Nature's rage, witnessing her hurl her worst, adds to the general drama. The scouring thump of water on sandstone is like watching erosion in action. The forest seems to be growing at visible speed. The smack of water on broad leaves and ornate edifice is near-deafening.

Cambodia – specifically, Angkor – in the monsoon is damp, yes, but offers thrills of the highest Indiana order. The jungle that threatens to (and occasionally succeeds in)

> Rice terraces glow in the rudest of health; cities are spring-cleaned of their usual dust; and waterfalls are in their fullest, most fabulous flows

reclaim the sprawl of Khmer temples is vivid green, the finery of the trees is fresh-washed and never more profuse. Plus the moats that enclose some of the ancient complexes are authentically full to bursting.

The best thing though – as with heading to any destination in the off season – is the paucity of other people. Of course, you're never completely alone; there are always other diehards braving the adverse climatic conditions. But queues are shorter, viewpoints less busy, and any crowds that

do amass are so much easier to lose. There's even, you fancy, a moist camaraderie. When a deluge hits and you find yourself cowering under a 10th-century cloister with a similarly wet-through traveller, you can strike up a conversation about the weather, and shelter in your shared resilience. You can also feel smug about the price tag: airfares, hotel rooms, taxi rides, even watermelon shakes, all cost less in the low season.

But it's not all plain sailing. There are distinct downsides to the wet – not least of all, the wetness. As dramatic as a storm can be, it would be nice to see a sunny sky, and to leave the brolly in your room. That said, a monsoon is not a constant drenching. Rain comes in bursts – an hour's shower here, an afternoon's torrent there; some days there is no rain at all. It's arguably better for your psyche this way. If you visit any destination in its dry season and get some unfortunate freak downpours, you'll be cross that your trip is a washout; visit in the wet, fully prepared for precipitation, and any dry days you have will seem like gifts from the gods. It's all a case of perspective.

Of course, getting around can be a bit trickier during the monsoon. Roads across much of Southeast Asia have improved in recent years, particularly in Thailand and Vietnam, but some backwaters remain tough to reach when the weather turns motorways to mulch. This is a downer; you must accept that some places may be off limits, unless you are tenacious, or have webbed feet.

But overall you're on to a winner: rice terraces glow in the rudest of health; cities are spring-cleaned of their usual dust; and cooling waterfalls, are in their fullest, most fabulous flows. Glowering skies might seem to dull your snapshots but actually they enliven them. Unmitigated sunshine washes out photos, while brooding clouds, and rays bursting through them, bring a landscape to life.

Rainy season? Nah, let's call it the brainy season. ●

WORK YOUR WAY

NO CASH? NO PROBLEM. BEG, BORROW OR STEAL THE AIRFARE AND MONTHS OF WORK AND PLAY AWAIT.

A*h, la France...* Morning lifts a curtain on a scene straight out of a Monet painting. You're in Le Breui, in beautiful Beaujolais. Vines march up rolling hills cloaked in mist, interspersed with proud stands of pine and oak. As you trudge through the mud breathing in the dewy dawn air, the first light spills like warm honey across patchwork fields of russet and gold, lighting up a stone village cupped in the valley below.

Allez! You set to work, secateurs in hand, slowing getting into the groove of clipping bunches of grapes and filling buckets. Before you know it, you are singing along to *vendange* (grape harvest) ditties with bonhomie and gusto. Or perhaps, if you are built like an ox, you'll be chosen as a porteur, where the backbreaking work of lugging a 50kg basket of grapes up and down a steep slope is eased by copious amounts of wine at the tractor from dawn to dusk.

While some aspects of the grape harvest in France are undeniably idyllic, you might not want to put on those rose–tinted spectacles just yet. It is hard graft, with early starts, long hours – typically 10 to 12 a day – no day off, and rock-bottom wages of around €50 a day. Oh, and a downpour can delay the harvest for days.

But hey, who cares? This is still living the dream. You get your bed and board thrown in, the scenery is gorgeous and you meet new friends from all over the world – trading stories and drinking deep of free wine under the stars. They tell you, through the grapevine, about other harvest work, from olives in Provence to oysters in Arcachon Bay. After a couple of hazy September weeks, you return home with better French, a healthy glow to your cheeks and a lifetime of memories. And you'll never look at a bottle of wine in the supermarket in the same way again. ●

HARVESTING GRAPES IN BURGUNDY, FRANCE   Getty/Ian Shaw

270

HANDS UP IN A CLASSROOM IN CHINA   Getty/Oktay Ortakcioglu

Working holiday in Oz
Working visa? Check. Return flights? Check. Sense of adventure? Check. A job? No worries, mate. Whether you dream of Sydney Harbour at sunset or swimming with whale sharks in Western Australia, travels here can easily be combined with casual jobs. Do your homework before setting off or just rock up and see what you can find as a fruit picker, bar tender, hostel worker, tour guide, even jackaroo.

Au pair in the USA
Stop California dreamin' and go see it for yourself. Or perhaps it's Manhattan's skyline or Colorado's rugged wilderness that make you swoon. Provided you have a knack with kids, common sense, a driving licence and clean bill of health, you could earn a decent crust slipping into Mary Poppins' shoes and staying with a host family pretty much anywhere in the States.

Ski season in the Alps
Skiing in the Alps is expensive, so working here for a winter season is a great way to pound powder for a few months, fund your lift pass and fondue dinners, and brush up your French, Italian or German. Think chalet maid, hotel and bar work, or, if you're a whizz on the slopes, ski or snowboard instructor.

Teaching in Asia
A TEFL (teaching English as a foreign language) qualification is your golden ticket to a decently paid teaching job in Asia. Not only will this throw you into the deep end of the culture and help you hone your language skills, you'll often gain much kudos from the local community. And you can use that pay cheque to see the temples of Burma, the teahouses of Japan or the beaches of Thailand.

PLAY A GAME OF CONKERS IN THE ENGLISH AUTUMN ● GET YOUR KICKS WITH A STORM-CHASING TOUR ON THE GREAT PLAINS OF AMERICA IN MAY, TORNADO HIGH SEASON ● TREK ALONG HIMALAYAN TRAILS COVERED IN BLOSSOMING RHODODENDRONS IN SPRING ● CATCH A DISPLAY OF THE AURORA BOREALIS IN TROMS, NORWAY, WHICH HOSTS THE NORTHERN LIGHTS FESTIVAL IN JANUARY FEBRUARY ● DIVE WITH LEVIATHAN MANTA RAYS FOLLOWING THE TRADEWINDS THROUGH THE MIIL CHANNEL IN YAP, A CLUSTER OF ISLANDS IN MICRONESIA, NOVEMBER MAY ● GO BLACK TRUFFLE HUNTING WITH A RABASSIER IN THE DORDOGNE, FRANCE, DURING JANUARY AND FEBRUARY, WHEN THE DIAMONDS OF PRIGORD ARE AT THEIR BEST ● TAKE UP VIZ MIGGING (VISIBLE MIGRATION), A FORM OF TWITCHING, WHERE BIRD ENTHUSIASTS WATCH MASS ARRIVALS AND DEPARTURES OF MIGRATORY SPECIES ● WATCH WHALES GO PAST AS YOU SURF ON WORLD-CLASS BEACHES IN ALBANY, WESTERN AUSTRALIA, MAY TO DECEMBER ● SEE THE RISING WINTER SOLSTICE SUN ILLUMINATE THE STONE AGE PASSAGE TOMB AT NEWGRANGE IN THE BOYNE VALLEY, IRELAND ● IN THE ENGLISH SPRING, WALK THROUGH VALLEYS OF BLUEBELLS AROUND HARDCASTLE CRAGS, YORKSHIRE ● GET YOUR GLOVES ON AND EXPERIENCE THE WINTER ICE-SCULPTURE FESTIVAL IN HARBIN, CHINA ● WATCH SURFERS DURING HAWAIIS WINTER BIG WAVE SEASON (NOVEMBER MARCH) ● SCARE YOURSELF SILLY ON KRAMPUSNACHT (6 DECEMBER) IN AUSTRIA AND GERMANY, WHEN THE ANTI-SANTA SORTS THE NAUGHTY FROM THE NICE KIDS ● SURF THE BEST BORE WAVES UP SEVERN ESTUARY BETWEEN ENGLAND AND WALES IN MARCH, SEPTEMBER AND OCTOBER ● BUILD A SNOWMAN IN CENTRAL PARK, NEW YORK ● BEHOLD THE PHANTOM FALLS OF THE BLUE MOUNTAINS IN NEW SOUTH WALES, AUSTRALIA, AN OPTICAL ILLUSION THAT TAKES PLACE IN THE SOUTHERN AUTUMN AND SPRING ● BETWEEN JULY AND OCTOBER, DRIVE SOUTH AFRICAS NAMAQUALAND FLOWER ROUTE ● ICE SKATE ACROSS THE FROZEN SEA BETWEEN ISLANDS IN THE STOCKHOLM ARCHIPELAGO IN SWEDEN ● GET INTO THE HEAD OF JAMES JOYCE AND WANDER AROUND DUBLIN UNDER THE LUKEWARM IRISH SUN ON BLOOMSDAY ● CHECK OUT THE STAIRCASE TO THE MOON IN ROEBUCK BAY, WESTERN AUSTRALIA, A PHENOMENON THAT TAKES PLACE ON CLEAR NIGHTS WITH A FULL MOON, MARCH OCTOBER ● HIKE THROUGH NEW ENGLANDS FORESTS AS THE LEAVES TURN INTO A KALEIDOSCOPE OF COLOURS ● EXPLORE KENYAS MAASAI MARA NATIONAL RESERVE FROM JULY FOR THE GREAT MIGRATION ● DO A WINTER OVERNIGHT STAY IN NORTH RONALDSAY LIGHTHOUSE IN ORKNEY, SCOTLAND, FOR THE ULTIMATE STORM-WATCHING EXPERIENCE ● WATCH GRIZZLY BEARS CATCHING SALMON AT BROOKS FALLS IN KATMAI NATIONAL PARK,

50 WAYS TO CELEBRATE THE SEASONS
By Patrick Kinsella

ALASKA, IN JULY ● PAINT YOUR WORLD PINK WITH CHERRY BLOSSOMS IN JAPAN ● GET YOUR CHRISTMAS SHOPPING DONE AT THE WINTER MARKETS IN PRAGUE ● CATCH THE BLOOMING OF THE TISZA, WHEN MILLIONS OF MAYFLIES EMERGE IN CLOUDS FROM HUNGARYS TISZA RIVER IN LATE SPRING ● LAY BACK ON A CLEAR MOONLESS AUGUST NIGHT ATOP SUGAR LOAF MOUNTAIN IN BRECON BEACONS NATIONAL PARK, WALES, AND CONTEMPLATE YOUR PLACE IN THE UNIVERSE ● JOIN A WILD-MUSHROOM FORAGING TOUR IN THE LUBUSZ LAKE DISTRICT, WESTERN POLAND ● SLEEP IN A SNOWHOLE IN THE CAIRNGORMS, SCOTLAND, IN THE MIDDLE OF WINTER ● DANGLE A FISHING LINE THOUGH A HOLE IN A FROZEN LAKE AT THE HWACHEON SANCHEONEO ICE FESTIVAL IN GANGWON-DO PROVINCE, KOREA ● TAKE A BOAT TRIP THROUGH BANGLADESH, ONE OF THE PLANETS LEAST-VISITED COUNTRIES, DURING THE COOL SEASON OCTOBER FEBRUARY ● OBSERVE MASS CORAL SPAWNING ON NINGALOO REEF IN WESTERN AUSTRALIA, TWO WEEKS AFTER THE MARCH OR APRIL FULL MOON ● GET YOUR GHOUL ON AND CELEBRATE DA DE MUERTOS (DAY OF THE DEAD) IN MEXICO IN EARLY NOVEMBER ● GO TIGER SPOTTING IN BANDHAVGARH NATIONAL PARK IN INDIAS SUMMER, WHEN THE ELUSIVE ANIMALS LOOK FOR WATER ● PACK A PICNIC AND WITNESS THE GREENING OF THE SOUTHERN TIP OF THE ARABIAN PENINSULA DURING THE KHAREEF, JUNE SEPTEMBER ● CUT LOOSE DURING FEBRUARYS FESTIVAL SEASON IN BRAZIL AND CHECK OUT THE ACTION AT THE CARNAVAL OF SALVADOR DA BAHIA ● CELEBRATE THE BOND BETWEEN MAN AND REPTILE AT THE SEPIK RIVER CROCODILE FESTIVAL IN PAPUA NEW GUINEA IN EARLY AUGUST ● SEE EVIL SPIRITS OFF AND EMBRACE A NEW YEAR AT THE COMRIE FLAMBEAUX, A PAGAN HOGMANAY FESTIVAL IN THE SOUTHERN HIGHLANDS OF SCOTLAND ● VISIT PUNTA NORTE, ON PENINSULA VALDES IN PATAGONIA, ARGENTINA DURING ORCA SEASON, LATE FEBRUARY-LATE APRIL, WHEN KILLER WHALES HUNT SEA LIONS ● GET A TEAM TOGETHER AND DO A 24HR-MOUNTAIN BIKE RACE UNDER THE MIDSUMMER MIDNIGHT SUN IN WHITEHORSE, YUKON ● LOAD YOUR WATER-RIFLE AND JOIN IN THE CHAOS SURROUNDING SONGKRAN IN APRIL, AS ASIA WELCOMES MONSOON SEASON ● CELEBRATE THE IMMINENT ARRIVAL OF SUMMER WITH THE OBBY OSS FESTIVAL IN PADSTOW, CORNWALL, ON MAY DAY ● AVOID THE CROWDS AND VISIT VENICE IN THE MIDST OF WINTER ● SEIZE A SUMMER DAY IN MILFORD SOUND IN NEW ZEALANDS FJORDLAND, AND DO A DIVE THROUGH 10M OF FRESH WATER BEFORE HITTING THE SALTY STUFF ● VISIT THE SERENGETI NATIONAL PARK IN TANZANIA TO WITNESS WILDEBEEST CALVING ● PUT YOUR PLAYING-OUT CLOTHES ON AND GET AMONGST IT DURING LA TOMATINA FOOD FIGHT IN THE VALENCIA TOWN OF BU OL ● SEE AUSTRALIA IN A NEW LIGHT DURING JULY AND AUGUST WHEN THE ALPINE AREAS OF VICTORIA AND NEW SOUTH WALES ARE CLOAKED IN SNOW ● GO KAYAKING AT THE BOTTOM OF THE PLANET, DURING A SUMMER BOAT CRUISE TO ANTARCTICA ● TAKE A 4WD ACROSS BOLIVIAS SALAR DE UYUNI DURING WET SEASON WHEN THE REFLECTION MAKES IT SEEM AS THOUGH YOURE DRIVING THROUGH THE SKY ●

THE THAMES, LONDON. Matt Munro

TO THE SOURCE

In 2010 Ed Stafford became the first person to walk the entire length of the Amazon, after an epic journey that lasted 28 months. But you don't have to pick one of the world's gnarliest rivers to follow to the source; even a minor river will usher you through enthralling landscapes. Many rivers make it easy: both the Danube and the Rhine can be cycled from source to sea or you can copy Jerome K. Jerome and take a boat up the River Thames. But Ed Stafford has some comforting words if you select a more remote river: 'I washed in the same river that I caught piranhas from every day, with no problems. I never got bitten by snakes either – I always saw them at the last minute, just as they were rearing up to strike.' So that's OK.

AY

Chapter
05

In which you quit your cubicle, take flying lessons,
ski sweet powder for twelve months,

YEAR

uncover your family's roots, and resolve to learn a new language.
Then, consider a sabbatical in the Caribbean
or the south of France, or even a round-the-world journey
with the perfect travel companion.

A Year

Chapter

05

REFUELLING THE CESSNA IN THE SERENGETI   Alamy/National Geographic

LEARN TO FLY

**TAKE THE CONTROLS AND FEEL THE THRILL
OF BEING IN CHARGE OF YOUR AIRBORNE DESTINY.
BUT DON'T GET TOO DISTRACTED BY THAT VIEW.**

It's *your first time* on safari in Africa. You're riding shotgun on a 12-seat charter plane when the young bush pilot asks if you want to fly. There's only one answer to that question. He explains that the U-shaped steering column works like the wheel of a car and points out which gauges to watch, then takes his hands off his steering column as you grasp yours. The plane rocks a bit as you find an equilibrium. And then – it's smooth and steady. You're doing it. You're flying!

You start paying less attention to the gauges and peek up over the dashboard to make sure the horizon remains horizontal and you're on course. Puffy cumulous clouds drift by gracefully below, and farther down, the majestic animals of Africa appear as specks on the dry savannah. If you turn too sharply, your fellow passengers suck in their breath, but you soon figure out how sensitive the steering is. You're disappointed when you have to hand over control so the pilot can land.

You come home from Africa raving not about the lions and elephants but about piloting the Cessna. You start joking that your plan-B career will be becoming an African bush pilot. People tell you about local flight schools, but you're not quite ready to commit to the many hours and considerable expense needed to quality as a fully fledged pilot.

And then someone who knows you well gives you the best gift ever: a combination scenic aerial tour and intro-to-flying lesson at a nearby flight academy. It turns out many schools offer these to entice would-be students; they're also able to feed a post-safari appetite for more. Most Western schools are more by-the-book than the average bush pilot, so your instructor asks you to demonstrate more fluency with the instruments and is more cautious about handing over the controls. No worries – once you feel the plane tilting in response to your touch and become aware that you're holding yourself aloft, the magic returns. ●

Heritage Flight Academy, USA
During the intro flight at this Long Island school, the instructor steers you over the Atlantic and up the Hudson River, with Manhattan's skyscrapers sparkling at eye level. When you get to the less-crowded airspace north of the city, you fly over the Long Island Sound.

Austrian Flight Academy, California, USA
The one-hour flight at this LA-area school has you and an instructor – and two friends, if you want – over Long Beach, Palos Verdes and California's stunning coastline and beaches.

IcelandAirclub, Iceland
Based at Reykjavik airport, this club offers piloted sightseeing trips over Iceland's fjords, glaciers, waterfalls and black-sand beaches, as well as arranging one-hour intro flights for anyone who wants a taste of the air.

Basair Aviation College, Australia
Australia's largest flight school, in a Sydney suburb, offers hour-long scenic trial instructional flights over the city in a Cessna 152. Students may even take off and land (with assistance from the instructor).

SAY YES

DAVID CORNTHWAITE IS THE 'YES' MAN

After an incredible 156 days and a sole-searing 5823km, I finally rolled into Brisbane, smashing two world records in the process. I'd traversed the whole of Australia, from Perth on the west coast, across the never-ending Nullarbor Plain, to the eastern shore. On... a skateboard.

Following my graduation from university, I had found a job fast, accepted it without thinking and lapsed into a disenchanted life of ennui and materialism. After 18 months I awoke with a feeling of moderate anger, something that drove me to a buy long skateboard – with the original intention of improving my snowboarding skills.

After two weeks of skating around town, I started to see my familiar world from a different perspective and I developed an urge to explore. I skated to work, put the keys on the desk, quit my job and promised myself that I'd skate further than anyone else ever had. One year later I became the first person to skate the length of Britain. And within two

I have fallen in love with the simple process of trying to make my life memorable. Not to others, just to me

years, I was setting off for Australia. Shortly after I arrived in Brisbane, my phone rang – and I was asked to write a book. I said yes.

And from there, I set about saying yes, a lot. I created Expedition1000, a project of 25 journeys of 1000 miles (1609km) or more, each using a different form of non-motorised transport. Among other endeavours, I said yes to paddling from source to sea down the Murray River, riding a tandem bike 2253km between Vancouver and Vegas, paddle-boarding over 3862km along the length of the Mississippi, swimming down the Missouri River, sailing across the Pacific on a 22m yacht, and riding an elliptical bicycle 3219km across Europe.

But adventure doesn't necessarily mean painfully long and difficult journeys. Saying yes doesn't mean you have to quit your job or sell your house or buy a tent. It's just a very effective means of slowing time, by weighing it down with experiences we really want to have, rather than those we feel we should. ●

A Year

507
years
age of an ocean quahog (Icelandic clam) called Ming, discovered when scientists killed it by prising it open to see how old it was.

4.2
years
length of time it takes light leaving Proxima Centauri (Earth's nearest star, beyond the sun) to reach your telescope.

21
years
length of time Horace Burgess has spent building a treehouse in Crossville, Tennessee.

3&12
years and days
length of time Bob Hanley spent pushing a wheelbarrow 14,500km around Australia between April 1975 and May 1978.

7
years
length of time it took Oskar Speck to paddle a folding kayak from Germany to Australia. He arrived in 1939, just in time to be interned for the duration of WWII.

50%
extent of decline
in performance level in crucial muscles after two years spent in a weightless environment, such as the space station.

8000

international tourists

who annually arrive in Moldova, Europe's
least-visited country.

6,961

pounds

of tea consumed per person per year in Turkey.

17

years

average time British people will spend on the sofa over
their lifetime, according to a 2008 study.

359

years

length of time the Rocky Hill to Glastonbury public ferry in
Connecticut has been continually running.

88

years

length of time a photography project has been documenting
ponderosa pine trees in Montana's Bitterroot National Forest.

93,363

passports

number of Irish passports issued by Irish embassies and
consulates in foreign countries in 2012 (when the in-country
population was 4.58 million).

A Year

FOOD FOR THOUGHT

GIVE THE DESK JOB THE SACK AND STEER YOUR CAREER OUTDOORS.

The hours are terrible, they said. And the conditions horrific. You'll never have time for yourself and you'll end up as fat as a butcher's dog – always snacking and eating leftovers. Friends were full of negatives when you quit your office job to go to catering college. But they weren't privy to your master plan. You never had any intention of working sadistic split-shifts in a sweaty restaurant kitchen or hellish hotel. Those that paid attention might have noticed that you'd also signed up to do a PADI openwater Scuba-diving course, and that should have given them a clue. Now, as you prepare a tasty seafood lunch for the divers beneath the luxury live-aboard boat – who will soon surface with happy, hungry and appreciative looks in their mask-ringed eyes – your mind wanders to later this afternoon. That's when you'll get a couple of hours off to hook up with one of the trainee dive instructors and go for your own daily dive. You're above Osprey Reef today – north of the Great Barrier Reef and several days' sailing time from mainland Australia – one of the best diving spots on this big blue planet. Yesterday a minke whale surfaced not 20m from the galley window while you were chopping onions. There's no way you could ever have afforded a trip like this, but here you are getting paid. The clients were up early doing a dawn dive, with a bit of luck you'll fit a night dive in later too – every hour underwater takes you a bit closer to the second part of the plan: to finish your divemaster course.

Live-aboard dive boats operate in Australia, Egypt, the US – they're always looking for gregarious and skilled crewmembers, from cooks and hosts through to diving instructors and boat handlers. ●

Cool callings
'Don't forget your bobble hat!' said the farewell card from your co-workers. You're not going to see those guys for some time – not where you're going. Telecommunications never felt like the sexiest of careers – until you saw an ad for a communications officer, in Antarctica. You passed the aptitude test and convinced them that you wouldn't crack up spending 6 months in a research station. The work is challenging, the pay is great, and where else can you go snow kiting in your lunch break? Monitor websites such as usap.gov and antarctica.ac.uk.

Career highs
Stopping for lunch you have a clear view of the pub on the corner, but there's no chance of sneaking off for a pint. Beer's not a great idea when you're working 23 storeys up. You're roped and harnessed, but this isn't the place to make mistakes. Can't beat the view though – you can even see the awful place where you used to work, before you turned the skills you'd acquired rock climbing into a new career as a high access specialist. Now, where's that Kit Kat gone? Visit irata.org for details.

Going with the flow
You push off from the bank, with a raft full of excited clients clutching paddles in their hands. The river still has more than a hint of winter about it and the levels are high, swollen by the ice melting up on the hills. You've been waiting for this moment since getting your RAJ (Japan River Guide Association) qualification, to go along with your IRF (International Rafting Federation) Award. You thought you'd be teaching English in Japan, but the only classroom you've been in has been the great outdoors. See internationalrafting.com.

On your bike
It wasn't easy watching your friends go to university while you were 'considering your options'. But kicking back in a bar in the French Alps, you think you chose wisely. You've always loved cycling, but it wasn't until a buddy scored a bike mechanic's job in Moab that you realised your passion could take you somewhere. After getting qualified, you picked up a gig here – with free accommodation and access to some of the best trails in world. Bike guides in Europe need to complete an International Mountain Leader award.

A Year

A YEAR IN PROVENCE

You wind down the car window and the scent of lavender wafts through on a gust of dry heat. Few places are as blessed with food, wine, sunshine and scenery as Provence in the south of France, and spending more than a couple of weeks here will help you get under the skin of the place. It's been about a quarter of a century since Peter Mayle's A Year in Provence was published. Mayle's best-selling memoir spawned a terrible TV series, a dire film and inumerable imitations. But despite all that, the idea remains as brilliant as ever.

THE HILLTOP VILLAGE OF ÉZE IN PROVENCE, FRANCE   Lottie Davies

A Year

THE UNQUENCHABLE FIRST

PATRICK KINSELLA EXPLAINS HOW TO LIVE FOREVER

***H**ow to achieve immortality?* It's an age-old question. You could try setting a world record, but records can always be broken. If you nail your name to a world first – that's yours for keeps.

Now you might moan that you've been born a hundred years too late and all the biggies have already been bagged. And in some senses you'd be right: it's been a busy century, with flags stabbed into most of our poor planet's extremities. But sometimes you have to think outside the square.

Roald Amundsen may have reached the South Pole in 1911, with a team of four men who had to eat their dogs as they went, but in 2013 Maria Leijerstam achieved a first by pedalling to the Pole on her own, without so much as nibbling her bicycle. And while Edmund Hillary and Tenzing Norgay were the first people to stand on top of the world on 29 May 1953, they did so fully clothed – not like 24-year-old Lakpa Tharke Sherpa, who straddled Everest's peak in the buff for three minutes in 2006.

Not everyone attempting a first is motivated by vanity. Consider Annie Taylor, a widowed schoolteacher who, on her 63rd birthday in 1901, became the first person to survive going over Niagara Falls in a barrel. Virtually destitute, Annie decided that risking death by taking the plunge (and hoping for fame and fortune in the process) was preferable to life in the poorhouse. Sadly the money never materialised, but her name has gone down in history. That is more than can be said for Robert Overcracker, who in 1995 died in his attempt to become the first person to ride a jet-ski over Niagara.

And therein lies a cautionary tale: you tread a thin line between becoming immortalised by achieving a 'first' and being remembered as a winner of a Darwin Award (annual anti-plaudits dedicated to people who die in stunningly stupid ways).

Some firsts are achieved by accident. In November 2013, when Sean Conway staggered ashore at John O'Groats as the first person to swim the length of Great Britain,

You only get one life, but there are ways to ensure your name lives on after you depart this mortal coil

his support kayaker Emily Bell discovered she'd inadvertently become the first woman to paddle the length of the island – albeit very slowly.

Achieving a first, even multiple firsts, doesn't guarantee fame, though. In the 1930s, German drifter Oskar Speck spectacularly kayaked from his home country to Australia. En route he knocked off the first paddling circumnavigation of Sri Lanka, but few people know about his efforts.

One last note of warning: if you do score a first, even a big one, the goalposts can change. In 2012, kayaking guide James 'Rocky' Contos was using Google maps to scout virgin river trips in Peru, when he discovered a 'new' source of the Amazon River, the Mantaro River tributary. His claim cast doubt over previous source-to-sea descents of the world's biggest river, which had all started on the Apurimac tributary, including the original 1985-86 expedition by Polish kayaker Piotr Chmielinski and American journalist Joe Kane, and British explorer Ed Stafford's epic Amazon walk completed in 2010. It also opened up a new opportunity to achieve one of earth's greatest firsts, a challenge which Contos bitterly fought with American paddler West Hansen, who he narrowly beat to the Atlantic by using motorised transport. If you want to bag a first, here are a few that remain unclaimed:

- Scale Gangkhar Puensum – at 7570m, this is the world's highest unclimbed peak
- Do a source-to-sea paddle along the Seine River in France
- Reach the real bottom of the Mulu Caves, deep in Sarawak's Gunung Mulu National Park on Borneo
- Swim the length of Lake Tanganyika (677km), the longest freshwater lake in the world
- Run the newly opened John Muir Way, which stretches 215km across Scotland, from Helensburgh to Dunbar.
- Unicycle the length of Ireland, 555km from Malin Head to Mizen Head
- Canoe the Tigil River on Russia's Kamchatka Peninsula
- Skateboard from Deadhorse, Alaska to Ushuaia in southern Argentina
- Paddle around Jamaica ●

A Year

ENDLESS WINTER

RECKON YOU CAN ONLY SKI FOR FOUR MONTHS A YEAR?
THINK AGAIN. EVERY WEEK OFFERS THE POWDER-HUNGRY
A CHANCE TO SATE THEIR APPETITE SOMEWHERE IN THE WORLD.
YOU CAN BASE YOURSELF IN THE HOTEL FROM THE SHINING,
BOUNCE DOWN MOROCCAN SLOPES, SKI UNDER SWEDEN'S
MIDNIGHT SUN AND SCOFF OCTOPUS SUSHI IN JAPAN:
THESE DESTINATIONS OFFER UP CULTURAL ADVENTURES
AS WELL AS SKI- AND BOARD-BASED THRILLS.

OUKAÏMEDEN, MOROCCO
JANUARY

There are more places to ski in Africa than you might think: Algeria, Lesotho and South Africa have pistes of varying quality. Oukaïmeden, which tops out at 3243m, is possible as a day trip from Marrakesh and offers one chair, several drags and bracing but skiable pistes. Donkeys also transport skiers and kit, although investment in a more automated system is planned.

SHIGA KŌGEN, JAPAN
FEBRUARY

Japan's highest resort offers varied terrain and – rarely for Japan – the chance to explore interlinked villages. The snow here is set off by Siberian winds and can be spectacular, but there's plenty more to enjoy: with saunas, slopeside sushi and Japan's famous snow monkeys to keep you occupied, Western visitors will find this an experience as well as a ski trip.

VALDEZ, UNITED STATES
MARCH

Alaska's Chugach Mountains get heaps of sticky snow – 25m a year falls here, and because of the salt water that blows off the sea, it results in precipitously steep slopes. Heli-skiing and snowmobiles are the only way to access the terrain. Packages don't come cheap, but if you want to rocket down the steepest off-piste in the world, this is where to do it.

BĔIDÀHÚ, CHINA
APRIL

Fuelled by China's rising prosperity, skiing in the country is growing rapidly, and Bĕidàhú, in Jílín province, northeastern China, is attempting to add 10km of trails every year. Most of the runs are appealingly tree lined, and the vertical drop is around 900m, with lodgings (many of them built for the Asian Winter Games) at the bottom of the mountain.

RIKSGRÄNSEN, SWEDEN
MAY

Riksgränsen is 300km inside the Arctic Circle in northern Sweden – it's so far north that the resort doesn't bother opening till February due to lack of daylight. By May, lifts stay open to catch the midnight sun and the snow is still plentiful. There's only a limited number of pisted runs, but for the experienced, there's a vast amount of off-piste to explore.

BLACKCOMB, CANADA
JUNE

Come June much of Blackcomb, Whistler's sister resort, is as green as you'd expect – and temperatures down by the lakes can be positively balmy. But the Horstman Glacier is open for around four hours a day, and has a substantial snow park served by two T-bars – perfect for honing those tricks in your sunnies.

ZERMATT, SWITZERLAND
JULY

A few high-altitude glaciers in the Alps offer skiing through the summer – meaning you can ride in your t-shirt in the morning and soak up the sun further down the mountain in the afternoon. The towering Theodul glacier in Zermatt offers surprisingly extensive skiing on blue and red runs throughout the summer, with views of the nearby Matterhorn.

PERISHER, AUSTRALIA
AUGUST

The Southern hemisphere's largest ski resort, south of Canberra, has its best snow depths in August and plenty of snow-making equipment (useful, since snowfall has been patchy in recent years). There are 47 lifts and there's varied terrain on offer, with alpine and cross-country runs, plus bowls to cruise through.

VALLE NEVADO, CHILE
SEPTEMBER

It's only 60km from Santiago, Chile's capital, but Valle Nevado is linked to two other resorts – La Parva and El Colorado – and offers the largest ski area in South America. Ski-in/ski-out accommodation, 45km of runs, a snow park and heli-skiing complete the high-altitude Andean picture.

NORTH ISLAND, NEW ZEALAND
OCTOBER

By October, the skiing is winding down in New Zealand, but the twin resorts of Whakapapa and Turoa, on either side of Mt Ruapehu on North Island, offer the country's largest ski area and one of its longest seasons. Expect precious few tree-lined runs, but well-priced skiing and relaxed après-ski – if you get some fresh powder, you'll find it hangs around for days.

TIMBERLINE LODGE, UNITED STATES
NOVEMBER

Timberline Lodge famously stood in for Jack Nicholson's haunted hotel in *The Shining*. Almost as freaky is the fact that you can ski at this Oregon resort twelve months a year – national teams train here in the summer, but the seven lifts and 700m of descent are open to anyone. It's only 100km from Portland.

VAL THORENS, FRANCE
DECEMBER

Europe's highest ski resort sits at 2,300m, with lifts heading up to 3,200m – making it a great place for guaranteed early-season snow. The functional town centre won't win any architecture awards, but with steep runs, vast stretches of off-piste, a lively bar scene and access to the immense Three Valleys area, you probably won't be worrying too much about the lack of dainty timber chalets.

A Year

START TICKING OFF A LIST

In 2014, Botswana's Okavango Delta became the 1000th addition to Unesco's list of World Heritage sites. In order to be selected for the list, sites must be considered of outstanding universal value. It is as good a measure of human genius or exceptional natural beauty as any. With stone circles, coral reefs, entire cities and precious wildernesses, there is, as the expression goes, something for everyone.

A Year

LEARN A LANGUAGE

BREAK DOWN BARRIERS AND CONNECT WITH A CULTURE LIKE NEVER BEFORE. A LITTLE LANGUAGE-LEARNING GOES A VERY LONG WAY.

You studied Spanish in school for years, but never managed to learn the difference between 'ser' and 'estar.' What's more, you didn't really care. It wasn't until you spent a semester in a small, dusy desert town – San Martin in Argentina – at the age of 17 that the language took root in your brain and began to blossom. Because learning a language isn't just about conjugating verbs. It's also about drinking maté tea with new friends and dancing at the discoteca, and chatting with the bakery ladies as you buy your dulce de leche pastries.

There are so many reasons to learn a new language. It unlocks new cultures and new experiences. It keeps your brain youthful and active. It even opens up professional opportunities: those who speak Mandarin as a second language, for example, now find themselves in high demand.

Snoozed your way through high-school Spanish class? Make up for it with a Spanish immersion in the handsome colonial city of Oaxaca in southern Mexico. The Intituto Cultural Oaxaca (ICO) offers Spanish classes, homestays with local families, and cultural courses on topics from cooking to salsa dancing to piñata making. ●

OAXACA'S CENTRAL ZÓCALO   Getty/Darryl Leniuk

Cantonese
Sure, Mandarin may be the dominant Chinese dialect, but Cantonese has better curse words! Plus, you can watch Bruce Lee movies without the subtitles. The Hong Kong Language School, in Hong Kong's neon-lit Wan Chai neighborhood, has classes ranging in duration between two and 16 weeks.

Danish

Want to read Kierkegaard in the original? Study Danish at Studieskolen in the heart of Copenhagen. It's got the royal seal of approval – the Crown Princess of Denmark, an Aussie who met her husband in a Sydney pub, learned Danish here. New courses start every six weeks.

Hindi

A great place to learn the world's 4th most widely spoken language is Language Must in Delhi, where native speakers will guide you through basic conversation skills. After just a few lessons, you'll be ordering your jalebis (syrup-soaked fried pastries) and chole bhature (spicy fried chick-peas with bread) like a local.

Swahili

Commonly used throughout southeast Africa, Swahili is considered relatively straightforward to learn. Find out whether or not this is true with a Swahili homestay in Kenya through Kenya Xperience. Spend the morning studying, and take the afternoon to roam Nairobi putting your skills to the test.

**CASS GILBERT PEDALS
PERU'S BACKROADS**

It had been one of those days. The kind that drag you out of your comfort zone, flip you upside down, prod you this way and that, and spit you out where you least expect. Our road had turned to quagmire. Gore Tex jackets had long soaked through. And my fingers clawed numbly at the brake levers of my bicycle. A tag team of electrical storms barrelled across the sky, chasing us 'like a pack of hungry grey wolves,' as my riding companion Kurt had put it.

In the distance, the outline of a corrugated shack signalled a blip of hope on this empty, unforgiving Peruvian plateau. We approached it with mounting excitement. It was unlocked and empty. Like prospective home-owners, we peered in, admiring the quality of its dry dirt floor and noting the rusty nails: perfect for hanging sodden clothes. Wasting no time in firing up our stoves, we were soon smiling contentedly, congratulating ourselves on our good fortune, hands cupped around warming brews like they were hard-earned trophies.

Some time later, after we'd made ourselves fully at home and the sprawl of our belongings marked our territory, voices could be heard carrying in the wind. Our luxury shack's owners had returned. Two young shepherd girls gingerly called to us from a distance, wondering what these strange, bicycle-riding gringos could want. When we brokered a deal to stay the night, they headed back to their family home across the plains. The following morning they returned, and when I asked if I could take their photo, they shyly brandished a documenting device of their own: a pink Chinese mobile phone, with which they video'd us waving hello, introducing ourselves and smiling sheepishly. Welcome to the road less travelled, where surprises lie around every corner.

Over the last few years, I've sought to follow this road whenever I can. It's taken me to a place where destinations cease to become the goal of a journey, displaced by the space that lies between A and B. In this case,

FINDING

ROAD

YOUR

> Part of the landscape, at one with the environment, these roads are the lifeblood of a country and they remind me of the reason I choose to travel

two weeks of riding Peru's remote mining roads, tracing a path along the faint veins and capillaries that course through its mountains, had revealed a succession of rugged Andean peaks and valleys of unfathomable beauty. Within, lay the most minuscule of pueblecitos,

where women wore fresh flowers in the brims of their sombreros, as if in defiance of the harsh reality of their surroundings. On these roads less travelled, our path was roughly chiselled into bare, impregnable rock. It wound its way up and over one mountain pass after another. Sometimes it unravelled slowly and graciously, in long and looping bows, as if tying one valley to next. At others times it marched forward with an unrelenting sense of purpose, grit and determination, like the mines that burrowed into the hillsides and pillaged from the earth, in this stark and buckled landscape.

For a thousand kilometres, Kurt and I pedalled our way onwards, passed herds of alpaca bred for meat and wool, to a land where condors glide and swoop. We dug deep within our reserves and conquered climbs that unfurled for over 2000m at a time. The forlorn and forgotten mountain villages, upon which we descended with such anticipation, felt undiluted and real, and we valued them

for what they were. They weren't destinations I'd necessarily recommend people visit. Rather, their appeal lay in their normality, and the context within which we discovered them.

And when we occasionally chanced upon larger settlements, promising bowls of hot soup, grizzled meat and all, or simply mounds of rice and fried eggs – the Peruvian mountain staple – then our lives felt complete. 'Entra gringitos,' said one restaurant owner with a smile. Come in, little gringos. Her words seemed all the warmer given our need to stoop through the doorway, and the way our lanky frames towered over all the local mine workers around. Like a favourite aunt, she invited us to platters of food and cups of steaming tea. When the time came to head back out onto the bumpy jeep roads of the sierras, she refused any notion of payment, bidding us instead a warm and heartfelt 'feliz viaje'.

But why go to all this trouble? After all, aren't there highways fashioned to save us hours on the road and deposit us neatly at our chosen destination? Why make life harder than it is? With every passing mile, with every experience and encounter, I've become increasingly convinced that it's these roads – and the connecting horse tracks, mule trails and footpaths – that reveal the essence of the land. Away from the brash whoosh of traffic and the sound of metal bluntly cutting through the air, they feel peaceful, organic and natural: worn gently and subtly into the earth from lifetimes of travel, like the stone steps of an old church that are grooved and polished by time. Part of the landscape, at one with the environment, these roads are the real lifeblood of a country, and they remind me of the very reason I choose to travel.

And they're everywhere. It's as easy as loading up your bicycle, and joining the dotted lines on your map. As sticking out your thumb, and engaging with the people around you. As choosing a bus because it's headed beyond the index of your guidebook. Next time you head out, pick the route that takes twice the time to reach the exact same place. Journey to villages that lie at dead ends. Investigate names that resonate.

Step out of your comfort zone, with the belief that it will all work out, and it will. Find your road less travelled. The experiences you'll earn will be unlike anywhere else you've been. ●

TRAVELLED

LESS

GET ON YOUR BIKE

'It is by riding a bicycle that you learn the contours of a country best, since you have to sweat up the hills and coast down them. Thus you remember them as they actually are...'
Ernest Hemingway

DEEP IN PERU Cass Gilbert

A Year

friends

with

Travelling

**KERRY CHRISTIANI DESCRIBES
THE PERFECT TRAVEL BUDDY**

***A**lone I would never consider* hitchhiking into the wild blue yonder. But give me a like-minded travel companion and suddenly the doors to adventure fling wide open. And so I find myself at the entrance to Khao Yai National Park in Thailand, on the edge of a track that slithers into a green haze of impenetrable monsoon forest. Hitchhiking Thai-style means waving with your palm down. Get it right and you're almost guaranteed a lift, we are told. We start waving like crazy, aware that time is ticking, with just a couple of hours of daylight left and the nearest campsite miles away.

Our chariot arrives after just five minutes: a battered Mitsubishi pick-up that grinds to a halt in a cloud of dust, its driver beaming at us with a toothless, whisky-fuelled grin. We climb into the back, where three women in skimpy shorts and with heavily lipsticked smiles welcome us like long-lost relatives. Between the peanuts and prawns they are shelling from 10-kilo-heavy sacks and broken conversation, we decipher that they are prostitutes, abandoning the red lights of Phuket for a night of national park wildlife-spotting. The driver, it would seem, is their pimp.

We pelt along the road, past mist-wreathed jungle and savannah alive with cackles and hoots, muffled growls and squeals. Every so often we stop for the obligatory thumbs-up snapshots at staggeringly beautiful waterfalls, my friend and I descending into fits of giggles at the randomness of it all.

Then it happens. We've read about the resident tigers, leopards, bears, gibbons and elephants. But on paper they seemed unreal, like fictional characters in a Rudyard Kipling story. But the three tons of muscle and flapping ears that is blocking the road now seems very real indeed. Instead of backing away or letting the elephant pass, the driver slams his foot down. The now angry adolescent elephant begins to trumpet and charge. It is close. Very close. And we are ridiculously exposed. My friend and I desperately cling on to the truck, as adrenaline, fear and excitement cartwheel through our bodies. It all happens so quickly.

The friend who stopped you drowning in New Zealand's rapids, or made you laugh when you had Delhi Belly will be a friend for life

We arrive in one piece at the campsite, a blood orange sunset creeping over the canopy as we pitch our two-person tent, listening to creatures move in the dusky shadows and laughing about a shared once-in-a- lifetime moment that neither of us will ever forget.

It is would-you-believe-it moments like these that make travelling with friends so special. Choose your travel buddy and your itinerary wisely and you'll strengthen the bond that already exists. The friend who stopped you drowning in the rapids in New Zealand, made you laugh when your insides were on fire with Delhi Belly, or called for oxygen when altitude sickness struck on the Bolivian altiplano will be a friend for life. Beyond the practical, friends can provide the sense of humour needed to overcome what would otherwise be a hellish experience if you were on your lonesome.

And whether it's to be a Thelma and Louise-style road trip through the USA or a multi-day trek in the Himalaya, sharing the experience with a good friend makes it that much more real. Get it right and you'll be the perfect double act – trading tips and suggestions, sharing stories and pooling your travel skills – haggling, map reading, getting to grips with the local lingo, you name it.

Of course, the bubble can burst, so it makes sense to test the water with a short break to make sure you are a good match before heading off together on a round-the-world trip. Common interests are key for successfully travelling with friends. After all, you don't want to venture to the other side of the globe only to find out that your travel buddy would rather watch Lord of the Rings at the hostel than tramp the Milford Track; that their budget means fine dining whereas yours allows for street food; or their idea of seeing Mexico is from the comfort of a hammock, Corona in hand, while yours is touring Mayan ruins. That irritating personality trait? It is going to be magnified when you spent 24 hours a day with someone, which is why breathing space and respect for personal space is so important when you travel as a duo.

'I have found out that there ain't no surer way to find out whether you like people or hate them than to travel with them,' Mark Twain once quipped. How right he was. ●

HADRIAN'S WALL, ENGLAND Justin Foulkes

BREAK DOWN WALLS

We're good at putting up walls. All over the world you'll find them: in China, the Middle East, the Southwest USA, the UK, Germany. But history shows us that walls don't stay standing forever. This is Hadrian's Wall in northern England. Building began in AD 122 and it probably seemed like a good idea at the time. Today, it's an even better spot for watching the sun set over Northumberland.

ALL AROUND THE WORLD

FROM THE TIME OF FERDINAND MAGELLAN IN THE EARLY 16TH CENTURY, CIRCUMNAVIGATIONS HAVE INSPIRED MANY TO SET OUT FROM THEIR FRONT DOOR TO SEE THE WORLD. OVER THE PAGE, DISCOVER HOW SOME HAVE SUCCEEDED (OR NOT) BY BOAT, PLANE OR BICYCLE. BUT YOU DON'T HAVE TO BE A GRIZZLED ADVENTURER TO JOIN THE GANG: ROUND-THE-WORLD PLANE TICKETS ARE EXCEPTIONAL VALUE. AND YOU CAN ALWAYS WARM UP WITH SOMETHING SMALLER THAN THE GLOBE; AN ISLAND LIKE ICELAND FOR EXAMPLE.

>

AROUND THE WORLD IN 80 DAYS
PHILEAS FOGG

Not all laps of the world actually happened. The popularity of Jules Verne's story, featuring globetrotter Phileas Fogg and his French valet Passepartout, is partly down to the rollicking good quality of the tale, but it's also attributable to brilliant timing. The novel was published in 1873, just after transcontinental railways had been completed in India and America, and the Suez Canal had opened: suddenly the world had become a much smaller place. This captured Verne's imagination and the French author's portrayal of an Englishman betting £20,000 (£1.5 million in modern terms) that he could circle the globe in 80 days was a winner with armchair adventurers. In the tale, Fogg and Passepartout travel mostly via train and boat. Fogg never existed but in 1889 an intrepid American journalist called Nellie Bly did a circumnavigation of the planet in 72 days (seven days faster than Michael Palin managed 100 years later) using the same methods of transport. ●

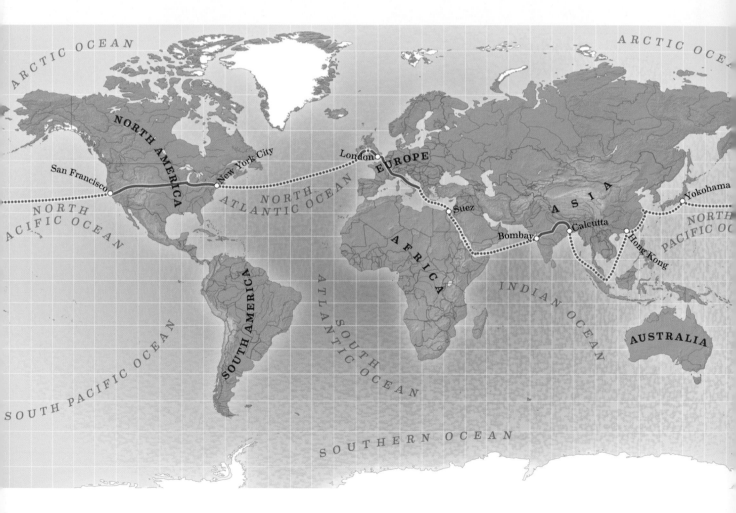

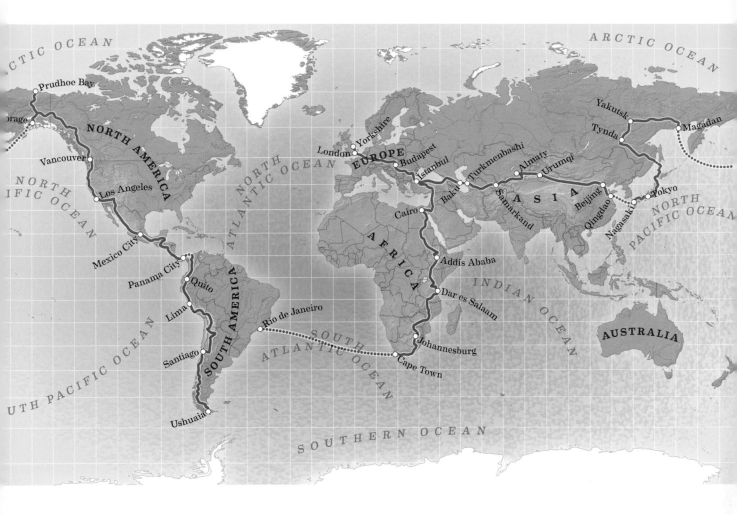

BY BICYCLE
ALASTAIR HUMPHREYS' TWO-WHEELED TRIP

Before he got into micro-adventures, British explorer Alastair Humphreys took on some major macro-missions, the first of which was a mammoth circumnavigation of the planet by bicycle. Starting from his back door in Yorkshire in 2001, he pedalled 74,000 km through 60 countries, traversing five continents to arrive back home in time for tea, just over four years later. His route was designed to take in countries that interested him, rather than to set any sort of speed record, as the map shows. He left his watch behind, rose with the sun and frequently collapsed into slumber in a wild camping spot at dusk. Humphreys made a point of having conversations with locals wherever he went, and along the way ate a sheep's head, guinea pig, bear, sea urchin, horse, fried worms and scorpions. He rode with a granny-style basket on the front of his bike, discovered that car drivers are far more dangerous than both lions and bandits, and picked up enough language skills to convince Japanese police not to arrest him for cycling naked. Mission successful. ●

A Year

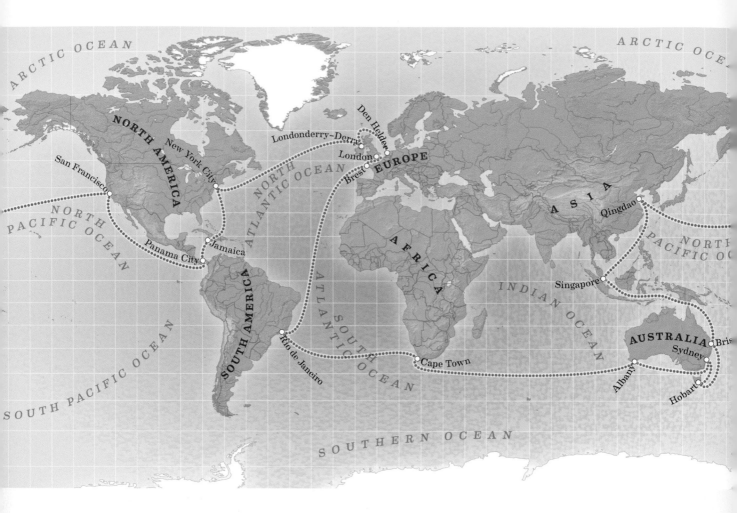

BY BOAT
CLIPPER ROUND-THE-WORLD RACE

For others it's about speed. In the Clipper Race, teams of amateur sailors go head-to-head in an epic 64,000km contest. Sailing identical yachts, the fleet departs from London's St Katharine's Docks and follows a set route back to Britain. The race was dreamt up in 1995 by Sir Robin Knox-Johnston, winner of the Jules Verne Trophy for being the first person to single-handedly sail around the planet without stopping. Competitors in the modern race are allowed to stop, and the last challenge (2013–14), saw 12 boats duke it out on a course that sent them to France, Brazil, South Africa, Australia, Singapore, China, the US, Panama, Jamaica, Northern Ireland and the Netherlands. En route there was drama aplenty; one sailor had a brush with death, falling overboard in heavy weather and floundering in the Pacific for 90 minutes. The threat of piracy plagued them on some stretches, while icebergs menaced in others, but all made it home. ●

BY PLANE
AMELIA EARHART'S LAST FLIGHT

Some circumnavigations don't succeed. On 2 July 1937, Amelia Earhart was two thirds of the way around the planet on a pioneering small-plane flight. As Earhart rolled her twin-engine Lockheed Electra down a jungle runway in Lae, New Guinea, the Americas were in her rear-view mirror, along with Africa, the Middle East and Australia. Next to her sat Fred Noonan, a specialist in celestial navigation, but the weather was dire and ahead lay 7000 miles of Pacific Ocean, punctuated only by slivers of terra firma. A smudge of land called Howland Island was their target. Three ships nearby were burning their lights to aid with navigation. One of these, the *Itasca*, had been receiving messages from Earhart for hours, but couldn't reply. At 7.42am they heard Earhart say, 'We must be on you, but we cannot see you. Fuel is running low.' An hour later, one more message: 'We are running north and south.' Then silence. The aviatrix disappeared without trace. ●

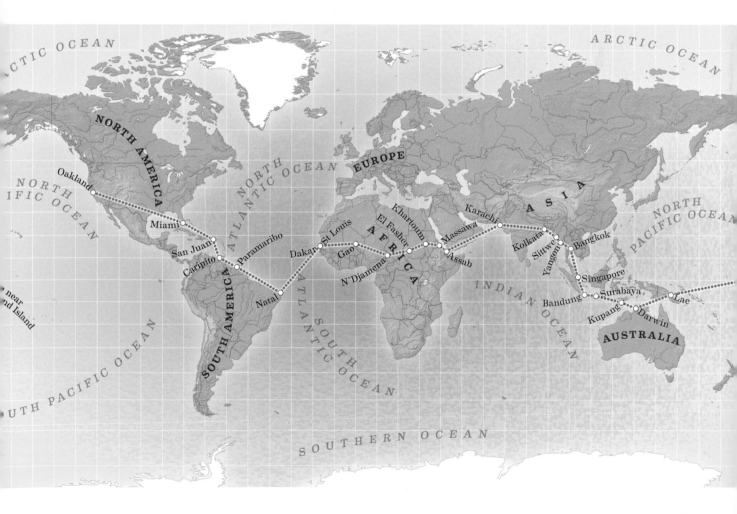

A Year

TAKE A PHOTO A DAY

Chronicle your year and all your adventures – far and near – by taking a photo a day and saving them in one place (several online communities allow this). For enthusiastic photographers it's a good discipline to observe. And at the end of the year, when you look back through the shots, expect to laugh, cry and be surprised at the memories attached to them.

**CLOVER STROUD
WRANGLES ON A
RANCH IN TEXAS**

Whenever *I'm feeling confined* – by domesticity, or penned in with deadlines – there is a place I journey to, in my mind's eye, to find my very own source of spiritual oxygen. That place is west Texas. England might be my home, but Texas is the place that remains in my heart.

The journey that took me to Texas propelled me far from my home in Oxford, to the arid, epic, legendary ranch-lands I'd dreamed of since I was a child. It was a journey that changed me. I only need to close my eyes, and I'm straight back there, surrounded by the bleached-out denim of a cowboy's shirt, the jingle of spurs on a bunk-house porch and the distant, lonely howl of a coyote under a starless sky. Texas is a part of me as much as the dense, wet,

green landscape of the southern England of my youth.

I was 22 and had spent much of the previous three years in the dusty, and occasionally very dull libraries of Oxford, studying for a degree in English literature. But after pursuing a life of the mind, I craved a tough physical challenge, somewhere far from home.

It was the late 1990s, and the dot-com bubble had yet to burst. While my friends from university all headed east to London, to pursue shiny dreams in air-conditioned offices, I packed a rucksack with three pairs of jeans, two T-shirts , my battered leather riding boots, and flew to America.

My unconventional parents had raised me on a diet of country music and a lot of western

> For a year and a half, a log cabin was my home, the cook house my kitchen and the back of a horse my place of work

movies. I was looking for big skies and an empty landscape with herds of horses, spikey green cactus and, hopefully, real live cowboys in leather chaps.

I first worked as a groom for a millionaire on a dude ranch somewhere near Denver. But I was looking for grit rather than glamour. Wasting time in a junk shop, I found a red t-shirt with TEXAS IS THE REASON printed across it in tiny gold letters, and knew I'd found my direction. I caught the next bus to Dallas, hired a car, and headed out to west Texas.

But I was soon to find out that dreaming is one thing and doing is another. I was young and fearless, unaware how ridiculous the idea of an English cowgirl was on a Texas ranch, where life is deeply traditional and very

patriarchal. A woman's place here is in the home, barefoot and pregnant, making beans and babies, not out under the huge blue skies of the range.

Finding a ranch to take me on was part of the journey I now value so much. I was laughed off more ranches than I can remember, and I might have given up if I hadn't met a cowboy called Lonnie at a rodeo near Amarillo. He kept a bottle of whiskey among old copies of Playboy under his pick-up seat, and drove me out onto the plains to give me my first lesson in roping. When his truck broke down, we slept in the pick-up, sheltering in the cab when an electric storm crackled through the dark blue sky.

He said I had cajones, and because he liked my spirit, he pointed me in the direction of a ranch in the Panhandle of Texas, where he thought I might be given a start. The cowboys I met there still laughed at me, but because I could handle a horse, and was willing to work very hard, for very little, I was offered a job.

For a year and a half a log cabin was my home, the cook house my kitchen, and the back of a horse my place of work. We branded cattle in searing temperatures in high summer, and fixed fences when an ice storm in darkest winter threatened to cut the power to the ranch. Big hearted and intensely practical, the cowboys taught me much more than simply how to throw a rope around a cow's neck, ride a bucking horse in a rodeo ring, or fix a barbed wire fence. Today I feel an intense gratitude for the fortitude, tenacity and bravery that my life beneath those huge Texan skies gave me.

But after almost two years, I understood that my fate didn't lie in Texas: I loved the place and the people, but England would always truly be my home. After I came home I got married and had two children in quick succession. By the age of 27, I was a single mother, facing a future supporting a toddler and baby entirely alone. The road that lay ahead of me was steep and rocky, but Texas had taught me how to cowboy-up. Today my home is Oxford but Texas is still, and will always be, the reason. ●

FREEDIVING WITH A MANTA RAY IN THE MALDIVES   Getty/Michele Westmorland

LEARN TO FREEDIVE

If skydiving is about the adrenalin rush of freefall, then freediving is the opposite: it's about finding and focusing on an inner kernel of serenity that comes through controlling your breathing and your emotions. This is one of the world's fastest growing sports, in part because of that feeling of empowerment that comes from defying human physiology. For many people, freediving is a lifelong obsession; not surprising if you can practise your skills swimming with manta rays in the Maldives.

A Year

CRUISE THE CARIBBEAN

RAISE THE ANCHOR AND GIVE THE KIDS AN EDUCATION ON THE OPEN WAVES, ISLAND-HOPPING IN THE CARIBBEAN.

'**D**olphins! Look! At the bow!' Your children groan. 'Not again. We're busy,' they reply. They have seen this marvel of nature countless times. Nonetheless, they drag themselves away from their games down below and climb into the cockpit. The lure of seeing these playful creatures is clearly just too great.

You are in the Caribbean on your own yacht with your family. You haven't worked for months. The sun is dazzling. Dolphins are dipping and diving through the translucent waves at the bow, darting this way and that, occasionally looking up to make sure their antics are being watched. The children laugh. It is difficult not to.

This may sound like a dream, but taking extended time out to cruise the Caribbean is easier than you think. Especially with little people in tow.

The benefits of travelling from the comfort of your own (floating) home are obvious: no lugging heavy bags across busy airports, no faceless hotels and plenty of space to stash all your possessions.

Sailing is an environmentally friendly way to get around, as long as the wind blows. Between December and April, outside hurricane season, trade winds in the Caribbean blow consistently from the east, taking you from one stunning island to the next.

You don't need to be experienced or break the bank to go cruising. Those new to sailing can master the art relatively easy on a course and the secondhand boat market will have something for any budget. Anchoring is free (and there hundreds of sheltered bays where you can drop the hook). If you can handle a fishing rod, your dinner could be free too.

There are literally thousands of islands to explore and all are surprisingly varied. If you're after stunning beaches and turquoise water, the Caribbean will certainly not disappoint. But there are also jungles to hike in Dominica, waterfalls to marvel at in Guadeloupe, a chocolate factory to explore in Grenada and history to learn in Nelson's Dockyard, Antigua.

Sailing these waters is safe, the scenery spectacular and the sun (pretty much) always shines. It is a lifetime experience you would be mad to miss out on. ●

1
Dominica, Roseau
Unspoilt, mountainous, jungle-covered island where locals greet you like old friends. The waterfalls are breathtaking and the snorkelling superb.

2
Union Island, Chatham Bay
Drop anchor in this picturesque forest-lined bay and you will struggle to find a reason to pull it up again. Pelicans dive into the sea, tuna jump out of it and turtles bob sleepily on the surface.

3
Bequia, Admiralty Bay
A yachty hangout and understandably so. This bay has shelter, markets to shop in, plenty of bars and restaurants along the water's edge, as well as an idyllic beach.

4
St Barth, Gustavia
Boasting the best croissants in the Caribbean, this French island is also a magnet for super-yachts. You will need your credit card but it is worth the trip for the relaxed, laissez-faire atmosphere alone.

A Year

CLIMB EVERY MOUNTAIN

START SUMMITING SCOTLAND'S MUNROS AND YOU MIGHT FIND IT A HARD HABIT TO KICK.

It's eight o'clock in the morning and your breakfast of eggs, bacon, mushrooms, tomato and a thick slice of black pudding is already finished. You're at Sligachan Hotel on the Isle of Skye and the reason for the rush is that you've got a Munro to bag and when the Scottish weather is favourable, it pays not to waste time.

A Munro is any hill in Scotland that is more than 914m (3000ft) high; they're not a single range but rather a collection named after a list kept by Sir Hugh Munro in the 19th century. There are rather a lot of them but the one with your name on today is Sgurr nan Gillean, Skye's most recognisable peak. This will be your first and if the hike goes well, perhaps it won't be your last.

Striking out from the hotel with a daypack filled with waterproofs food and water, a compass, a map and the wherewithal to use them, you head up to Coire Rhiabhach, the curved head of the valley. The 12km walk gets tougher now, becoming more of scramble then a balancing act along a snow-crusted ridge. Up here the views of wild Skye are staggering. And so is the wind. You hug the rock at the summit limpet-like before turning round, exhilarated.

For many, collecting Munros becomes an obsession; people compete to climb them all as quickly as possible (the quickest 'round' took less than 40 days). For you, perhaps it will just be something to do when you're next in Scotland. One down, 282 to go. ●

SGURR NAN GILLEAN ON THE ISLE OF SKYE   Getty/Chris Hepburn

Corbetts, Scotland
Daunted by the number and altitude of the Munros? Then perhaps start peak-bagging with the Corbetts, which is the collective name for Scottish hills from 2500 to 3000 ft in height. There are just 221 of them.

Fourteeners, USA
Colorado and California are home to most of the peaks in the US higher than 14,000ft (4270m), though the highest is Mt McKinley in Alaska. Ticking off Colorado's 53 Fourteeners is a popular pastime for climbers.

The Aussie 8, Australia
To scale the highest peak in each of Australia's eight states you won't be climbing higher than 2228m (that's Mt Kosciuszko in New South Wales' Snowy Mountains) but you will be journeying vast distances between them.

Eight Thousanders, Nepal, China, Pakistan & India
Of the 14 peaks higher than 8000m on earth, the most famed is Mt Everest; the others are also in the Himalaya and the Karakoram. Summit all 14 and you'll join an exclusive club of 30 climbers, led by the legendary Reinhold Messner.

We humans are restless. More than a billion international travellers cross borders annually, while over 200 million of us are migrants, living outside our country of origin. The urge to migrate seems embedded in our collective DNA. With so much frenetic motion, 'home' can just as easily signify the cloud where we store our Instagrams as it can a physical address or country of origin.

I'm a 4th-generation American. My great-grandfather, Peter Pearson, left the village of Tvååker, Sweden, in 1883, to start a new life in the mining and logging boom town of Tower, Minnesota. Legend has it that the Norway pines were so tall on this frozen frontier that they blocked the sun.

In the spring of 1909 my great-grandfather, his wife Josephine, also a Swedish immigrant, and their nine children moved into a farmhouse, 10 miles south of Tower. The house was 6m by 8m, a storey

Northern Minnesota is the antithesis of progressive or exotic, but it is the place where I still feel a tangible link to my family's past

and a half, and built on wooden blocks, with a kitchen, dining room, and living room downstairs, and one low-ceilinged giant bedroom upstairs.

'On the cold winter nights to keep from freezing it was necessary to sleep in our long woollen underwear, plus German socks which extended over one's knees.' my Great Uncle Morrie wrote in his diary. 'There was no ceiling upstairs and the roof was not insulated, the rafters were visible and white with frost. When the temperature got down to -40°F, the jack-pine logs in the walls boomed like a rifle shot as they cracked open.'

The summer was short, but the giant garden would still sprout potatoes, cabbage, lettuce, carrots, cabbage, squash and raspberries. In late June the field to the east would bloom with thousands of daisies, buttercups, and Indian paintbrushes.

'On nice, warm sunny Sundays,' Morrie wrote 'the family would pack a picnic basket and follow a narrow path to the crest of the hill where we would sit on the ground and enjoy the most delicious food ever served, listening to the birds and the wind playing a tune through the needles of the pine trees. Their pungent fragrance added to the taste of the food.'

More than a century later, I live 1500 miles south in Santa Fe, New Mexico. But my parents still spend summers on a lake 30 miles from the homestead. When I return in late June, I ride my bike to the farmhouse. It's a wreck. Falling in on itself and infested with mice, it's been condemned as a fire hazard. But if I time my visit correctly, the blooming buttercups, daisies, and Indian paintbrushes still overtake the adjoining field.

I often dream of tearing down the farmhouse, erecting a modern, light-filled cabin, and re-rooting the Pearson name to this place. It's an irrational impulse. The farm was never my own home and I visited my Great Uncle Arnold, who took it over from my great-grandfather, only a few times a year as a child. Northern Minnesota is the antithesis of progressive or exotic, but it is the place where I still feel a tangible link to my family's past. And, for me, that makes it one of the most desirable destinations in this wide, restless world. ●

A Year

SOW SOME SEEDS

By taking part in one of the
many tree-planting schemes
worldwide or purchasing your
very own parcel of Amazonian
rainforest you can sow seeds
literally. But metaphorically,
this is about the adage 'you get
out of life what you put into it'.
As they say in Australia, from
little things big things grow.

A Year

OPEN DOORS

The Peacock Gate in Jaipur's City Palce is perhaps the most beautiful doorway in the world.

THE PEACOCK GATE, JAIPUR, INDIA   Matt Munro

APPRECIATE THE DETAILS

Azulejo has been a form of decorative ceramic tilework in Portugal for 500 years. The overall effect, as seen on many of Lisbon's buildings is mesmerising but look closer to appreciate the beautiful details of the tradition.

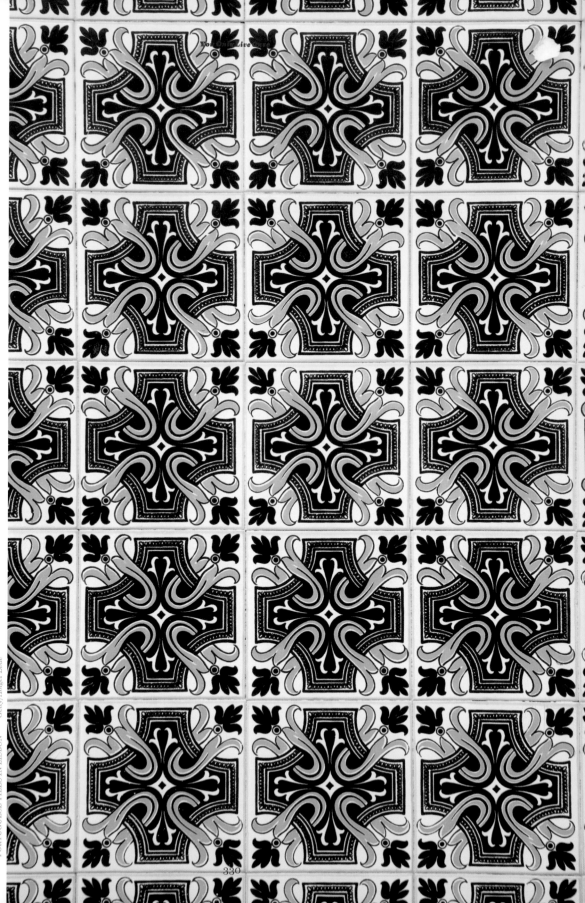

LIFE GOES ON

Even in Death Valley, one of the most inhospitable places on earth, with extreme heat and drought, life persists. Occasional rainstorms cause wildflowers to bloom across the Mojave Desert, for as far as the eye can see.

JOSHUA TREES UNDER THE MILKY WAY IN DEATH VALLEY NATIONAL PARK, USA

Getty/Marc Adamus

ACKNOWLEDGEMENTS

PUBLISHED BY LONELY PLANET GLOBAL LIMITED

Managing Director
Piers Pickard

Associate Publisher &
Commissioning Editor
Robin Barton

Art Director
Daniel Tucker

Editors
**Sally Schafer, Karyn Noble,
Jessica Crouch**

Illustrator
Holly Exley

Cartographer
Wayne Murphy

Authors
**Ann Abel, Sarah Barrell, Robin Barton,
Sarah Baxter, Greg Benchwick, Lucy
Burningham, Garth Cartwright, David
Cornthwaite, Cass Gilbert, Sam Haddad,
Ben Handicott, Patrick Kinsella, Emily
Matchar, Karyn Noble, Stephanie Pearson,
Manfreda Penfold, Adam Skolnick, James
Smart, Nicola Williams**

Print Production
Larissa Frost, Nigel Longuet

Published June 2016

ABN 36 005 607 983
ISBN 978 1 76034 259 3
PRINTED IN CHINA
10 9 8 7 6 5 4 3 2

STAY IN TOUCH
lonelyplanet.com/contact

AUSTRALIA
The Malt Store, Level 3,
551 Swanston St, Carlton,
Victoria 3053 T: 03 8379 8000

IRELAND
Unit E, Digital Court,
The Digital Hub, Rainsford St,
Dublin 8

USA
150 Linden St, Oakland,
California 94607
T: 510 250 6400

UNITED KINGDOM
240 Blackfriars Road,
London, SE1 8NW
T: 020 3771 5100

Paper in this book is certified against the
Forest Stewardship Council™ standards.
FSC™ promotes environmentally responsible,
socially beneficial and economically viable
management of the world's forests.